THE SKILLFUL
TEAM LEADER

For Pop.

THE SKILLFUL TEAM LEADER

A Resource for Overcoming Hurdles to Professional Learning for Student Achievement

ELISA B. MACDONALD

A Joint Publication

CORWIN
A SAGE Company

FOR INFORMATION:

Corwin

A SAGE Company

2455 Teller Road

Thousand Oaks, California 91320

(800) 233-9936

www.corwin.com

SAGE Publications Ltd.

1 Oliver's Yard

55 City Road

London EC1Y 1SP

United Kingdom

SAGE Publications India Pvt. Ltd.

B 1/I 1 Mohan Cooperative Industrial Area

Mathura Road, New Delhi 110 044

India

SAGE Publications Asia-Pacific Pte. Ltd.

3 Church Street

#10-04 Samsung Hub

Singapore 049483

Acquisitions Editor: Dan Alpert

Associate Editor: Kimberly Greenberg

Editorial Assistant: Heidi Arndt

Permissions Editor: Karen Ehrmann

Project Editor: Veronica Stapleton

Copy Editor: Ashley Horne

Typesetter: C&M Digitals (P) Ltd.

Proofreader: Wendy Jo Dymond

Indexer: Sheila Bodell

Cover Designer: Edgar Abarca

Printed in the United States of America.

Library of Congress Cataloging-in-Publication Data

MacDonald, Elisa.

The skillful team leader : a resource for overcoming hurdles to professional learning for student achievement / Elisa MacDonald.

pages cm
Includes bibliographical references and index.

ISBN 978-1-4522-1883-0 (pbk.)

1. Teaching teams. 2. Professional learning communities. 3. Educational leadership. I. Title.

LB1029.T4M33 2013
371.14′8—dc23   2012043755

This book is printed on acid-free paper.

14 15 16 17 10 9 8 7 6 5 4 3

Contents

This chapter outlines the key components of a skillful approach to overcoming hurdles to team learning for student achievement. It also provides valuable information to readers about the unique format and organization of this resource book.

This chapter intends to heighten awareness of the roles that mindset and adult development play in team learning for student achievement. It addresses the hurdles a team leader can face when she or her team members have a fixed mindset, and it suggests strategies for fostering a school culture rooted in a growth mindset.

Collaboration is fundamental to professional learning, but what
does a team leader do with a group that is a team in name only?
This chapter applies a skillful approach to hurdles that can
obstruct collaborative inquiry. It offers suggestions to solve common dilemmas facing team leaders as they work to build a cohesive team that has a high impact on student learning, sometimes
up against a school "culture of alone together."

Professional learning relies on the foundational value of shared
leadership. This is more than sharing the workload; it is sharing
responsibility for learning. But what if leaders and teachers are
unaccustomed to sharing? This chapter applies a skillful approach
to the hurdles a team faces when leading each other. It offers solutions to complex dilemmas for team leaders who seek to foster
shared responsibility for learning within a team and school. It
examines the gap in school culture between believing in shared
leadership and putting it into practice, and it offers strategies for
team leaders to begin closing the gap.

5. **Seemingly SMART: Overcoming Hurdles to Set and Attain Impactful Goals**   **79**

Schools value goal setting and attainment as a means to achieve professional learning for student achievement, but how can a team uphold that value when investment in goals is low and accountability is high? Building upon Anne Conzemius and Jan O'Neill's work around SMART goals, this chapter applies a skillful approach to dilemmas encountered when setting and advancing toward long-term goals and small student-learning targets. It offers team leaders strategies to engage a team in a process for goal setting in order to maximize impact on teacher practice and student learning. It explores the challenges of goal setting in schools where a "scapegoat culture" exists, and it suggests actions team leaders can take to shift to a culture of mutual responsibility.

6. **Off-Course Discourse: Overcoming Hurdles to Lead a Team in Rigorous Discourse**   **103**

Professional learning requires teams to engage in rigorous discourse, but what if discourse is just talk? This chapter applies a skillful approach to overcoming hurdles brought about by challenging conversations about data sometimes laden with blame, excuses, and assumptions. It offers strategies to team leaders to facilitate discourse that is evidence based, dialogic, culturally proficient, reflective, and actionable, even in schools where the "culture of nice" keeps talk superficial.

7. **Inertia: Overcoming Hurdles to Lead an Action-Oriented Team for Continuous Improvement**   **131**

In professional learning, teams strive for continuous improvement, but how does a team do so when there is resistance to change? This chapter applies a skillful approach to hurdles put forth by internal and external obstacles to change. It offers strategies to transform team learning into actions that yield sustainable results for teachers and students, even when a school's culture seems acidic to change.

Dilemma
Questions Index

CHAPTER 7

How do I lead an action-oriented team when

List of Figures and Tables

Acknowledgments

I am fortunate to have had wonderful people in my life influencing my approach to this work and the writing of this book.

To the educators I have met through my consulting work:

The administrative leadership teams, teacher leaders, teacher teams, and faculties in more than twenty-five districts who welcomed me into their schools. I am honored to have worked alongside such incredible, dedicated professionals; Sue Freedman, whose confidence in me and my writing helped me believe in myself; John D'Auria, president of *Teachers*[21] who gently nudged my thinking with his nuanced understanding of school culture and leadership; Jill Mirman, who first gave me the opportunity to work in a formal role as a leader of adult learners and supported me with wisdom and encouragement as I learned the ropes from her masterful approach; colleagues Karen Engels, Pam Penna, and Jenny Miller, who are an incredible network of skillful leaders of adults.

To my former colleagues:

The outstanding administrators and teachers of Brighton High and the former William H. Taft, who graciously permitted me to learn as I led, and whose passion for education ignite me to this day; Charlie Skidmore, who believed in my potential to lead my colleagues in learning; Joyce Campell, the most incredible teachers' teacher; Cathleen Kral, who created a phenomenal network of coaches and gave me opportunities to lead and grow; Shannon Baker, Jo Ann Rogers, and my literacy coach network, whose mastery as team leaders elevated my own learning; Elizabeth Hale, who agreed to meet up with me at an outdoor café, despite barely knowing me, to share with me her publishing experiences and encourage me; Britta Heister, an outstanding teacher, mother, and friend who gently reminds me of the importance of balance.

To my new Teach Plus, T3 family:

Meghan O'Keefe whose rock-solid leadership inspires me each day; Daryl Frischling Campbell, who is an effervescent spirit of love, encouragement, and a darn good facilitator of adult learners; Toby Romer and Lisa Lineweaver, outstanding educators who have had a tremendous influence over my thinking and understanding of data and instruction; and the coaches and teacher leaders with whom I now work and whose every day excellence makes me strive to be better.

To the Boston Athenaeum and Calderwood Writing Initiative for the opportunity to take what began as some ideas on a torn out piece of notebook paper into the start of something real; Judith Goleman, who provided me with sound wisdom and encouragement during my time in the fellowship; the amazing cohort of fellows with whom I began this writing journey, many of whom have gone on to publish extraordinary articles, plays, and books themselves; Sarah Davis, who by divine fate I met as a fellow, who is one of the most insightful, articulate, generous people I know, and who for five years gave up many a Saturday morning and late evenings to read and respond to draft after draft of my writing.

To my dear friends:

Emily Becker and Elizabeth Belkind, outstanding educators and friends with heart, soul, and smarts; Jenna Rubenstein, who brought her psychology eye to my work; My ACES, Amanda Hennessey and Sheryl Faye, whose immense talent and tenacity I greatly admire and whose generosity and friendship I could not be without; Ashot Gheridian, Amy Thorne Allison, and Vanessa Foster, my long-time friends and diner buddies, who made sure I didn't fall too far off the map in my own secluded writing world, and Barbee and J. J., dear friends for life.

To the amazing professionals at Corwin and Learning Forward who have helped to bring the best version of my writing to a wide audience; Heidi Arndt, editorial assistant, who helped ensure a smooth transition to production; Veronica Stapleton, project editor, who coordinated the production schedule and kept the project on track; Ashley Horne, copy editor, whose eye for detail is like no other, and Dan Alpert, my editor, whose calming presence and encouragement helped me "birth" my first book.

To the Robbins Library in Arlington, Massachusetts, where weekend after weekend I was provided with the perfect writing nook, and to my local Starbucks where I sat for hours typing away, hot cocoa in hand.

To my family:

My mother, who made extraordinary sacrifices to instill in me a love for learning at a young age, whose courage and strength inspire me, and who continues to hold an unwavering belief in my abilities. My father and stepmother, who provided me with a strong moral compass . . . and for telling me to "finish the book." My sisters, Carmen and Marcy, whose amazing accomplishments and genuine hearts inspire me each day; Oma and Uncle Walter, who supported me with love, encouragement, endless hours of babysitting, and time-saving trips to the grocery store. My Uncle Roger and my beloved Pop—the greatest educators in and outside of the classroom; my Nana, who brought joy to my childhood and now to my children; my husband's family, who treats me as their own and has many times jumped in to help without hesitancy; my mother-in-law, Donna, who showed unrelenting faith in me during my writing process, reading draft after draft, helping me stay true to my voice; my now three year old twins, Liam and Grace, who make my heart dance every day and make me giggle when they tap their precious little fingers, pretending to "write like mommy"; and above all, my husband, Bobby, my dearest love and an outstanding father . . . much deserving of a golf weekend.

PUBLISHER'S ACKNOWLEDGMENTS

Corwin gratefully acknowledges the contributions of the following reviewers:

Roxie R. Ahlbrecht
Math Intervention Specialist Substitute Teacher,
Sioux Falls Public Schools 49–5
Sioux Falls, SD

David G. Daniels
High School Principal, Susquehanna Valley Schools
Conklin, NY

Freda Hicks
Assistant Principal, Orange County Schools
Hillsborough, NC

Linda Jungwirth
Educational Consultant, Pepperdine University
Los Angeles, CA

Angela Mosley
Assistant Principal, Richmond Public Schools
Richmond, VA

Tanna Nicely
Assistant Principal
Knox County Schools, TN

About the Author

Photo by Ky Winborn

Elisa MacDonald is a former teacher, literacy coach, AP of instruction, and consultant. She has recently joined Teach Plus, T3 as the director of teacher leader development, where she supports, coaches, and teaches leaders in underperforming schools by developing them as purpose-driven instructional leaders, evidence-based decision makers moving through data inquiry cycles, skillful facilitators of adult learners, and schoolwide change agents. Elisa has consulted with numerous school districts, launching districtwide professional learning communities, coaching and leading courses for team leaders, leading school-based inquiry teams and workshops in literacy and classroom management. She has received numerous grants and awards including the Calderwood Writing Fellowship and English Speaking Union Treadwell Scholarship, and she was featured as a teacher in *Middle Ground Magazine* in December 2001. Elisa is author of "When Nice Won't Suffice: Honest Discourse Is Key to Shifting School Culture" (*JSD*, June 2011). She has coauthored several articles, including "Buoyed on all Sides: A Network of Support Guides Teacher Leaders in High-Needs Schools" (*JSD*, December 2012), and is a contributing author to the third edition of *Beyond Mentoring* (*Teachers*[21], 2010). She earned an MA in critical and creative thinking from UMass Boston and graduated with honors from Brandeis University with a BA in psychology and education. In addition to being passionate about teacher and student learning, Elisa loves the theater and has performed professionally in Boston. Elisa lives in Arlington, Massachusetts, with her husband, Bob, and their twins, Liam and Grace.

Part I

Foundations

A Skillful Approach 1

This chapter outlines the key components of a skillful approach to overcoming hurdles to team learning for student achievement. It also provides valuable information to readers about the unique format and organization of this resource book.

A Note From One Team Leader to Another

Three weeks into my first year as a teacher, I am standing in the hallway at dismissal when the director of instruction gently approaches me and says, "Elisa, the principal wondered if you could lead your team's meeting?"

"Today?" I ask, slightly panicked that the meeting starts in fifteen minutes, and I have never led a team of adults before, let alone five colleagues with more experience than me.

He musters up his best smile and says, "For the year." He adds, "Just put a couple things down on paper as the agenda and try to get people to stick to it. You'll be fine."

My entrypoint into team leadership is what I call an instant coffee approach: Start with a group. Just add leader. And as you might imagine, this approach yielded as much richness as, well, instant coffee. I am so grateful to the first team of teachers that I led, but I would hardly call what I did leading learning for student achievement.

Since that fall day in 1995, I have had opportunities to develop my capacity to lead teams as a teacher, coach, consultant, and administrator. These experiences and my coaching of other team leaders in numerous districts have led me to appreciate the craftsmanship of leading a team of adults. This book comes from years of listening to team leaders' dilemmas and reflecting on my own. It comes from mulling over moments when my response succeeded in overcoming a hurdle to team learning or unintentionally created another. It comes from an ongoing quest for practical solutions grounded in theory and research. It comes from the belief that although hurdles can seem impossible to move past, they can in fact be catalysts for greater learning when we approach them skillfully.

A dear friend calls the content of this book "revolutionary common sense." If you lead a team and discover, like me, that the more you work to develop impactful professional learning, the more you need to learn, then I ask you to join me to revolutionize team leadership . . . and what better place to start than with our own common sense.

—Elisa

THE NEED FOR SKILLFUL TEAM LEADERSHIP

The well-intentioned advice from my administrator to write an agenda and try to stick to it does not begin to prepare a team leader for the complexity of leading colleagues in learning. Regardless of who is leading or being led, every team seeking to improve student achievement comes up against hurdles. These hurdles generate distinct dilemmas for a team leader.

For instance, a team leader might succeed in getting teachers to regularly look at student work together, but her team withholds critical feedback essential for learning and growth. This presents the team leader with the dilemma, *How do I facilitate rigorous discourse when we can't move beyond superficial talk* (Ch. 6)? Or a team leader may find she is able to foster rigorous discourse, but her team gets stuck at implementation in the classroom, leaving her to wonder, *How do I lead an action-oriented team when intentions don't align with actions* (Ch. 7)?

Team hurdles often crop up because of what is going on inside the team, but often outside factors contribute as well. School leadership, for example, can help or hinder a team's learning and impact on students. For instance, a team leader may be designated to lead a team, but when the principal is still making all of the team's learning decisions, the team leader is faced with the dilemma, *How do I foster shared leadership for learning when no one has authority to lead (including me)* (Ch. 4)? School culture can also contribute to the hurdles a team must overcome. For example, *When a "culture of alone together" exists, where people are grouped together but act alone, a team leader must find a way to bring people together to collaborate* (Ch. 3).

No matter how much experience a team leader has, she is likely to be confronted with team hurdles, creating a dilemma of what to do. What distinguishes the skillful team leader from a less-effective leader is her approach to overcome these hurdles. This approach is rooted in the leader's values, mindset, intelligence, and skill.

AN INTRODUCTION TO A SKILLFUL APPROACH: VALUES, MINDSET, INTELLIGENCE, SKILL

Values

Values provide guidance for the work teams do. They ground a team leader in what is important. They remind a team leader of what matters. When faced with hurdles to team learning the skillful team leader relies on her strong commitment to five foundational values[1]:

1. Collaboration

2. Shared leadership

---

[1]These five values stem from the work of experts, namely, DuFour, Hord, and Fullan; leadership gurus Heifetz, Wagner, Kegan, and Lahey; and experts on organizational change, Argyris, Schein, and Senge.

3. Goal setting and attainment

4. Rigorous discourse

5. Continuous improvement

To anyone versed in professional learning community (PLC) literature, this list should sound familiar: in fact, perhaps so familiar that the meaning is watered down. The skillful team leader has an elevated, nuanced understanding of these five foundational values, and she fully commits to putting them into practice. A glimpse into what each value looks like follows. Each chapter in Part II of this book provides a more detailed understanding.

The skillful team leader values the following:

1. *Collaboration.* She believes learning together yields better results than does working alone. She is not satisfied with a group that meets regularly and calls itself a team when the members neither learn from one another nor advance student learning. She continuously assesses and advances her team's function (*how* they work interdependently) and impact on student learning (*what* they are working on and the outcomes achieved) (Ch. 3).

2. *Shared leadership.* He does not simply share leadership within his team by rotating roles of facilitator, notetaker, timekeeper, and the like. Instead, he insists that team members share the lead for each other's learning, including his own (Ch. 4).

3. *Goal setting and attainment.* She does not set and implement team goals out of compliance but works diligently with her team to attain impactful goals that deeply matter to teachers, students, and the school. Driven by purpose, the team leader advances her team through the inquiry cycle to achieve measured gains for students (Ch. 5).

4. *Rigorous discourse.* He does not settle for team discourse that promotes more of the same talk and practice, but he gently and purposefully prods his team to engage in evidence-based discourse that challenges cultural assumptions held by leaders, teachers, and students so that actionable knowledge is gained (Ch. 6).

5. *Continuous improvement.* She is not satisfied with team learning that doesn't result in replicable, long-lasting change (Ch. 7).

Mindset

What a teacher believes in his core about every student's capacity to learn impacts his effectiveness in the classroom. What a team leader believes in her core about every teacher's capacity to learn and improve impacts her effectiveness in leading a team. Carol Dweck's (2006) research (explained further in chapter 2) highlights the distinctions between fixed and growth mindsets and the impact each has on an individual's effort and success. Applied to leadership, the skillful team leader approaches hurdles from a growth mindset with a belief that every student and every teacher can improve as can her own ability to lead them. Being able to recognize both a teacher's mindset and one's own is a necessary skill for any team leader to facilitate ongoing learning. Being able to *influence* mindset brings about desired change (Chapter 2 explores the roles mindset and adult development play in team learning).

Intelligence

The intelligence with which the skillful team leader approaches her work is not IQ but EQ, emotional intelligence. A term coined by Daniel Goleman (2002), *emotional intelligence* is one's ability to be attuned to and respond to emotions in self and others. Skillful team leaders access "a potent emotional guidance system that keeps what they say and do on track. . . . They listen carefully, picking up on what people are truly concerned about, and they respond on the mark" (p. 50). Jack London's (1916) description of surfing in his short story, "The Kanaka Surf," seems a perfect metaphor for the emotional intelligence the skillful team leader exhibits. He wrote that "[It] requires wisdom of waves, timing of waves, and a trained deftness in entering such unstable depths of water with pretty, unapprehensive, head-first cleavage, while at the same time making the shallowest possible of dives" (para. 39). Like the surfer, the skillful team leader possesses wisdom, timing, and deftness as she navigates the hurdle-filled waters of leading a team. She is highly attuned to the emotions of the group and is aware of how her own emotional response can impact others. She manages these emotions with skill.

Skill

A skillful approach to overcoming hurdles to professional learning for student achievement requires a team leader to anchor her leadership in the five foundational values, to hold the mindset that every teacher has the capacity to learn and change, and to read and respond effectively to the emotional climate that a hurdle creates. Executing this approach requires skill. The skillful team leader is able to do the following.

Identify the hurdle. Like pausing a movie at a critical point, the skillful team leader has the keen ability to detect a hurdle when it is almost unnoticeable to anyone else on the team. He recognizes when a team encounters an obstacle to learning and consciously proceeds to uncover where it is coming from.

Explore possible causes. The skillful team leader does not react to a hurdle but instead thoughtfully analyzes it as if looking through a telephoto lens of a digital video camera. She is able to zoom in to causes found at the team level and then zoom out to see causes posed by her own leadership and the school.

Respond. After careful analysis of possible contributing factors to the hurdle, the skillful team leader thoughtfully considers her options for response. She not only decides which responses to use but also when to use them. She makes use of four types of responses:

- *Proactive response.* What the team leader says and does can often prevent the team from coming up against the hurdle in the first place. For example, one of many proactive responses suggested throughout each chapter is "norming," also known as crafting a group agreement. Chapter 3 recommends that teams norm not only for how a team functions (e.g., We will agree to disagree) but also for the team's impact on teacher and student learning (e.g., We will invite others to question our assumptions, beliefs, and values).

- *In-the-moment response.* The skillful team leader makes the decision to respond to what is happening as it is happening. For example, one strategy offered in multiple chapters is to *"find an entry point."* This response requires the team leader to listen keenly to team members, sifting through the conversation to pull out a key thought, idea, or concern that needs to be explored further.

- *Follow-up response.* The skillful team leader's words and actions after a meeting assures the team is able to sustain gains made without creating another hurdle to learning. For instance, several chapters reference the *"check-in"* strategy, when a team assesses how well they function and the impact they have on student learning.

- *School leadership team response.* The skillful team leader mobilizes others, particularly the principal and administrators, in helping her team move beyond a given hurdle. Finding solutions to team dilemmas is not a one person job, and often if one team encounters hurdles, others will too. Tony Wagner et al. (2006) suggest districts form "leadership practice communities" where leaders commit to "helping one another solve problems of practice related to the school's teaching and learning challenges together" (p. 17). This type of learning leadership team is also beneficial at the school level. One strategy suggested throughout the book for school leadership teams is to *"model."* The team leader together with other school leaders demonstrate the desired team behavior in their own leadership team meetings, which is sometimes easier said than done.

Consider school culture. The skillful team leader views hurdles as obstacles to overcome but also as windows into the complex world of school culture. Often described as "the way we do things around here," school culture is chock-full of beliefs, values, customs, and traditions that suggest how people have interacted in the past and are the basis for how they interact in the present (and likely will in the future unless deep-rooted change is made). Schools that don't address the deeper cultural issues at hand only go through the motions of being a PLC, and they will struggle to achieve *sustainable* student improvement (Fullan, 2009). The skillful team leader knows that addressing a problem specific to her team without a deep look at how school culture contributes will only give rise to the hurdle again. For a team leader, this means considering not only causes from within the team but also looking for signs of a "gap" in school culture. Based on Edgar H. Schein's work, this culture gap is when an espoused value doesn't align with visible evidence in the organization (as cited in Senge, Kleiner, Roberts, Ross, & Smith, 1994, pp. 268–269). The school may have a healthy culture otherwise, but a gap creates a hurdle that teams have trouble moving past.

For example, the team leader faced with the dilemma, *How do I facilitate rigorous discourse when my team can't move beyond superficial talk* (Ch. 6), might attribute the problem to a team's discomfort with using a "looking at student work" protocol. But she must also question if the *culture of nice*—where educators censor what they say because open, honest discourse is discouraged throughout the school—is negatively impacting the team's ability to speak candidly (MacDonald, 2011).

Teams who are content to be pockets of success in a system where school culture gaps go unaddressed find themselves struggling to sustain the positive impact they have. It's as if the team is working hard to knit a beautiful sweater while someone is on the other end unraveling the yarn. The skillful team leader not only works with her team to navigate around the hurdles that school culture gaps cause, but also works to close those gaps so all teams can succeed.

Closing school culture gaps is not easy. People are often "deeply invested (sometimes even just by habit and not ideology) in preserving the rhythms and practices in place" (Pappano, 2010, p. 9). Others hold so tightly to assumptions about student and adult learning that it is difficult to get them to even listen to different perspectives, let alone be influenced by them. Beliefs so strongly shape the policies, procedures, and everyday life of individuals in a school, even when leaders and teachers leave, their beliefs stick around (Schein, 1985/1992). It's particularly difficult to close a gap in an otherwise healthy school culture when no one talks about it publicly. But the skillful team leader notices when a gap exists between what a school says it values and what it practices. She is not only able to navigate around hurdles created by a gap in school culture, but also able to lead her team to positively influence the school culture.

As team leaders master the skills—identify the hurdle, recognize possible causes, respond, and consider culture—they are able to have a greater impact on professional learning, which results in student achievement.

IMPORTANT INFORMATION REGARDING THE WRITING AND ORGANIZATION OF THIS BOOK

This book is divided into two parts:

> Part I: *Foundations* provides the reader with a skillful approach to leading teams of adult learners for student achievement. Chapter 1 provides an overview of a skillful approach: values, mindset, intelligence, skill. Chapter 2 delves deeper into the role of mindset in team learning.

> Part II: *Hurdles* consists of five chapters, each named for a substantial hurdle that teams encounter when putting one of the five foundational values into practice: collaboration, shared leadership, goal setting and attainment, rigorous discourse, and continuous improvement. Each chapter follows a consistent format as outlined in the following:

> *What Is (the Foundational Value), and Why Is It Important?* Defines the foundational value in focus, specifically what it is and the literature that speaks to the benefits of effectively putting that value into practice.

Hurdles to (Putting Foundational Value Into Practice). Names the hurdles a team might encounter and three to five increasingly complex dilemma questions[2] that arise for a team leader as a result of the hurdles.

Dilemma. Zooms in to one dilemma question presented in the previous section.

Snapshot. One or two paragraphs (shown in *italics*) frame the dilemma followed by a snapshot of a hypothetical team experiencing it. Snapshots are intended to be relatable, concise, and nonjudgmental. They illustrate a specific problem while still having a broad enough application to the reader's own specific issues. All snapshots are intended to resonate with the reader and are garnered from a collection of real experiences, but none are retellings of actual events. They may sound familiar because the hurdles to team learning are universal (In fact, I have had some team leaders read them and say, "This just happened to our team last week."), but the actual team members described are fictional.

It is also important to note that each hypothetical snapshot is just that— a snapshot in time. I intentionally write about one small moment in a team's work together, like a snapshot captured on film, for the purpose of demonstrating a specific dilemma. The snapshot does not define the team. In other words, teachers who show reluctance in one snapshot are not to be labeled resistant, a struggling team leader is not to be thought of as inept, and a team is not to be branded dysfunctional. Even the most consistently high-functioning, high-impact teams (explained in detail in Ch. 3) come up against hurdles to learning and achievement.

Identify the Hurdle. Specifies the hurdle to team learning encountered in the sample snapshot of a team.

Explore Possible Causes. Considers a wide array of possible causes for the hurdle.

Respond. Provides the team leader with field-tested, proactive, in-the-moment, follow-up, and school leadership team responses.

Consider School Culture. Assumes that school culture is generally healthy but can have a gap that might contribute to the team hurdle (e.g., a "culture acidic to change," Ch. 7). Readers learn recognizable indicators that a gap exists, and they take away suggestions on how a team, together with others, can help shape the school culture to its' healthiest state so team learning can thrive.

Application to Your Own Practice: Connect, Observe, Explore, Act. Each chapter concludes with an action-planning tool to apply the learning from the chapter to the readers' own team(s). This section is particularly useful if a school team or cohort of team leaders is reading and discussing a chapter. It is also useful for those leading a course on team leadership to foster reflective thinking and action.

Note: Resources that a team leader may find useful can be found at the end of the book.

---

[2]I address dilemmas that have been most frequently asked by the hundreds of team leaders with whom I have worked and that have no simple answers. This book does not answer basic questions such as "How do I find time for my team to meet?" Dilemma questions within each chapter are designed to grow increasingly more complex, so the reader can turn to the level of complexity as needed.

This book is intended for formal and informal leaders who facilitate professional learning in teams. Team leaders may be responsible for or may be in training to lead any type of learning team such as district K–12, school-based instructional leadership, departmental, grade level, data, study groups, and inquiry groups. Although the term "team leader" is used in the singular throughout this book, it is understood that some teams rotate the role or have coleaders. This book can be valuable to whoever is holding the role for any duration of time.

Program directors, staff developers, and professors who provide instruction and training to team leaders may also find this book useful in a course or book study.

This book is intentionally designed as a resource. When picking up a professional text for the first time, I tend to do a brisk read cover-to-cover to get the lay of the land and then sit it prominently on my shelf, pages dog-eared, sticky notes protruding so that I can go back to particular sections as needed in my work. Consequently, I have designed this book for that purpose. This book is easy to read, written in a consistent format so that team leaders can read it from start to finish or select chapters that speak to the current hurdles they are encountering. Both the chapters and the dilemmas posed as questions within each chapter build on prior ones but also stand well on their own. In this way, a team leader can reference relevant sections as needed, and she can even share portions of the text with her team or colleagues in a course.

This book is not a manual. It provides numerous possible causes for the hurdles described in each chapter, as well as a variety of effective responses for a team leader to consider. It is not intended as an "if this happens, say or do this" type of book. It requires the reader to tap into her own emotional intelligence, to read the waves of her team and school culture, and thoughtfully and selectively use this book as a resource to work through her own team dilemmas.

The title of this book is a tribute to the teachers and team leaders with whom I have worked alongside and coached, who remind me that leading teams requires skillfulness that we can and must continuously develop in order to foster learning for teachers and students. It is also a reverent nod to Jon Saphier, who founded the nonprofit *Teachers*[21] for whom I have consulted for fifteen years and who authored *The Skillful Teacher*, which has had a tremendous impact on my own teaching and that of my colleagues.

Why a Whole Book About Hurdles?

When writing this book, I toyed with a number of words before committing to *hurdles*. *Roadblocks* was a consideration, but the word sounded too impassable—like the closed street by my house that crews have been working on for months. *Obstacles* was a contender but made me think of cones I used to have to run around as a teenager on field day—seems more like an inconvenience than the angst I feel when I'm face-to-face with a hurdle. And the word *problems* seemed too depressing. I settled on *hurdles* because of the onomatopoeia—the word sounds as huge and intimidating as the actual thing—and because I have this inspiring image in my head of the team leader as a runner, leaping over one hurdle after another. Sometimes the race is a sprint, and the runner makes it through speedily and unharmed. Other times, it's the long hurdle race where it just seems like as soon as she gets over one hurdle another is waiting, and another, and another. Regardless of the height of the hurdle or how many are in the runner's path, the only way to get beyond them is to run toward them. This is frightening. Seeing the hurdles that lie ahead can make her want to quit. But the more she runs the course, the more she learns to anticipate what is coming and, more important, how to respond. Once the runner makes the leap, she is encouraged.

Hurdles to professional learning for student achievement come from people we care about, cultures we are proud to work within, and oftentimes from ourselves. A skillful approach can help us make the leap.

Mindful About Mindset 2

This book sets forth to help team leaders overcome specific hurdles to professional learning using a skillful approach. It is designed for the reader to flip around to specific dilemmas relevant to her work; however, none of the suggested responses will be effective if a team leader is not attuned to the mindset of the teachers she leads and her own. Consequently, this chapter is intended to heighten awareness of the roles that mindset and adult development play in team learning for student achievement. It addresses the hurdles team leaders can face when they or their team members have a fixed mindset, and it suggests strategies for fostering a school culture rooted in a growth mindset.

MINDSET

I remember being at a meeting with other leaders when I voiced my belief that every teacher has the capacity to learn and change. A colleague I respect turned to me and said, "Oh, c'mon, Elisa. You don't really believe that?" It got me thinking: why do I believe that, and can I be an effective team leader if I don't?

The work of leading teams does not begin with setting agendas or finding the right protocol. It begins in the minds of both the learners and those responsible for leading learning. Our minds house our beliefs about our own and others' capabilities, and this, in turn, influences our actions and what we are able to accomplish. Mindset can make a person receptive to learning or act as an internal obstacle to change (Kegan & Lahey, 2009). What a student believes about her intelligence influences what she ultimately achieves (Dweck, 2006). The same is true of the adult learner. What teachers believe about their own capacity to learn and change will determine their actions and response to failure. What team leaders believe about other adults' capacity to learn and change will determine their effectiveness as leaders. The skillful team leader is always mindful about mindset.

Carol Dweck (2006) has done extensive research on how people's mindset about their intelligence can influence their performance. She primarily looks at why some students reach their potential, while others do not, and she maintains two types of mindset: fixed and growth.

A person with a fixed mindset believes that ability in a specific domain is limited. For example, a student is either good in math or not. His talent can't be developed. This belief impacts the student's effort, causing him to put looking smart above learning. Consequently, he will not take learning risks. This student is less likely to work hard at getting better in math because he doesn't think it will make a difference.

On the contrary, a person with a growth mindset believes that ability can be cultivated through effort, study, and persistence. For instance, the student who is not performing in math pictures her brain as a muscle that gets stronger each time she learns something new. With effort and perseverance, she can acquire the skills needed to be high performing in math, regardless of her innate talent. For this student, learning is more important than looking smart. Consequently, she is willing to fail publicly for the sake of learning.

Apply Dweck's findings to the domain of adult learning, and a team leader gains insight as to the impact mindset has on team learning and achievement.

The Impact of the Adult Learner's Mindset

A team member's mindset influences how receptive he is to learning and change. A teacher with a fixed mindset does whatever he can to continue to look and feel competent among his colleagues. He shies away from team tasks at which he might fail. When he does fail he is likely to blame external factors or deem himself a failure.

On the contrary, a team member with a growth mindset views setbacks as necessary for growth. Failure doesn't become her identity; instead, it is merely an incident from which she must learn and persevere. This team member is comfortable taking learning risks, even if it means failing in front of her colleagues, because she views it simply as an indication that she hasn't achieved success *yet* but knows she will.

The skillful team leader pays close attention to the mindset of those she leads, knowing its influence over their words and actions in a team. She looks for evidence to answer fundamental mindset questions: What does the teacher believe in his core about (1) students' capacity to learn and (2) his own capacity to learn and improve as a teacher (see Figure 2.1)?

Discovering one or more team members have a fixed mindset about either students or their own capacity to improve as educators leads to a deeper understanding of why some individuals exhibit resistance to team learning. It alerts the team leader to the need to initiate a shift toward a growth mindset.

The Impact of the Team Leader's Mindset

The skillful team leader is not only attuned to the mindset of those she leads but also to her own. Her belief about learners, both children *and* adults, influences those she leads. She must reflect critically. A team leader who has a growth mindset as a teacher would not put a cap on what children can learn, but would she for adult learners? She would not stop trying in multiple ways to help a student learn, would she do the same for an adult learner? Successfully leading others requires a growth mindset about the learner, regardless of age, experience, or motivation to change. This is not always easy. It requires a team leader to believe that regardless of how steep one's learning curve is, every teacher can improve.

Often, hidden beneath the fixed mindset about a teacher is the team leader's own fixed mindset about her ability to lead. To reveal her own mindset about herself and the adult learners she leads, the team leader must answer fundamental mindset questions: What do I believe in my core about students' capacity to learn, teachers' capacity to learn and improve, and my own capacity to lead others in learning and change (see Figure 2.1)?

Figure 2.1   Fundamental Mindset Questions

1. What does the teacher believe in his core about • Students' capacity to learn? • His own capacity to learn and improve as a teacher?	2. What do I believe in my core about • Students' capacity to learn? • Teachers' capacity to learn and improve? • My own capacity to lead others in learning and change?
3. How do our mindsets impact our team's learning and achievement?	

DECONSTRUCTING THE FUNDAMENTAL MINDSET QUESTIONS

What Does the Teacher Believe in His Core About Students' Capacity to Learn and Achieve?

Dweck (2006) says that students with a fixed mindset view themselves as failures when they fail and perceive effort as something required only of people who aren't capable. Teachers with a fixed mindset about students hold the same view, and it comes out in their praise or criticism. For example, the teacher might be heard saying something like "Lisa is just not a math person. Jane will never get an A in my class. Jamaal is so smart; he doesn't even have to try. Kate needs to work hard because she'll never be as good as everyone else. Dan is college material; Pia is not. It's OK that Chris flunked calculus; not everyone has a mind for numbers."

The teacher with the growth mindset, however, believes his or her students are capable of high achievement regardless of the ability they bring to the task. With effort and practice, ability can improve.

Teachers' words and behavior in their teams and classrooms are influenced by their mindset about their students' capacity to learn and achieve (see Figure 2.2).

What Does the Teacher Believe in His Core About His Own Capacity to Learn and Improve as a Teacher?

Although not always the case, a teacher's fixed mindset about a student's ability can reveal a fixed mindset about his own capacity to learn and improve

Figure 2.2   Teacher's Mindset Toward Students

Mindset	Belief	Might Sound Like	Might Look Like
Fixed	Some students do not have the capacity to learn and achieve in a particular subject area. Regardless of effort, students' ability is limited.	A teacher says, "Every paper I get from Doug shows that he just isn't capable of thinking critically about text. I've tried everything and nothing works. There's nothing more I can do."	• Avoids changing instruction • Exerts minimal effort in trying to help the student succeed • Interprets constructive feedback on his instruction as a personal attack • Downplays or discredits other teachers' success with the student
Growth	Every student has the capacity to learn and achieve in all subject areas. With effort and practice, students' ability is unlimited.	A teacher says, "Every paper I get from Doug shows that he is not yet able to critically think about text. I've tried everything I know how to do up until this point, and I am ready to learn alternative practices that can work.	• Eager to teach all students regardless of beginning ability • Persists with unrelenting effort to help all students • Invites constructive feedback about his teaching • Inspired by other teachers' success

as an instructional leader. For example, a poorly performing teacher might say, "Jane will never get an A in my class," because that teacher does not believe in his own ability to get her to that goal. Teachers with a fixed mindset see limits to what they can learn and do as an instructor of students, and thus shy from learning in a team. They do not want to expose their shortcomings. They put in little effort to change because they don't believe it will improve their teaching or the student outcome.

Highly effective teachers can also have a fixed mindset about their own capacity to learn, in fact sometimes more so than poorly performing teachers. A look at Dweck's (2006) research about why gifted students underperform provides a clue. Gifted children do not need to work hard at that which they are born doing well. Consequently, when they do face a challenge they are likely to give up or avoid it all together for fear of diminishing their gifted image to others or even themselves.

Like gifted students, those teachers for whom teaching has always seemed like a natural fit, who are regarded in high esteem by colleagues and administrators, have a lot to lose if they fail. Since team learning requires risk and exposes failure, a highly effective teacher with a fixed mindset might close off to team learning in order to protect his image.

On the contrary, a teacher with a growth mindset has the desire to learn how to be a better practitioner and believes in his capacity to learn how. He is not only willing to risk failing in front of his colleagues because he is on a quest to improve, but he sees risk as necessary for his own improvement.

A teacher's beliefs about his capacity to learn and improve is reflected in his behavior in a team and in the classroom (see Figure 2.3).

Figure 2.3 Teacher's Mindset Toward Himself

Mindset	Belief	Might Sound Like	Might Look Like
Fixed	Teacher does not believe he is capable of learning how to develop into a better instructional leader for all students any more so than he already is. There is a limit to his teaching ability.	A teacher says, "It's impossible to expect me to get all of my students who are currently getting a zero on open response to increase to a one."	• Avoids challenges and high-stakes goals • Avoids putting too much effort in a team that seems as if it will fail • Disregards feedback • Threatened by other successful teachers
Growth	Teacher believes he is always capable of learning how to develop into an increasingly better instructional leader for all students. There is no limit to his teaching ability.	A teacher says, "I don't know how to get all of my students who scored zero to a one, but I am going to schedule observations and debriefs with colleagues who have done so in order to learn to do it too."	• Learns from setbacks in teaching • Puts in effort to improve his own teaching practice • Invites constructive feedback • Inspired by successful teachers

What Do I (the Team Leader) Believe in My Core About Students' Capacity to Learn?

Most likely, the skillful team leader believes that every student has the capacity to learn, and she will go to whatever lengths necessary to make certain of this. If a student lacks motivation and does not want to try, the teacher makes it her mission to uncover the causes for the lack of effort, considering that the student may in fact have a fixed mindset about his own ability in that subject area.

If the skillfull team leader does doubt a student's ability to improve, she finds the courage to learn where the doubt comes from and shares this doubt and learning with her colleagues, as well as her struggle to adopt a growth mindset. Applicable to team leaders who are teachers, Figure 2.2 defines each mindset and provides examples of what a team leader might say or do.

What Do I (the Team Leader) Believe in My Core About Teachers' Capacity to Learn and Improve?

Answering this question is where the work of being a team leader gets complex. A team leader who holds a fixed mindset about teachers believes that no matter what effort a teacher puts forth only some teachers can learn to be highly effective with students. On the contrary, the skillful team leader approaches the work with a growth mindset rooted in the belief that teaching ability can be cultivated through effort, study, and perseverance. Adult learning is developmental. If a teacher lacks motivation to change his instruction, the skillful team leader does not dismiss that teacher as someone who can never be highly effective, but instead uncovers why, keeping in mind that the teacher's own mindset about his ability might be the hurdle to overcome. With a growth mindset, she fosters team learning; with a fixed mindset, she shuts it down. Her words and behavior with teachers reflect whichever mindset she possesses (see Figure 2.4).

What Do I (the Team Leader) Believe About My Capacity to Lead Others in Change?

I have heard the argument "I believe teachers have the capacity to learn and change but only if they want to" (from the same people who believe it is a teacher's responsibility to tap into what motivates a child to learn). This, to me, indicates a team leader's fixed mindset about her own ability to lead.

Leading adults in learning for change is difficult and no one is born knowing how to lead skillfully (Lambert, 2003). Coming up against hurdles to team learning is part of the work, and it challenges team leaders with more and more nuanced dilemmas (as can be found throughout this book). Each dilemma can spin a team leader into self-doubt about her own abilities as a leader and can even make her want to relinquish the leadership role.

The skillful team leader holds a growth mindset about her own leadership and makes her growth as a leader a priority. She persists until her team excels. She perceives hurdles, such as resistance, as opportunities to develop and learn. If she believes that she can learn how to reach all adult learners, team learning is inevitable. If she does not, she won't persist in the way that is needed to achieve the learning and impact desired (see Figure 2.5).

Figure 2.4   Team Leader's Mindset Toward Teachers

Mindset	Belief	Might Sound Like	Might Look Like
Fixed	Team leader believes some teachers do not have the capacity to learn and develop into highly effective instructional leaders. There is a limit to their teaching abilities.	A team leader hears a teacher make a negative assumption about students and does not respond because she believes that teacher will never change.	• Avoids changing leadership style • Exerts minimal effort in trying to help the teacher succeed • Interprets feedback on her leadership as a personal attack • Downplays or discredits other leaders who have success leading teachers
Growth	Team leader believes every teacher has the capacity to learn and develop into a highly effective instructional leader. There is no limit to his or her teaching abilities.	A team leader hears a teacher make a negative assumption about students and investigates the assumption without judgment, saying, "I'm curious to learn more about what you mean by that statement." "What has informed your thinking?" "What positive and negative effects might this assumption have on our actions toward students?"	• Eager to lead all teachers in learning • Persists with unrelenting effort to help all teachers • Invites constructive feedback about her leadership • Inspired by other team leaders' success

Figure 2.5   Team Leader's Mindset Toward Herself

Mindset	Belief	Might Sound Like	Might Look Like
Fixed	Team leader does not believe she is capable of learning how to lead any adult team better than she already can. There is a limit to her leadership ability.	A conflict breaks out at the last team meeting causing the team leader to dread meeting again. She says to another team leader, "No matter what, I'll never be able to lead this team."	• Shuts down when hurdles arise • Avoids putting too much effort into a team • Disregards feedback • Threatened by successful team leaders
Growth	Team leader believes she is capable of learning how to lead any adult learning team more effectively with effort and practice. There is no limit to her leadership ability.	A conflict breaks out at the last team meeting, causing the team leader to dread meeting again. She approaches team members individually before the next meeting to hear feedback on her own leadership of that meeting. "I recognize that conflict in our last team meeting prevented us from reaching our desired outcomes. Could you share with me on why you think this happened and what I can do better as the team leader to help our team function better?"	• Learns from hurdles • Puts in effort to improve her own leadership • Invites constructive feedback • Inspired by successful team leaders

How Do Mindsets Impact Our Team's Learning?

Mindsets have an impact on team learning. As will be seen in subsequent chapters, even one person's fixed mindset can create hurdles for the whole team. However, teams do not need to be paralyzed by this. Mindsets can change (Dweck, 2006) and, in fact, must. "We can learn and reflect as much as we want, but the changes we hope for, or that others need from us, will not happen because all the learning and reflecting will occur within our existing mindsets" (Kegan & Lahey, 2009, p. 5). This does not mean the team has to wait for everyone to have a growth mindset before it is able to learn and change. In fact, Michael Fullan (2006) states that behaviors sometimes need to change before beliefs; once a teacher sees improvement is possible, his mindset shifts (p. 10). A skillful approach to leading teams begins with a heightened awareness of the impact that a team leader's mindset, and the mindsets of those she leads, has on team learning for student achievement.

THE DEVELOPING MIND

It's worth mentioning the work of two other prominent researchers in this field, Kegan and Lahey (2009), who provide a deeper understanding of the role of the adult mind and who I reference throughout the book. They present a developmental model that illustrates three stages of mental complexity, applied in the following to teachers in a team: the socialized mind, self-authoring mind, and self-transforming mind (see Figure 2.6).

A teacher with a socialized mind is strongly concerned with what others in the team think and consequently censors what he says and does. He is a good team player—pulling his weight and following the decisions that the team leader or others make—but doesn't put forth his own convictions. When members of a team have a socialized mind, the team leader is challenged with bringing forth diverse perspectives that will lead to better results for teaching and student achievement.

The next developmental stage is the self-authoring mind. A teacher at this level has strong convictions and holds steadfastly to his views. He shares his ideas and opinions freely, even if they are different from the team. This teacher is focused and self-assured and seeks opinions and ideas that fit with his direction and agenda.

Having a team made up of members with a self-authoring mind is good for team learning, but it can also present a challenge to a team leader, namely, conflict. A teacher with a self-authoring mind can struggle to see flaws in his own ideology and often disregards others' methods and values if they don't fit in with his own. The team leader is challenged with building a cohesive team that makes collective decisions on what is best for students even when opinions conflict.

The highest developmental level one can reach is the self-transforming mind where a teacher has strong convictions and clear direction but is not pigeonholed by them. He elicits feedback from colleagues that modifies his lens in order to refine it.

> The self-transforming mind can stand back from its own filter and look *at* it, not just *through* it. . . . [it] values and is wary about any one stance, analysis, or agenda. It is mindful that powerful though a given design might be, this design almost inevitably leaves something out. It is aware that it lives in time and that the world is in motion, and what might have made sense today may not make as much sense tomorrow. (Kegan & Lahey, 2009, pp. 20–21)

When team members possess a self-transforming mind, they are able to navigate new information, challenges, and change while using their ideology as a compass—always with the goal of deepening their understanding of the complexities of their work, even if it means thoughtfully shifting direction.

The skillful team leader possesses a self-transforming mind. She has well-formed convictions like someone with a self-authoring mind, but she approaches the team as a learner, constantly seeking a more complete picture. She does not force her beliefs on others, but she looks to expand her own notions of teaching and adapts to the challenges of attaining measured gains for students in a constantly evolving environment. She recognizes the developmental stages of members of her team and responds in ways, such as modeling, that helps the team develop a more self-transforming mind. Throughout this book, I share examples of teams encountering hurdles that may be caused by a team member's socialized or self-authoring mind and provide strategies for development.

Figure 2.6 Levels of Mental Complexity

Mental Complexity	Description	Might Look Like
Socializing mind	A person who faithfully follows leadership, a good team player	A teacher sees flaws with the team goal and action plan but goes along with it for team harmony.
Self-authoring mind	A person who authors and holds steadfast to a view, a problem solver	A teacher identifies a problem area from his own student data and sets a goal. Others in the team see more pressing issues in the data, the teacher listens only to rebut each point and defend his position.
Self-transforming mind	A person who can critically examine his own view and "re-author a more comprehensive view" (Kegan & Lahey, 2009, p. 26)	A team identifies a goal and action plan for students. Formative assessments reveal that the strategies the team has implemented in the past are not working. The teacher elicits feedback on not only how to do the strategy better but presses the team to implement a change in strategy—one that requires a major shift in how things are done.

Source: Adapted from Kegan, R., & Lahey, L. L. (2009). *Immunity to Change: How to Overcome It and Unlock the Potential in Yourself and Your Organization.* Boston, MA: Harvard Business Press.

CAN WE CHANGE OUR MINDS?

I opened this chapter with a reflective question, *Why do I believe all teachers can learn and change, and can I be an effective team leader if I don't?* I know my answer now, but before learning about Carol Dweck's work, I was unaware of the mindset I held or of the impact it had on those I led.

Over the course of my eighteen years leading adult learners, I have developed a growth mindset, but I did not start with one. As I reflect on my early years, I see evidence of my fixed mindset. At times, I lowered my expectations about what some teachers could achieve, and consequently, I didn't nudge and support them as I should have. Similarly, I didn't feel confident in respectfully challenging teachers who were considered outstanding; I believed they had nothing more to learn and would balk at anything our team or I suggested. In addition, I mistook some teachers' concerns about changing as an indication that they were just being resistant. Even as a teacher, I possessed a fixed mindset about my own abilities, sometimes quick to challenge my team leader when asked to implement something I didn't think I could do.

So how did my mindset change? As a teacher, I listened and learned from my colleagues, hearing their growth mindset about students—going to all ends of the earth to ensure that their students learned. I followed suit with my classes and ultimately realized that the adults I lead are learners too, needing the right conditions for growth.

As a team leader, I worked with teachers who at first were reluctant to make changes to their practice and later became champions of the change.

I noticed that when I responded differently to someone who had a fixed mindset about his own teaching, his mindset and actions began to shift. Instead of dismissing someone who showed resistance, I believed in his abilities, came to understand his concerns, and followed through with action. When he began to achieve, he began to believe.

Research taught me that adult learning is developmental (Helsing, Howell, Kegan, & Lahey, 2008; Kegan & Lahey, 2009). We are not born into our ability, and there is no cap to what we can learn (Dweck, 2006). Through tests of adversity, learning over time, and collaboration with others, we develop highly effective teaching practices. I am certainly living proof of this. I was faced with many challenges my first few weeks of teaching. Many thought I would not make it. And yet because an administrator had a growth mindset about my ability and put in time and effort to show me how to be more effective, I learned to view failure differently. Teachers who fail are not failures.

These experiences shaped my current belief that every teacher has the ability to learn and grow. It is also why I believe it is my responsibility as a team leader, entrusted with leading others in learning, that I (along with others) must maintain this growth mindset. If a team leader discovers that she possesses a fixed mindset about those she leads, she withholds judgment or self-deprication and instead works at developing a growth mindset about all learners. It is a journey, but one worth taking.

HURDLES TO MAINTAINING A GROWTH MINDSET

An individual's fixed mindset can show up in many forms, creating hurdles to team learning. Sometimes it causes a person to withhold from collaboration for fear of exposing her failures (Ch. 3). Other times, it shows up as a teacher reluctant to offer help to a colleague because the teacher doesn't believe his effort will make a difference (Ch. 4). Occassionally, it impacts a teacher's willingness to commit to a team goal when he thinks he can't attain it (Ch. 5). Frequently, a fixed mindset or a self-authoring mind can spawn resistance to implementing a new practice or adapting to change (Ch. 7). Throughout this book, I share snapshots of teams facing hurdles that are likely because of the presence of a fixed mindset and offer strategies on how to initiate a shift to a growth mindset.

CONSIDER SCHOOL CULTURE: SHIFTING FROM A FIXED MINDSET CULTURE TO A GROWTH MINDSET CULTURE

It is not uncommon to find people who possess a fixed mindset in schools. Students, teachers, and leaders who hold fixed beliefs about themselves and/or others exhibit that mindset through their words and actions, thereby shaping the culture of the school. Instead of creating an environment with Dweck's (2006) underlying message, "learning at all costs," the culture encourages people to hide their deficiencies, avoid learning risks, and blame other factors for failure. Although the school may set up teams and profess that they are a professional learning community (PLC), learning is discouraged.

Recognize the Signs of a Fixed Mindset Culture

- Master teachers are excused from professional development.
- Teachers who need the most improvement are excluded from professional learning teams for fear that they will be toxic to the group or hold the team back from making gains.
- Teachers reluctant to change are labeled "resistant" or "difficult."
- Leaders, parents, teachers, and students label teachers as "good" or "not so good" with no room for growth.
- Team leaders are thrown into the role without any leadership development.

Where Does This Fixed Mindset Culture Come From?

It is not easy to maintain a growth mindset about teachers when our current educational culture seems to perpetuate a fixed mindset, where teachers are labeled either "good" or "not so good." This Harry Potter "sorting hat" practice is dangerous because it creates a false dichotomy with no account for the role learning and growth play in the profession of teaching. Make no mistake, all teachers must be accountable to maintain high teaching standards for students and like all professions must have formal evaluations to measure their success at doing so. Any teacher who is presently harming children academically, emotionally, or physically should not be permitted to teach. A principal, even one with a growth mindset, needs to make hard decisions about a teacher's readiness to work with students, but a team leader must be wary about a school culture that thinks of teachers in an either/or fixed mindset way.

For one thing, team leaders are charged with leading adult learning. They cannot do this well if they believe in their core that some teachers can learn and change and others can't. Nor can they have an impact if they shirk responsibility for those teachers whom a school believes have potential but "just don't want to change." Their mindset impacts their effectiveness as leaders.

Additionally, a school culture that operates under the fixed mindset that some teachers "have it" and others "don't and won't" creates an additional hurdle for team leaders. Teachers told they are "good" are susceptible to thinking they have reached their potential and can't get any better, causing them to avoid risk for fear of failing and losing their "good" status in the eyes of others. Those teachers who are considered "not good" are often viewed by others and themselves as hopeless, written off as "resistors" or those who can't change.

Difficult as it may be, the team leader must hold a growth mindset about all adult learners, even when the school culture operates under a fixed mindset. The skillful team leader works with others to create a team space that fosters continuous learning for teachers in order to ultimately make measurable learning gains for students. To promote a growth mindset culture in school teams, the skillful team leader together with administrators and colleagues can do the following:

Trade labels for the word yet. Although it is part of school language for students, parents, teachers, and administrators to refer to others as a "good teacher" or "not so good teacher," schools must shift to specific descriptors that will help teachers grow. For example, instead of Mr. K saying, "I'm a failure as a teacher," he might say, "I am not yet capable of getting students with learning disabilities to read at grade level." Or someone might resist labeling Ms. J a resistant teacher and instead say, "Ms. J is not yet on board with this new initiative." This is more than semantics. Removing labels from our language fosters the belief that a person can change and become better, and it shares responsibility for that person's learning.

Create conditions for growth. The skillful team leader does not just offer moral support or encouragement to a teacher experiencing failure (e.g., "I believe you can"), but instead she accesses resources and creates conditions necessary for that teacher's success. If a teacher fails, the team leader might analyze the teacher's data with him, model a lesson for the teacher, arrange for peer observations, or find a relevant book to help him succeed. The team leader's belief in the teacher's capabilities drives her committed actions to help the teacher learn.

Foster a growth mindset in evaluators. The mindset an evaluator holds about a particular teacher influences the action she takes. If she does not believe in a teacher's capacity to learn (fixed mindset), she is likely to remove the teacher. If she does believe in that teacher's capacity to learn and change (growth mindset), she will likely create conditions that will result in swift teacher learning. Having a growth mindset about teacher learning does not mean that a teacher will stay on in the role he is occupying (as it ultimately might not be the right fit at the right time for that teacher and students), but it does mean that the evaluator, through her actions and words, respects that all teachers need the conditions and opportunity to be highly effective, instructional leaders, and fosters a learning environment for them to succeed, not a culture of fear.

The skillful team leader might facilitate a discussion at a school leadership team meeting where evaluators read about mindset and discuss fundamental mindset questions (see Figure 2.1) as it pertains to their roles.

Model. Leaders who are also learners demonstrate the importance of every educator seeking continuous improvement. An administrator or team leader can share his own learning challenges and seek input from others to improve.

Provide team leadership training. Just as teaching is not a fixed trait at which someone is born knowing how to excel, neither is leading (Lambert, 1998). Team leaders need to learn how to develop into skillful leaders. Forming a cohort, where team leaders meet regularly to learn from their own and each other's hurdles, can help. Observing live or recorded team meetings can be the basis for discussion about applying a skillful approach to overcoming hurdles. Leaders may also wish to use thought provoking questions for team leaders to reflect and create an action plan for improved leadership, as found at the end of each chapter in this book. Having a coach who provides feedback to team leaders on improving the function and impact of their teams can also help. Partnering with a local university who offers certificates for teacher leadership is another valuable support for team leaders.

A FINAL WORD

I believe that teachers vary in skill and ability throughout their career, developing mastery as they learn. A PLC believes in and invests in teacher development, always with the goal of achieving measurable gains for students. The skillful team leader believes every student, every teacher, and every leader has the capacity to learn and improve. Yes, there are moments when one might question this belief. I think that's only human. But these moments typically come on the heels of a challenging hurdle: When an internal or external obstacle to learning and student achievement presents the team leader with a dilemma, and when the team, said to be the "engine" (DuFour, DuFour, Eaker, & Many, 2006, p. 3) of a PLC stalls or breaks down. Regardless of the hurdles that come our way, team leaders are entrusted with leading learning for student achievement. The skillful team leader approaches the work with a growth mindset and self-transforming mind.

This book explores some of the most common hurdles that test our beliefs about adult learning. I reference fixed mindset, socialized mind, and self-authoring mind throughout the book as possible contributing factors for team hurdles, and I offer strategies on how to continuously advance team learning. As you read and lead, I invite you to hold to the fundamental core belief: Every person has the capacity to learn and achieve continuous improvement.

APPLICATION TO YOUR WORK: CONNECT, OBSERVE, EXPLORE, ACT

Think and write independently. Then, discuss with colleagues.

Connect	Observe
Remember a time as a leader or participant when you or a colleague exhibited a growth mindset. What behaviors did you see in the team? In the classroom? What impact did it have on student learning? On teacher learning?	Of what mindset are teachers on your team? How do you know? What mindset do you hold about teachers on your team? How does it impact your leadership of them? What evidence do you have that you hold a growth mindset about your own capacity to grow as a leader?
Explore	**Act**
What hurdles prevent you or teachers on your team from holding a growth mindset about student learning? About teacher learning? What have you done to overcome them? What have you not tried yet?	What will you and your colleagues do to foster a growth mindset about student and teacher learning? Name next steps and support needed.

Part II
Hurdles

Alone Together 3

*Overcoming Hurdles to Foster a
High-Functioning, High-Impact
Collaborative Team*

FOUNDATIONAL VALUE: COLLABORATION

Collaboration is fundamental to professional learning, but what does a team leader do with a group that is a team in name only? This chapter applies a skillful approach to hurdles that can obstruct collaborative inquiry. It offers suggestions to solve common dilemmas facing team leaders as they work to build a cohesive team that has a high impact on student learning, sometimes up against a school culture of alone together.

WHAT IS COLLABORATION, AND WHY IS IT NEEDED?

Teaming has become the primary vehicle for professional learning in schools. If one were to look at any school's professional development program, it likely includes many hours of time for teachers to collaborate. The collaboration most teams hope to achieve, but only some do, is that in which team members work well together, learn from one another, and implement change that yields measured gains for students.

Grouping people together and calling them a team does not necessarily result in collaboration that transforms a school. Just about any book on the subject of educator collaboration speaks of the importance of high-functioning teams. Team members must know how to work with one another. Teaming tools such as group agreements (also called "norms"), agendas, and protocols are known to move a low-functioning team forward.

Although improving a team's function is critical, it is not the only criterion by which a team's collaboration should be measured. Just as important as *how* a team collaborates is the measured impact the team's collaboration has on student

In support of collaboration:

- "Throughout our ten-year study, whenever we found an effective school or an effective department within a school, without exception, that school or department has been a part of a *collaborative* professional learning community" (Milbrey McLaughlin as cited in DuFour & DuFour, 2005)
- Forty thousand preK–12 teachers surveyed named *time for collaboration* as the second most important factor in retaining good teachers after *supportive leadership* ("Teachers," 2010).
- "A leader skilled in collaboration . . . know(s) how to balance the group's focus on the task at hand with its attention to the quality of members' relationships. They naturally create a friendly but effective climate that lift's everyone's spirits" (Goleman, 2002, p. 15).
- Huffman and Kalnin (2003) found that when science and math teachers engaged in collaborative inquiry, they not only changed their instruction but also began to impact schoolwide change.
- Collaboration is a critical factor in ensuring school reforms and mandates succeed (Hargreaves, 1994).
- "Improving schools requires the creation of collaborative cultures. Without the collaborative skills and relationships, it is not possible to learn and to continue to learn as much as you need to know to improve" (Fullan & Hargreaves, 1991).

learning. This requires teams to take a close look at what they are collaborating about and the outcomes they achieve. "In their most rigorous, robust (and somewhat rarer) forms, collaborative cultures . . . extend practice critically, searching for better alternatives in the continuous quest for improvement" (Hargreaves, 1994, p. 195). High-impact collaboration requires teacher team members to do more than just search; they must have evidence that their collaboration results in a change in instruction that brings about greater learning for students. The skillful team leader ensures his or her team is not only high functioning but also high impact (see Resource 3.1: Function vs. Impact).

The Team Function, Impact Matrix in Figure 3.1 illustrates four possible types of collaborative teams. Beginning in the top right quadrant and moving counterclockwise, they are Quadrant I: high functioning, high impact; Quadrant II: high functioning, low impact; Quadrant III: low functioning, low impact; and Quadrant IV: low functioning, high impact.

The ultimate place for a team's collaboration to fall is in Quadrant I: high functioning, high impact. Represented by a star in the matrix, the high-functioning, high-impact team works well together and produces measurable gains for students. Members have a shared purpose for collaboration with goals. They utilize teaming tools such as agendas, group agreements, roles, and protocols effectively. They voice different opinions but still come to consensus, produce action plans, and follow through on those actions. They not only engage in constructs like the inquiry cycle, but they use those constructs to continuously assess their impact on student learning and adjust their instruction. Members in high-functioning, high-impact teams are generally proud of their team and highly invested in the team's work. They continuously transform teaching and learning and have evidence to show for it.

Diagonally across from Quadrant I and represented in the matrix by a symbol of a sad face, Quadrant III: low functioning, low impact is the least desirable state of collaboration for a team. Members of a low-functioning, low-impact team not only struggle to work productively, but their collaboration has little to no impact on student learning and achievement. They typically lack purpose, disagree over goals, have unresolved conflict, consistently break norms, and have no real systems or

> **Figure 3.1** Team Function, Impact Matrix

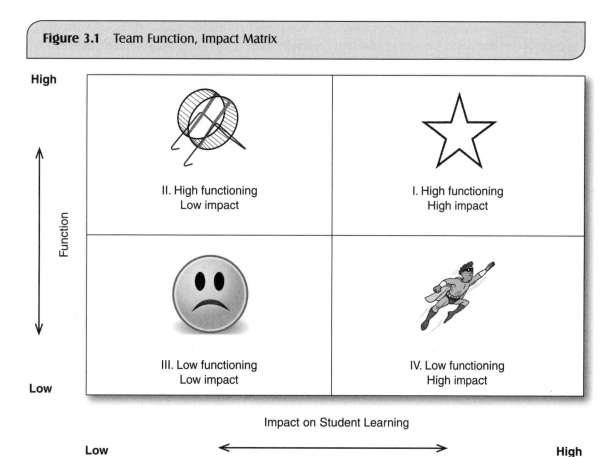

High

Function

II. High functioning
Low impact

I. High functioning
High impact

III. Low functioning
Low impact

IV. Low functioning
High impact

Low

Impact on Student Learning

Low ←——————————→ **High**

protocols to structure their collaboration. They seldom come to an agreement on decisions, and those decisions they do agree upon (i.e., picking a date to give midterms or determining a book rotation) have little to do with measurable student learning. Members in a low-functioning, low-impact team, as well as people outside of the team, are aware that the team needs significant improvement.

To the right of Quadrant III in the matrix is the low-functioning, high-impact Quadrant IV. A team whose collaboration falls here is peculiar in that its members function poorly as a group and yet still manage to achieve team goals and advance student learning. They meet together, but they struggle with interdependence. This can take the form of extreme independence or extreme dependence. The former is when individuals accomplish a lot but work in isolation. Acting in a culture of alone together, each member is a superhero in his own right, not a cohesive team. The low-functioning, high-impact team who takes the form of extreme dependence, relies heavily on a member, the lone hero, to carry and sustain high-impact results for the team. In neither case do the team members function well together: When the superheroes leave, so do the results. Any attempt to foster interdependence where team members learn from and rely on one another in a low-functioning, high-impact team often results in conflict, gossip, or withdrawal. Members in low-functioning, high-impact teams who single-handedly take on the goals of the team can feel resentful or can burn out quickly, while others who depend on them can feel helpless. When these feelings are not constructively expressed, tension can rise in the group, further dividing the team. Although the team achieves impact on student learning, results are likely not replicable because no one learns from one another (and members likely don't want to work together again). This quadrant is appropriately marked with a symbol of a superhero.

A team in Quadrant II: high functioning, low impact is deceiving to the untrained eye because it is extremely productive, yet what it produces yields little to no measurable gains for student learning. The team is efficient. Members utilize all the tools necessary for a high-functioning team such as group agreements, roles, protocols, and agendas. Their collaboration enables them to accomplish any task; however, the task on which they choose to collaborate has little to no impact on student learning. For example, the high-functioning, low-impact team might walk away with a better system for filing kids to lunch, a teacher coverage schedule for administering midterms, or even an instructionally related task such as a consistent way to collect homework, but the learning challenges students had when the team started collaborating remain. Represented in the matrix by a symbol of a gerbil wheel, the high-functioning, low-impact team appears to be advancing, but in matters of student learning, it gets nowhere.

Because this type of team works so well as a group, they are often not aware that the team's collaboration is not transforming teaching and learning. Members in high-functioning, low-impact teams are typically deeply invested in the work of the team and enjoy meeting. This leaves a team leader wondering how to shift to collaboration that will yield greater student-learning results without breaking the spirit and momentum of the team.

Key Considerations

The Team Function, Impact Matrix helps teams assess which quadrant they are in either on a given day, in a given cycle, or over the course of the year. It provides a framework for teams to talk about how they collaborate and how to do it better to achieve their student-learning goals (see Resource 3.2: Team Function, Impact Matrix Indicators). When using the Team Function, Impact Matrix, a team must keep three key points in mind:

1. It can be expected that levels of collaboration may vary over time. For instance, a team may be high functioning, high impact in one inquiry cycle and high functioning, low impact during another.

2. Although the categories are labeled "high" and "low" teams often fall along a continuum on either axis. This is why the matrix has arrows. For example, a team who has cocreated group agreements and reads them at every meeting, but doesn't respond when someone breaks one, might be considered "high functioning with area for growth" or "moderately functioning." What a team chooses to name the different levels of collaboration is less important than ensuring the team members are aware of their strengths and areas for growth in both function and impact as a team.

3. A team's placement in the matrix is not fixed. With skillful team leadership, every team has the ability to evolve into a high-functioning, high-impact team.

HURDLES TO FOSTERING A HIGH-FUNCTIONING, HIGH-IMPACT COLLABORATIVE TEAM

Collaboration is more than teaming people together. Any reality TV show today in which individual competitors are forced to collaborate on a team project, quickly reveals the challenges of attaining a high-functioning team. Many spend more time at odds than working interdependently as a team to achieve a shared goal. While school teams may not function as poorly as a team on Donald Trump's *The Apprentice*, they can have their fair share of functioning hurdles to face.

Even when the team leader is able to navigate group dynamics and create systems and protocols for working as a cohesive team, collaboration is insufficient unless the team's high function yields high impact for student learning. The skillful team leader is attuned not only to the function of a team, but also to its impact. Teams face hurdles in both domains, and the leader must have the skill to identify where the problem lies and work with the team members to improve their collaboration. Hurdles are exacerbated when a culture of alone together exists, where teachers are teamed but still think and act as if they are isolated.

A team leader might wonder, How do I foster a high-functioning, high-impact collaborative team when

1. we struggle to get along,

2. we are not working interdependently, or

3. we work well together but have little to no impact on student learning?

Dilemma 1: How Do I Foster a High-Functioning, High-Impact Collaborative Team When We Struggle to Get Along?

The idea of collaborating with colleagues is exciting for some and dreadful for others. Concerns around why a team is together and what it is working toward, combined with the micropolitics of working as a group can bring collaboration to a halt before it is even given a chance.

Consider the following snapshot of a team:

Jacqui leads a math team comprised of existing members from the previous year and new members to the team. Despite an agreement to start on time, a longtime member chronically comes late. The team's agenda is to analyze results of a common word problem assessment, but a side conversation erupts about logistics for an upcoming open house. Jacqui tries to bring the group together by asking, "Why do you think 60% of students got question three wrong?"

"They don't read the question," a longtime member responds.

"I think they just got confused in determining what the problem was asking them to do. We need to teach them key words," says a newer member.

"You're new to our group, but you'll soon learn that we have taught it every way possible. Why are we talking about this anyway?" says the longtime member. "I thought we were going to leave here with a plan for open house."

"If you came to our meetings on time," the new member mumbles, "you'd know our agenda."

The longtime member overhears and says, "I was working with a student. I think that's more important than coming here to do whatever we seem to be doing."

The new member does not speak again and time runs out without the team making any instructional decisions from the data. After the meeting, members split off—venting about others. Jacqui is concerned that unless she is able to foster a cohesive team, the bickering will continue, and the team will have no impact on anyone's learning.

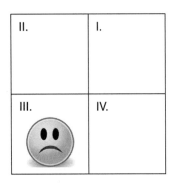

Identify the Hurdle

The team in this snapshot is a classic example of a low-functioning team: broken group agreements, off-the-agenda conversation, poor time management, and unresolved conflict. Add to this the challenge of blending new and existing members, and the team is bound to struggle with how it works together. This team spends more time bickering than problem solving. Although some low-functioning teams are able to achieve gains for students, this team is unlikely to have an impact since any attempt at an evidence-based discussion about student performance or math instruction is stunted by the dysfunction of the team. In order to get this low-functioning team to a place where they can have an impact on each others' and students' learning, Jacqui must uncover why the team fails to function.

Explore Possible Causes

It's a phase. Teams go through various stages in their life cycle together (Goleman, 2002; Tuckman, 1965). According to Tuckman (1965), teams move through five developmental stages: forming, storming, norming, performing, adjourning (see Figure 3.2).

The team in this snapshot is experiencing an "Us and Them" dynamic, characteristic of Tuckman's second stage in teaming called *storming*. It is here where a group might lack a shared purpose or have varied interpretations of why they are teamed together and what they intend to accomplish. People push for position, mistrust intentions, personally attack in a meeting or behind closed doors, and form cliques. In this snapshot, some members think they are collaborating about open house, others about a math word-problem assessment. One team member shuts down another's suggestion, causing her to withdraw from further participation. Following the meeting, team members form cliques further dividing the team.

Group disagreements. Group agreements, commonly referred to as "norms," serve to govern individual behavior, facilitate conversation, and keep the team productive (Champion, 1993). They create an environment safe for collaboration. When team members do not come to an agreement on how they

Figure 3.2 Five Stages of a Professional Learning Team (Based on Tuckman's Model)

FORMING	STORMING	NORMING	PERFORMING	ADJOURNING
• Unclear purpose • Superficial interactions, polite • Lack of established trust • Hesitant to share ideas and feedback • Members dependent	• Unclear purpose or clear with varied interpretations • Cliques, fight for position, mistrust • Shutdown of ideas • Resist feedback • Members independent	• Shared purpose, shared understanding • Agreed-upon approach to working together and solving conflict • Initial trust • Openness to ideas • Welcome feedback • Members interdependent	• Shared mission to achieve shared purpose • High trust, high risk • Seek alternate opinions and ideas • Invite feedback • Members interdependent • Evidence of influencing student achievement	• Achieved share purpose • Team dispersed but learning and implementation are sustained • Members interdependent

Source: Adapted from Tuckman, B. W. (1965). Developmental Sequence in Small Groups. *Psychological Bulletin, 63*(6), 384–399.

will interact as a team, they are more likely to be low functioning. In this snapshot, the team actually has some group agreements on how to work together such as starting on time, but one person chronically comes late. No one constructively addresses it.

Additionally, although the team has at least one group agreement about function, they lack agreement on behaviors that will ensure impact on student learning. Teams need to both norm for function and norm for impact.

Avoidance. One person breaking a group agreement might be a random event that resolves itself, but when someone chronically breaks an agreement, it could be a sign of a greater problem. In this snapshot, the longtime member prioritizes other things above the team's collaboration, consequently causing her to be consistently late to meetings. While the cause might simply be that she has too much to do in a day and not enough time, it might also be an indication that she is avoiding collaboration. Perhaps she is uncomfortable analyzing a common assessment with her colleagues as it might expose her own challenges as a teacher. Perhaps the team has been storming for several meetings, and she wishes to avoid further conflict. Or maybe the team regularly begins meetings late, flooded with announcements, and the teacher doesn't want to waste her time. Whatever the teacher's reasons, chronically coming late to a meeting might indicate more than a team member just needing to improve her own time management.

Contrived collegiality. Some teams struggle to function well because their collaboration is contrived. A term coined by Hargreaves (1994), *contrived collegiality* is when collaboration is administratively regulated, compulsory, focused on implementing others' mandates, scheduled formally, or with team members having little voice in purpose and outcome (p. 193). When teams do not have the ability to form organically, they may not all have clarity in why they are grouped together, as indicated by the longtime member's comment in this snapshot, "Why are we talking about this anyway?" Even if they are told why they are together, investment in collaboration is likely to be initially low.

Subculture. There is an unspoken code of how a team is supposed to function, and new team members pick up on it quickly. Even when a group just forms, a subculture is quickly established. In this snapshot, newcomers are perceived as an addition to an existing team, needing to learn the ways of the team as opposed to team members redefining themselves as a new, cohesive team.

Respond

Proactive response: To prevent a low-functioning team and maximize the potential for impact, a team leader can do the following:

Define purpose. The skillful team leader anticipates that when a team is forming, members are likely "concerned with defining the directions the group will pursue" (Tuckman, 1965, p. 8). Having clearly articulated, shared goals (Ch. 5) keeps the team focused and helps them move swiftly through the hurdles of working as a team. In this snapshot, Jacqui may have been able to prevent some of the dysfunction in the team by ensuring new and existing members understood that they were collaborating for the purpose of improving students' ability to answer word problems, not to talk about a low-impact issue like open house.

Preview Tuckman's stages. A team stuck in the storming stage is low functioning and at risk of being low impact unless they can learn how to work together. The skillful team leader makes her group aware of the stages so that they can anticipate expected challenges and move through them. For instance, a team might discuss how a high-functioning team versus a low-functioning team disagrees, and they may create structures to ensure their disagreements do not affect the impact the team has on student learning.

Appreciate different group styles. People need different things when they are learning in a group. The skillful team leader not only facilitates tolerance of different learning styles but fosters an appreciation of them. For instance, some people need to always have the big picture in mind, while others can't move forward with vision until the details are ironed out. Some members feel collaboration is not worthwhile unless it results in a product, while others are uncomfortable with deciding on a next step when not everyone has had a chance to voice his or her ideas and perspectives. Multiple styles in a group can generate conflict. The skillful team leader facilitates a means for members to express how their needs might differ from others. One effective and lighthearted way to do this is through the Critical Friends Group activity, Compass Points adapted in this book for teams (see Resource 3.3).

Get a new identity. It is important for the cohesion of the group to make those bringing a different perspective feel welcomed and valued. Together, the team can create new group agreements, adapt goals and action plans, or get input on existing ones. As the team looks and feels different, existing members will see the team as a whole and not as "our team from last year plus the newbies," and new members will take ownership too.

Norm for function and impact. The recommendation to establish group agreements early to ensure that the group functions well is not likely breaking news to any team leader. Statements such as "keep to time agreements" and "agree to disagree without being disagreeable" are just some ideas that often make up a group agreement list. But the skillful team leader norms for high impact as well as high function. For example, "Always bring evidence of student learning." Jacqui's team could norm for impact with the agreement to "leave every meeting with actionable instructional steps." The skillful team leader considers several suggested guidelines when setting group agreements to ensure high function and high impact (see the textbox on p. 38).

In-the-moment response: If function hinders the potential for impact, a team leader can do the following:

Assess and take action. The skillful team leader uses Tuckman's stages of a team or the Team Function, Impact Matrix to increase awareness of a team's function so that team members may identify what they need to move toward becoming higher functioning. Jacqui might ask, "Where in Tuckman's stages of a team are we now, and how do you know? What, if anything, might be keeping us from reaching Tuckman's performance stage?" Or she could lead the team in an assessment activity in which members individually place sticky notes on the Team Function, Impact Matrix. If the sticky notes don't all fall in the same quadrant, the team discusses why they marked the team where they did and name the challenges the team faces in becoming a high-functioning, high-impact team. Whichever assessment tool the team uses, the purpose is to promote dialogue that results in action steps team members agree to take to improve the team's function and impact.

Clear the air. When the elephant in the room is trumpeting, someone needs to say something. Daniel Goleman (2002) believes it is important to "short circuit the trouble rather than letting it smolder" (p. 184). Creating time for team members to express their feelings up front in a meeting might be enough to have them clear the air and move forward. The skillful team leader is transparent about the purpose of clearing the air and keeps to a strict time limit so as not to monopolize the meeting. A simple protocol based on "I statements" can move the group forward. Jacqui or another member could lead by saying, "*When* our team meeting ends without setting next instructional steps, *I feel* frustrated because I'm unclear as to what I am responsible for doing with our students. *I need* our team to better manage time so that we leave each meeting with clear follow through." After each person shares one statement, the conversation shifts to problem solving; what will the team commit to doing or changing? (Note: If problems are more complex than originally thought, the team leader can schedule additional time for the group to work through the

CONSIDERATIONS FOR GROUP AGREEMENTS

Co-construct. Groups feel more ownership if they write their own agreements (Richardson, 1999). Even if a team leader presents an initial list, she can foster ownership by providing time for team members to decide which items to keep, toss, revise, or add. Norms are intended to help the team accomplish their work, not take time from the work. The skillful team leader is thoughtful about scheduling time in the agenda for crafting group agreements and is careful that it does not monopolize the meeting.

Come to consensus. Once all have a chance to voice suggested agreements that will promote a high-functioning, high-impact team, members can reach consensus in which all members may not agree wholeheartedly with a decision but are willing to live with the decision, satisfied that their contributions were heard. Without consensus, expectations may be ambiguous, thereby opening the door to different standards of behavior. The skillful team leader ensures that each member commits to live by the agreements for the duration of the meetings.

Check for understanding. On paper, a group agreement can seem straightforward; however, unless the team assesses understanding, varied interpretations can reveal different expectations for different people, which results in conflict. Often, the discussion around the interpretation of the group agreement is more valuable than the words that make it to the paper.

For example, the agreement to "take risks" for some might mean trying a new practice once, but to others it means failing publicly, questioning a colleague who is "playing it safe," or risking judgment from colleagues by saying the unpopular thing. The skillful team leader facilitates short but meaningful discussion that defines broad, generic agreements.

Norm for broke. It is common for someone at some point to break a group agreement. The skillful team leader anticipates this and helps teams agree on a system for calling attention to a broken agreement and addressing it. Deciding on how to respond to a person who breaks an agreement before it happens shifts responsibility away from the team leader and onto the whole group. It permits the team to acknowledge the broken agreement and recommit to it. Some teams opt to speak out when an agreement is broken, while others prefer to give an agreed-upon silent signal during a meeting to heighten the group's awareness without disrupting the flow of the meeting. Whatever the team decides, having the discussion up front reduces angst that can occur when everyone knows an agreement has been broken but doesn't know how to address it.

Norm for self. It can be uncomfortable for one member to point out when someone else is breaking a group agreement. In addition to generating a short list of group agreements, a small team may choose to set personal norms of behavior (commitments) to which they ask the group to keep them accountable. For instance, "I know I often monopolize a conversation. My personal commitment is to listen more than talk. Please signal me when you hear me talking for more than two minutes." Someone else in the team is more likely to call attention to a broken agreement if the individual has requested that others make him aware of his behavior.

Revisit. Teams revisit agreements regularly throughout the course of a team's work: reviewing their meaning, assessing if they still work for the team, and redefining and adapting as needed. The skillful team leader might say, "These meetings are designed by us to enhance our learning as professionals so that we may better help our students. What we do here must be real and connected to what we are doing in the classroom. Our group agreements are in place to help us achieve our goals. If they are getting in the way of our work, we must revise them. If they aid us in reaching our goal, we must recommit to them." She also reads the emotions of team members to ensure that there isn't so much talk about group agreements that momentum for the work is lost.

problems on a different day, cautious that time spent clearing the air does not detract from time needed to collaborate on high-impact work.)

Agree and zoom in. The skillful team leader explores comments that create tension and responds in a way that will de-escalate the conflict. Instead of outright disagreeing with the speaker, she starts from a place of agreement that will allow the team to explore differences respectfully and productively. In this snapshot, the longtime member's comment, whether intentional or not, shuts down the discussion and silences the new member. Jacqui might reopen dialogue saying to the existing member, "That's a good point; we did teach it. Let's talk further about how we taught it." Then she can invite everyone's thoughts, including new members, on how the team can proceed.

Use humor. The skillful team leader lightens conflict with humor, particularly if the team leader has a good relationship or something in common with a member who has made a shut-down comment. She is cautious if using sarcastic humor—this might get a laugh but at the expense of another team member, which will likely create new tension.

Repurpose. The skillful team leader calls attention to the group's purpose for collaboration. A gentle reminder helps a team bond toward a common mission, refocus on students, and put differences aside. In this snapshot, Jacqui might say, "We agreed that the focus of our collaboration is on improving students' performance on word problems. Although planning open house is time sensitive, let's not lose sight of our purpose for meeting." If there is pushback she can schedule another time for the team to plan open house or carve out a portion of that day's meeting with specific outcomes for it. She might say, "I am proposing we use ten minutes now to create a list of logistical decisions needed, and who will make them, rather than taking time away from our team's purpose to make all the decisions jointly. Is there anyone who can't live with that?"

Follow-up response: To sustain a high-functioning team with potential for great impact on student learning, a team leader can do the following:

Approach individually. When a team is newly blended, the skillful team leader privately approaches new team members to inquire about how they are adapting to the team, offers support to make the transition smoother, and sincerely lets them know that the team is lucky to have their perspectives. If a comment by another team member is mean spirited or is a personal attack, the skillful team leader privately and with genuine curiosity approaches the teacher who made the comment. The team leader can then ask the teacher how he feels about the new makeup of the team and what he meant by the comment.

Respectfully inquire. The skillful team leader does not assume the reason for a team member who chronically breaks a group agreement, but instead states her observation of the broken norm without judgment. She then inquires what the difficulty is to help the teacher problem solve. In this snapshot, Jacqui might say, "I noticed you have come late to the past three meetings (pause)." Often, once prompted, the teacher will share the reason. If not, the skillful team leader might follow up by saying, "Is our start time working for you or do we need to adjust it? What can the team or I do to help keep our group agreement?"

Observe teams. Some teams are truly unaware of any dysfunctional aspects of a team until they see a high-functioning, high-impact team. The skillful team leader arranges for group members to observe how other teams work together (even low-functioning ones) and then comes back together to create action steps for the team to improve their own collaboration. This can be done through video, live observation, or a written transcript of a team.

School leadership team response: To foster high-functioning collaboration, team leaders, the principal, and administrators together can do the following:

Look schoolwide. Chances are likely that if storming is occurring at the team level, it is also happening schoolwide. The school leadership team examines collaboration throughout the school through questions: Are there specific individuals competing for position in teams and negatively affecting the culture of the school? Do teachers mistrust colleagues or administrators? Are teacher cliques dominating meetings? Are there times when members don't follow group agreements for our meetings that we lead?

If the answer is yes to any of the preceding questions, school leaders redirect the faculty to the purpose and urgency of the school's work and ask them to envision the culture that needs to exist for teams to be successful. Questions to pose might include the following: What are we here to do? Why? What conditions do we need to get there? What behaviors must we hold each other accountable to? What must we do and say in our interactions with each other, administrators, families, and students to achieve our purpose? What must we not say and do? What is destructive to our purpose?

If a team cannot, despite support from others, shift from low to high function and maximize impact, it might be in their best interest to reconfigure teams in a subsequent cycle.

Dilemma 2: How Do I Foster a High-Functioning, High-Impact Collaborative Team When We Are Not Working Interdependently?

It is somewhat expected that a low-functioning team will also be low impact. But what about the team that does not work well together yet somehow is seeing measured growth for students? Team members who rely too heavily on one person to attain results or who rely only on themselves, creating a circumstance where they are grouped together but act alone, are not a collaborative team. Consider the following snapshot:

> *Ellen leads a team of humanities teachers who regularly come together to analyze common unit quizzes that assess each student's grasp of specific concepts taught. Results are consistently good but conversation about them is typically stifled and awkward. Teachers often multitask during the meeting with minimal sharing. In looking at the results of a recent quiz, Ellen draws attention to one concept that a few students struggle with and asks, "What can we do differently?" Ellen hears audible sighs and sees some members grading papers and others texting. She says, "I'm wondering if we need to step back for a moment and check in to see how people think we are functioning as a group."*

One teacher responds, "Obviously, we are doing fine. We're getting better results than all of the other teams."

Another teacher speaks up. "Look, we all know what we have to do. Instead of talking about it, let's just go and do it."

A third teacher interjects, "Actually, I have four students that I'm not sure how to help, and I would love to hear more about what you do."

The first teacher responds, "Just send your kids to my classroom during lunch. I'll take care of it."

Ellen is pleased that quiz results have been good, but she is concerned about how long the team can have an impact when they don't collaborate.

Identify the Hurdle

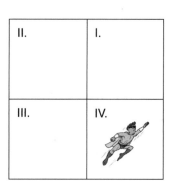

This team is having a positive impact on student learning, yet it is not functioning well. Collaboration is most frequently defined as a positive, interdependent relationship where members are mutually reliant on each other for every member's professional learning and the success of all students (DuFour, DuFour, Eaker, & Many, 2006; DuFour & Eaker, 1998; Senge, Kleiner, Roberts, Ross, & Smith, 1994). Ellen's team is low functioning, high impact because team members do not work interdependently. Most teachers on her team want to work independent of the group, relying on no one. The few who express interest in collaboration are thrust into a dependent circumstance where they must rely on one teacher to solve their problems for them. Jacqui is aware that although the team is achieving desired results for students, the members' inability to work interdependently is inhibiting their ability to become even better instructional leaders. Unless the group learns how to mutually rely on each other, teacher learning will flatline. Over time, the team's struggle to work together can limit the impact it has on student learning. Additionally, if one teacher is carrying the results for the team by taking on the superhero role, tension in the group is likely to build as the one teacher becomes overburdened and others increasingly feel disempowered. In order to understand why the team can't function interdependently, the skillful team leader considers causes for both types of behavior: extreme independence and extreme dependence.

Explore Possible Causes for Extreme Independence

No perceived need. Collaboration can be mistakenly viewed as something people who need help do; if a team is getting results for students, its members do not need to collaborate. Those operating under this assumption do not see how collaboration can be of value when a team is achieving its student-learning goals. Consequently, they are more likely to resist relying on others and learning publicly.

Dysfunction junction. If the team leader has not yet been able to facilitate a collaborative conversation where all members are co-constructing knowledge in a productive way, it is possible a teacher will get to the point where he resists working with others. When discourse is consistently awkward and unproductive, some members lose patience and opt to act independently of the group.

Preserving autonomy. It's not uncommon for a team to have one or more members prefer to work alone. Once considered the sole decision maker in the classroom, a teacher might have concerns that collaboration will result in loss of autonomy. In this snapshot, the notion of collaborating with others on teaching strategies can bring up concerns that teachers must conform their practice. If a teacher is passionate about a way of doing things, and is confident in its effectiveness, he or she is more likely to advocate working alone than learning new instructional methods from others.

Fixed mindset. Resistance to collaboration often shows up when people must "'expose' themselves" (Tuckman, 1965). Collaborating about instruction puts teachers' shortcomings out in the open. People with a growth mindset are open to this exposure, knowing they will become better practitioners because of it. But people with a fixed mindset are confident in what they can do and are less open to learning how to improve, concerned that they will lose credibility with the group if they can't maintain high results. In this snapshot, it is possible that the teacher who encourages others to pass along their students to him is actually trying to preserve his good standing among his colleagues and protect himself from having to reflect on his own practice publicly.

A teacher who is reluctant to work interdependently may have a fixed mindset, but not necessarily. It's possible he has a growth mindset about his own capacity to improve as a teacher, but holds a fixed mindset about his colleagues' abilities. In this snapshot, the teacher might offer to take his colleague's students because he doesn't believe that other teachers are capable of achieving the results that he can. His response actually encourages others to depend on him.

Results override learning. A strong focus on student-learning results is what collaboration must be about; however, teams must not lose sight that it is professional learning that will permit the team to be high impact year after year. In this snapshot, the team sees no problem with the way they interact because of the student results they achieve. They are not focused on how they and others in the team can learn more effective instructional methods from each other.

Explore Possible Causes for Dependence

Discouraged contributions. Although the teacher in this snapshot who offers to take others' students may have the best of intentions, he is actually limiting his colleague's contributions to the group. Frey, Fisher, and Everlove (2009) make observations about students that can apply to adult learners as well. They write, "They [students] are not going to have a positive picture of themselves as learners if they are not contributors to achieving the group goal. If students realize that they are not full participants, their self-talk is likely to turn negative: *I can't do this because I'm too stupid.* Fear of failure and embarrassment then creeps into the learning process and can form an invisible barrier" (p. 24). When team members do not feel like their contributions are valued, when they feel intimidated by another member, or when they are not being heard, they may begin to judge their own ideas and hold back.

Respond

Proactive response: To promote interdependence, a team leader can do the following:

Define the "why" and the "what" of interdependence. The skillful team leader engages team members in an early discussion about what it means to be interdependent and how it is critical to the team's function. The group articulates how to ensure each person is viewed as indispensable to the team. In this snapshot, Ellen might prompt team members to reflect on a previous team experience that either was or was not interdependent, share out, and then collectively decide how they will function interdependently.

Norm for interdependence. Once a team defines interdependence, they can create a group agreement to keep each other accountable to acting as such. They might agree to "equally contribute to ideas and actions" or "trust yourself, trust others."

In-the-moment response: If a team struggles with interdependence, a team leader can do the following:

Capitalize on success. The skillful team leader acknowledges the team's success and relates it back to collaboration. In this snapshot, Ellen might respond to her team members by saying, "Our quizzes indicate that our results are better than other teams' results. What value then does meeting together bring? How are we taking advantage of the great expertise in the room for sustainable student learning? How are we taking advantage of the great expertise in the room for our own learning?"

Access fears. Teachers need to voice concerns about collaboration safely, particularly if they have not worked together before as a team. The skillful team leader leads them in a process that surfaces individuals' hopes and fears about collaboration (see Resource 3.4: Hopes and Fears). For example, a teacher on Ellen's team might say, "I fear that if we use this time to collaborate on instructional strategies, I will be expected to change what I know works for my students. I hope we will be able to work together in a way that honors individuality." Airing expectations and concerns up front helps the team avoid hurdles that could generate conflict later.

Extend learning. The skillful team leader looks for moments when she can create professional learning opportunities. In this snapshot, Ellen might thank the teacher who offers to instruct other teachers' students and invite the teacher to model a live or videotaped lesson. (Note: So as not to put him on the spot, asking the teacher privately may improve the likelihood of him agreeing.)

Follow-up response: To sustain interdependent collaboration, a team leader can do the following:

Check in. The skillful team leader keeps a pulse on the team's interdependence. At different check points in a team's work she asks, "In what ways is our collaboration supporting your learning or limiting your learning? What evidence do you have of students benefitting from our collaboration? Do we have the right balance of independence from and dependence on each other? How do you know?" The skillful team leader also circles back to the team's definition and expectations of what it means to act interdependently and asks, "How are we staying true to this? What needs to change?"

School leadership team response: To facilitate interdependence, team leaders, the principal, and administrators together can do the following:

Model. If school teams operate too far to the left or right of interdependence, there is a likelihood that the school leadership team does too. If the school leadership team is only made up of a few "superheroes," and those are the people having the greatest impression on school decisions that impact student learning, a principal might need to invite school members who do not usually attend. If the school leadership team consists of members who act completely independent of one another, the principal or other leader can encourage individuals to rely on each other for solutions to common dilemmas using a protocol like the Consultancy (to access this protocol go to www.nsrfharmony .org/protocol/doc/consultancy_dilemmas.pdf). When the school leadership team made up of team leaders acts interdependently, team leaders experience a high-functioning team and have a model for the teams they lead.

Distinguish between consistency and conformity. Collaboration is an opportunity for teams to achieve consistency across content and grades, but it does not have to resemble every teacher abandoning their teaching style and individual decision-making ability. The school leadership team can hold frank conversations about what should be common (i.e., standards, benchmark assessments) and what can be distinct (i.e., daily in-class assessments to check for understanding). By putting less importance on listing what goes in each column and more on the purpose of what needs to be accomplished and what will help students achieve what is set out by the school's goals, school leaders are able to give teams decision-making ability over how they will achieve the goals.

Dilemma 3: How Do I Foster a High-Functioning, High-Impact Collaborative Team When We Work Well Together But Have Little to No Impact on Student Learning?

It's somewhat of a no-brainer that a low-functioning team needs a make-over. Teams who don't have a shared purpose for collaborating, who struggle to follow group agreements and agendas, who communicate through storming, or who can't find the yin and yang balance of interdependence, need a team leader who can find more sustainable ways of working together. So if a team does work well together, can it be left alone?

Consider the following snapshot of a team:

Carmen's ninth-grade English team starts every meeting on time, reading the agenda for the day and reviewing group agreements. Teachers equitably rotate roles. Recently, their department head charged them with improving reader's response notebook grades. Carmen leads her team in looking at notebooks to discover that 60% of students were not completing the required three entries per day. The team resists the urge to vent about previous teachers and instead follows their group agreement of "owning responsibility for all students." Teachers agree that getting 90% of students doing the minimum required entries would be a success. They give themselves six weeks to achieve this goal. They come to the consensus that students lack motivation and agree that raising the weight of the notebook would get more students to complete their responses. Team members respectfully debate if students should receive points for entries that are not written in complete sentences, eventually generating a rubric distinguishing between full and partial completion.

In today's meeting, the team is doing a notebook check to see how students are improving. Since they began four weeks ago, teachers see a 10% increase in completion. Motivated by the gain, teachers collectively agree to use this meeting to create a points system to incentivize students further. They volunteer to work through their lunch so they can begin implementing right away. Carmen is inspired by their commitment yet is concerned that although more students are completing more entries, the quality is poor. Students are not meeting the common core standard RL.9-10.1 to "cite strong and thorough textual evidence to support analysis of what the text says explicitly as well as inferences drawn from the text." When she suggests that the team hold off on adopting the incentive system and instead reflect on how the team's work is improving students' ability to respond with evidence to text, teachers object, saying, "We don't need to reflect; we're working great as a team."

Another teacher adds, "We've been looking at the responses and using the rubric and kids are starting to get higher grades. Let's keep working on the new points system; we're getting so much done."

Identify the Hurdle

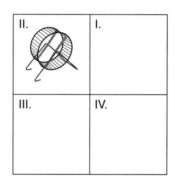

Carmen's team is classic high functioning; they cocreate agendas, keep to their group agreements, and come to consensus on a goal and action plan. They even work through disagreement to craft a rubric to assess students' completion of responses. They are adept at working together, and yet to what impact on student learning does their collaboration yield?

DuFour and Eaker (1998) recommend schools assess their teams not by asking the question, "Are we collaborating?" but instead by asking, "*What* are we collaborating about?" A team can be high functioning yet what they are collaborating about can have little to no impact on student learning. The most obvious "what" that teams must put in check is collaborating on operational tasks such as field trips, open house, fire-drill protocols, fund-raisers, book-rotation schedules, science-lab procedures, and the like. It's not that this type of collaboration is not real. In fact, Hargreaves (1994) points out that collaboration is valuable so long as it achieves its purpose. Different teams collaborate for different purposes, and if a team sets out to plan a book rotation and accomplishes it, they have collaborated effectively; however, teams that strive to make gains in student learning cannot only collaborate on book rotations, open houses, and the like. According to DuFour and Eaker (1998), collaborating on operational tasks may achieve improvement in the function of a school event or procedure, but it will not transform learning.

It makes sense that a team focused on operational tasks won't have an impact on student learning, but what about teams like Carmen's? They are not planning field trips or the next bake sale. Their goal is student centered and connected to instruction: to improve students' reader's response notebook grades. However, their productivity yields no advancement in learning. This team is high functioning, low impact. Carmen must uncover why a team that works well together and accomplishes each task they set out to do has no impact on student learning. Then she can begin to determine why the team seems reluctant to address the problem and shift the team toward higher impact.

Explore Possible Causes

Seemingly SMART goal. A high-functioning team has a shared purpose for collaboration; however, their impact on student learning is determined by the goal(s) they have chosen. While Carmen's team has a goal and even a rubric to measure progress toward that goal, the goal is Seemingly SMART. Further explained in Chapter 5, a Seemingly SMART goal specifies and measures an outcome for students, but it does not name or measure a learning outcome. Carmen's team sets out to achieve greater completion of reader's response notebook entries (and they do), but students don't get closer to mastering the learning standard. The team gets deeper into the pitfalls of a Seemingly SMART goal by focusing their collaboration on the development of an incentive system to encourage greater completion. Even if they accomplish this task (which is likely since they are so high functioning), they won't have any impact on how teachers' teach or what students are learning.

High impact, high risk. Collaborating for high impact on student learning requires each team member to dive deep into their individual effectiveness as a teacher. For some team members, this is a risk they don't want to take with their colleagues. Developing a points system for students, such as the one designed by Carmen's team, does not require anyone to engage in rigorous discourse (explained in detail in Ch. 6) about their instruction. Fear of discovering (or being discovered) that their instruction is ineffective and needs to change or having concern that sharing one's struggles might not be kept in confidence may be a cause for the team to remain low impact.

Momentum. High-functioning teams are highly productive teams. They get things done. And this makes for highly invested, motivated members. Teachers in Carmen's team are enthusiastic about their progress and their plans. They are even willing to extend the meeting through their lunch time to finalize their incentive points system. With team momentum charging ahead, it's no wonder that Carmen's suggestion to pause and readjust their plan is met with polite opposition.

Respond

Proactive response: To prevent a team from becoming high functioning, low impact, a team leader can do the following:

SMARTen up. The skillful team leader starts with a goal that specifies and measures a student learning outcome. If the team seems to settle on a Seemingly SMART goal (explained in greater detail in Ch. 5), the team leader skillfully guides members to focus on learning. For instance, Carmen could say to her team, "Currently, we are determining student success by a rubric that measures students' rate of completion. Is it possible for students to show improvement on our rubric, yet not improve on learning standard RL.9-10.1? We can continue to monitor completion, but we must also determine how to measure improvement of students' ability to respond to text with evidence."

Norm for confidentiality. In order for a team to collaborate for greater impact on teacher and student learning, teachers need to feel safe looking at student work and talking about instruction. The skillful team leader creates a safe space for learning. Adopting a confidentiality norm such as the "Vegas" norm, "What happens in the team stays in the team," can allow team members to take risks that can yield greater learning.

In-the-moment response: If a team is high functioning, low impact, a team leader can do the following:

Name the learning outcome. If a team's outcome for a meeting is not focused on student learning, the skillful team leader finds value in it and shifts the team. For example, Carmen might say, "Creating an incentive system for students to complete their notebook entries will likely help some students who know how to do the work but are underperforming because of low motivation. What do we need to leave with today that will help students who don't know how to do the work—those who might not be completing entries not because of low motivation, but because they aren't able to write with evidence from the text yet?"

Assess impact. The skillful team leader aids the group in assessing the impact of its collaboration on student learning. The Team Function, Impact Matrix Indicators (found in Resource 3.2) is a tool team members can use to assess where they are, discuss why, and strategize what they need to do (and stop doing) to be higher impact. In this snapshot, once Carmen's team members identify themselves as high functioning, low impact, they can take action steps, reworking their goal and agenda, to see which tasks will yield the greatest impact on student learning.

Craft a team vision. Just like a school crafts a vision for what success will look like, the skillful team leader guides his or her team to craft a vision of itself as a high-impact team. Carmen might ask teachers, "If in three weeks we are a high-impact team, what would a video capture us saying and doing in a meeting? What would it not show us saying or doing?"

Engage in inquiry. Teams who are not seeing the impact on student learning that they expect are likely in need of an evidence-based inquiry cycle (see box on pages 48 to 49). Carmen's team might investigate why the increase in students' written responses is not yielding better evidence-based writing.

Collaborative inquiry is the vehicle teams in a professional learning community (PLC) use to improve teaching and learning. "An inquiry approach . . . calls on all teachers to bring all students up to grade-level standards. Teachers are asked to diagnose the learning needs of struggling students and design instructional responses and system changes that meet their learning needs" (Talbert, 2011, pp. 131–155). If one Googles the "inquiry cycle," over three million images come up (including a slug—not sure how that one fits). Essentially, most versions speak to the same process, which Richard DuFour and Becky DuFour (2007) lay out neatly. "Teams in a PLC:

- Set results-oriented goals specifically linked to school and district goals;
- Analyze interim assessment data;
- Identify areas in which students are struggling;
- Build shared knowledge on how best to address those areas;
- Develop and implement short-term action plans to improve students' performance;
- Analyze data to see what worked and what didn't;
- Help each other as they work toward their goals;
- Continue this process in an ongoing cycle of improvement" (pp. 27–28).

A version of the inquiry cycle that I have adapted from multiple sources[1] is shown in Figure 3.3.

Teams engage in the following cycle over a period of time (typically 4–8 weeks, depending on the frequency of meetings):

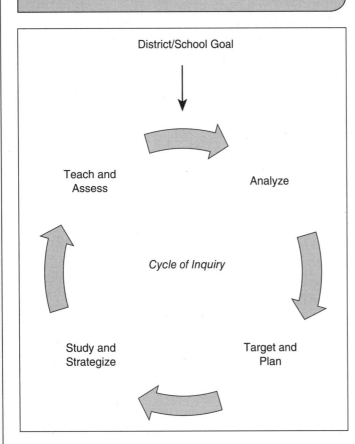

Figure 3.3 Cycle of Inquiry

District/School Goal

Teach and Assess

Analyze

Cycle of Inquiry

Study and Strategize

Target and Plan

- *Analyze.* The team analyzes instruction and various forms of student data to investigate a teaching question or learning problem aligned to the school goals. The team uses data to determine strengths and needs of students. The team members discuss how a skill, concept, or standard has been taught, inferring causes for why students perform as they did.
- *Target and plan.* If this is the first inquiry cycle for the team, members set long-term SMART goals. If long-term SMART goals have already been set, the team decides on small SMART learning targets for specific groups of students that will advance the team toward its long-term goals (Ch. 5). The team members set a timeline for when students will master the targets. They determine interim assessments

to monitor progress and create or select a postassessment to measure gains at the end of the inquiry cycle.

- *Study and strategize.* The team consults current research and texts and shares best practices to gain strategies that will ensure students achieve targets. The team decides what actions to implement, when, how, and what resources it needs.
- *Teach and assess.* The team implements strategies and action plans. The team collects data to monitor student progress and teacher implementation. A predetermined postassessment is administered to determine which students met learning targets. Team determines next steps.
- Cycle repeats.

Simply engaging in an evidence-based inquiry cycle does not ensure a team will have a high impact on student learning. As can be seen throughout the snapshots in each subsequent chapter of this book, it is common for a team to encounter hurdles at each stage. The skillful team leader anticipates these hurdles and works with the team to navigate around them to maximize its impact on student learning.

[1]*Sources:* Boston Public Schools (2003); CES National (1999); Deming's Plan-Do-Study-Act Cycle in DuFour, Dufour, Eaker, and Many (2006); Scaffolded Apprenticeship Model (SAM) in Scharff, Deidre, DeAngelis, & Talbert (2010); Talbert (2011); The Leadership and Learning Center's Six Step Data Team's Meeting Process in Leadership and Learning Center (2012).

Follow-up response: To sustain a high-functioning, high-impact team, a team leader can do the following:

Observe and assess. The skillful team leader arranges time for the team to observe themselves through video or other teams to determine where they are in the Team Function, Impact Matrix. Having an evidence-based discussion, team members are able to notice areas of strength as a team and moments that hold them back from having a greater impact on student learning.

School leadership team response: To foster high-impact teams, team leaders, the principal, and administrators together can do the following:

Multipurpose. Not every team meeting must be high impact. Teams need time for collaborating for different purposes—the nuts and bolts of an open house are important. School leaders work with team schedules to provide meeting time for both operational tasks and collaboration that yields a high impact on student learning—monitoring to ensure the former doesn't outweigh the latter.

Model. Just as it was advised in the prior dilemma that the school leadership team be a model of a high-functioning team, so should they be high impact. Members should be able to point to measured learning outcomes for students. For instance, the team should not only work on testing schedules for the school, but it should also analyze test results, looking for trends and patterns, determining priorities for the school, and determining next instructional steps for underperforming students. In doing so, team leaders experience being a part of a high-impact team and can improve their own.

CONSIDER SCHOOL CULTURE: SHIFTING FROM A CULTURE OF ALONE TOGETHER TO A COLLABORATIVE CULTURE

Teams striving to be high functioning, high impact have an additional hurdle to overcome when there is a gap between what a school values as collaboration and what is actually practiced. When a school culture of alone together exists, educators are physically teamed together, and they may even be collegial, but remain guarded in their collaboration. Instead of building collective strength to continuously improve learning for both adults and children, individuals in this school culture hold on to assumptions that dictate who, when, about what, and why people would collaborate. These assumptions can limit the learning potential of teams.

Recognize Signs of a Culture of Alone Together

- Pockets of collaboration exist. For example, "Our middle school math department collaborates so well; I'm so glad I'm not at the high school where no one even talks to each other."
- Teachers within a team might collaborate but competition or isolation keep teams from learning from one another.
- Collaboration is not reciprocal or mutually beneficial. A teacher might offer help without realizing she has an opportunity to learn as well. For instance, a teacher might say to another, "I heard you were teaching X next semester. Here is my curriculum binder. You're welcome to use anything in it. If you have any questions just ask" rather than discussing the curriculum together so that both teachers improve.
- PLC is something people do; it is not something they are. Teachers come together during scheduled team time but rarely when not scheduled. For instance, a teacher might say, "When is our PLC meeting this week?"
- Teachers opt out of participation in a team. It might sound like, "You guys work it out. My kids did fine."
- Administrators view collaboration as something for *teachers* to do, not them. During time when teams meet, administrators are doing nonlearning tasks (i.e., writing reports at their desk, calling parents, etc.)
- The principal gives praise to an individual or team, and others poke fun or are jealous.
- Another in-district school has strategies for success but does not share.

Where Does the Culture of Alone Together Come From?

Teaching has always been, and to some degree still is, an isolating profession. One does not have to go back to the days of the one-room schoolhouse to see examples of teachers having little opportunity to interact. Numerous schools have made efforts to promote collaboration through the structure of teacher teams, but this does not immediately change assumptions and behaviors.

People in a school where a gap between valuing collaboration and doing it well exists, might assume that collaboration is for novices who need help. Educators embrace it as a tool to support someone new to teaching or a curriculum. They will gladly collaborate in a mentoring or coaching capacity. Teams are even willing to cross-collaborate when it is for the purpose of helping each other, such as an English language arts team helps a science team to teach students how to write better research reports.

Collaborating for the purpose of helping is beneficial, but this definition is limiting for two reasons: First, if someone is not a novice and needs help, he or she may not ask for it. Asking for help can make people feel inferior and vulnerable (Schein, 2009). Second, once someone gains expertise, he or she no longer sees value in collaborating.

Limited beliefs as to who can learn from whom also promote a culture of alone together. On one hand, an experienced teacher may dismiss collaborating with a beginning teacher assuming the novice has little to offer. Along the same logic, a new teacher may assume her newly learned methods are more current and relevant than those of a longtime practicing teacher who has been out of school for years. Similarly, a content teacher might not see value in meeting with a specialist teacher (i.e., physical education) simply on the assumption that the specialist can add no value to the content teacher's learning. The same type of assumptions can hide in administrator–teacher relationships, where a principal may think he can learn nothing he didn't already know from collaborating with a teacher and vice versa. Assumptions about from whom one can learn (and from whom one can't) can cause friction and resistance within teams.

Assumptions about which individuals can function together as a group and which can't add to the complexity of collaboration. The thought that collaborating with friends will yield higher functioning, higher impact teams instead of putting people with different perspectives together is actually a misperception (Kain, 2006). In fact, it is the differences that lend to a richer learning experience.

On the surface, these assumptions dictate how people respond to collaborative teams. Mistrust can often be found underlying the assumptions in a school culture of alone together. Teachers and leaders are guarded. They hesitate to share their "special sauce": that which makes them unique and irreplaceable to the school. They place their individual accomplishments above the collective. Paradoxically, when an individual is recognized for an accomplishment, others are jealous or discredit the accomplishment by putting the individual down, consequently isolating the individual from the team even more. Instead of fostering a culture of collaboration where successes are genuinely celebrated, individuals in a school culture of alone together shrink from public recognition or being labeled experts.

To make the shift from a culture of alone together to a collaborative culture is a challenging, ongoing effort. When a school culture is collaborative, collective learning is valued. Being a learner is not viewed as a weakness but instead as something that is essential for the growth of every educator regardless of experience. Everyone is a learner and a leader of others' learning. Healthy competition with oneself drives the work for continuous improvement instead of pitting one person against another. Like an ensemble in a successful theater production, each person is unique and important to the whole, but it is the performance as a group that gets the standing ovation.

When a school discovers they are collaborating in a culture of alone together, a team leader together with other school members can do the following:

Foster trust schoolwide. Patrick Lencioni (2003) coined the phrase *vulnerability-based trust* and defines it by saying, "Members of a cohesive, functional team must learn to comfortably and quickly acknowledge, without provocation, their mistakes, weaknesses, failures, and needs for help. They must also readily recognize the strengths of others, even when those strengths exceed their own" (p. 36). The only way to make admitting mistakes and asking for help common practice is to examine how a school responds to the person who speaks up. People need to be both praised for being vulnerable and supported in learning from the mistake or failure. If anyone is humiliated, the school can bet that the next person is less likely to ask for help.

Open the market on sharing. A collaborative culture neither withholds good ideas and effective practices from each other nor loots people of their unique contributions. Members in the school community honor intellectual property, but they don't build a fence around it. Establishing a practice of giving credit to individual teachers that includes bylines on handouts and recognizes teachers as professionals paves the way for teachers to feel encouraged to share what makes them uniquely successful.

Make celebration a tradition. "Find the good and praise it," Annette Bailey, a former assistant principal, once told our staff. Schools unafraid to celebrate student-learning accomplishments create a culture ripe for collaboration. People want to know how others achieve success. A public shout-out at a staff meeting about a teacher having a measurable impact on student learning or a bulletin board highlighting students' growth as a result of a team's work together can spark uncontrived collaboration.

Note: Just as Rick DuFour noticed when he first began celebrating small academic wins publicly, teachers may initially be uncomfortable, but once public celebration is a routine and they partake in the nomination of individuals and teams, the tradition will become the new status quo (Deal & Peterson, 1999).

Ask courageously. Having conversations that challenge an existing culture of alone together is not easy. School leaders and teachers looking to shift the culture need to initiate courageous, reflective conversations about collaboration. Some question prompts include the following:

- Why do we meet in teams? What percentage of our teams are high functioning, high impact? How is team collaboration improving learning for adults and students? When does it work? When does it not work? What school and team conditions support or impede collaboration for high impact? How can each of us take responsibility for engaging in continuous learning in order to have a high impact on student learning?
- Individually rate one to five (one being the lowest, five being the highest) how much you trust collaborating with your team? Other teams? Administrators? District leaders? What level of trust do teams need to be high functioning, high impact? What do we need to do as a school to attain or sustain high-functioning, high-impact teams?

APPLICATION TO YOUR WORK: CONNECT, OBSERVE, EXPLORE, ACT

Think and write independently. Then, discuss with colleagues.

Connect	Observe
Remember a time as a leader or participant when you engaged in a high-functioning, high-impact team. What did collaboration look and sound like?	Where does your team fall on the Team Function, Impact Matrix now? What do you see and hear that informs your assessment?
Explore	**Act**
What hurdles prevent your team from being high functioning, high impact? What have you done to overcome them? What have you not tried yet? Why?	What will you and your colleagues do to be more high functioning, high impact? Name next steps and support needed.

Not It 4

Overcoming Hurdles to Achieve Shared Leadership for Learning

FOUNDATIONAL VALUE: SHARED LEADERSHIP

Professional learning relies on the foundational value of shared leadership. This is more than sharing the workload; it is sharing responsibility for learning. But what if leaders and teachers are unaccustomed to sharing? This chapter applies a skillful approach to the hurdles a team faces when leading each other. It offers solutions to complex dilemmas for team leaders who seek to foster shared responsibility for learning within a team and school. It examines the gap in school culture between believing in shared leadership and putting it into practice, and it offers strategies for team leaders to begin closing the gap.

WHAT IS SHARED LEADERSHIP FOR LEARNING, AND WHY IS IT IMPORTANT?

Not too long ago, there existed a "Mighty Mouse" view of leadership—bring in a single, dynamic principal to "come and save the day." But many now agree that this leadership model is flawed. If the outstanding leader leaves, the school flounders, and if the leader stays but does not live up to his heroic image, he is blamed for failure, while others can abscond from responsibility.

Today, many schools emerging as professional learning communities (PLC) are structured in teams ripe for shared leadership. The principal trades in his solo act for collaboration with a team of leaders who lead others in realizing the school's vision. Building capacity in this way has the potential to transform a school when every member of the school community has a "shared responsibility for a shared purpose" (Lambert, 2005). While a principal or administrator might share leadership with teachers for the purpose of creating an exam schedule, designing a student award ceremony, or executing a school fundraiser, in a PLC the purpose is always learning.

Schools that share leadership *for learning* uphold the following six beliefs:

1. Good ideas about how the school can achieve its vision and goals can come from anyone. One doesn't need the title of "leader" to lead learning. The ideas generated should influence decisions about student learning.

2. Leadership is clearly defined. Clear expectations are set for leaders with formal roles and understood by the school community. Expectations of those without formal leadership titles are well defined as skillful contributors.

3. Shared leadership for learning is more than distributing roles and responsibilities to a few individuals (i.e., a principal shares with a few team leaders or a team leader spreads responsibility among her team with roles like note taker and timekeeper). Designated leaders mobilize their colleagues to make teaching decisions that align to the school's vision and goals.

4. Teachers and leaders are responsible for their own *and others'* professional learning in order to improve student achievement. They actively participate in the design and implementation of individual, team, and school-wide learning goals. If a professional learning experience does not provide what that teacher needs to best meet her students' needs, she acts to change it. If a colleague is reluctant to learn how to improve his instruction for the benefit of his students, teachers and leaders support him.

5. Learning is reciprocal. Leaders learn alongside teachers. All share responsibility for student failure as well as success.

6. Formal leaders in successful schools don't share leadership for learning as a courtesy to teachers, as a means to generate support for their own agenda, or to lessen the load of their own responsibilities. They do it because they can't achieve high impact on student learning without it.

Source: based on Lambert (2009), pp. 12–13.

HURDLES TO ACHIEVING SHARED LEADERSHIP FOR LEARNING

Principals in schools with high-leadership capacity know that sharing the lead with team leaders is not enough. In fact, it can have a negative effect on a school by creating an "Us and Them" culture where the "chosen" lead and others are left to follow. Instead, team leaders have the responsibility to foster shared leadership for learning within their teams. This can prove challenging.

Sandwiched between administrators and teacher teams, a team leader who is a teacher must often overcome hurdles from two angles—sharing the lead with colleagues and sharing the lead with school leaders. A team leader may struggle to get teachers to lead learning causing her to feel overwhelmed with responsibility. Another team leader might have teachers enthusiastic to take on team responsibilities, but they lack the leadership skills necessary to keep the team advancing. Or a team leader might find team members are comfortable taking on leadership tasks but uncomfortable leading learning when colleagues show resistance. And perhaps the most challenging hurdle a team leader can face is when her team is willing and capable of leading learning, but a principal or administrator is not—when mistrust between those with authority and those without permeates the culture.

A team leader might wonder, How do I foster shared leadership for learning when

1. everyone expects me to take the lead, or

   - *on the flip side . . .* no one is the designated leader;

2. some members are ineffective at moving the team forward;

3. individuals are willing to lead tasks but not learning; or

4. no one in the team has authority to make decisions (including me), or

   - *on the flip side . . .* I have authority, but it works against me?

Dilemma 1: How Do I Foster Shared Leadership in a Team When Everyone Expects Me to Take the Lead?

In support of shared leadership:

- A 2010 study funded by the Wallace Foundation finds that "collective leadership has a stronger influence on student achievement than individual leadership. Almost all people associated with high-performing schools have greater influence on school decisions than is the case with people in low-performing schools" (Wahlstrom, Louis, Leithwood, & Anderson, 2010, p. 8), and "when principals and teachers share leadership, teachers' working relationships are stronger and student achievement is higher" (Wahlstrom et al., p. 39).
- Distributed teacher leadership is critical to sustaining success of student learning (Jacobson, 2011).
- Teachers who lead other teachers are often more able to get buy-in for reforms than educational officials or principals (Margolis, 2009).
- Better decisions are made when those affected by them have a voice in making them (Lambert, 2005).
- "It (shared leadership) increases the chances that the alternative ways in which problems can be formulated and resolved will be scrutinized and act as a control against premature closure and the tendency to think that there is only one way by which problems may be viewed and handled" (Sarason, 1971, p. 161).
- There is shared mutual responsibility for shared purposes and outcomes (Senge, Kleiner, Roberts, Ross, & Smith, 1994). Teachers are more likely to take responsibility for the outcome of a decision when it is one they helped to make.
- Sharing leadership enhances teacher morale, job satisfaction, and feelings of empowerment (Dinham & Scott, 2000; Leithwood, Louis, Anderson, & Wahlstrom, 2004).
- "When teachers have a genuine part in making decisions and implementing changes, they become more committed to reform efforts. In a collaborative culture, reform is not imposed upon teachers but created by them" (Lummis, 2001, pp. 4–5).
- Building capacity through teacher leaders sustains improvement as higher-up leaders come and go (Lambert, 1998).

According to Lambert (2000), "Every person has the potential and right to work as a leader" (p. 12), but what if no one is eager to? Although research demonstrates that having a team leader improves a team's performance, it can discourage other members from leading each other in learning.

Consider the following snapshot of a team:

> *The principal asks Nadia to be the team leader of the seventh-grade math team because of the results she achieved on last year's state exam. He expects Nadia to share her expertise with her colleagues so that other teachers can get the same results. Whenever Nadia shares something she does well in her class, teachers in the*

> *team get quiet. She asks, "How could this strategy work in your own classrooms? Does anyone else have a successful strategy to share or know of a professional text that could inform us further?" For an uncomfortable minute, the teachers just look down at their papers. Nadia is concerned that her leadership title is keeping others from stepping forward.*

Identify the Hurdle

Leadership cannot be limited to a few chosen people. All members of the school community must be empowered to lead in learning. Nadia provides multiple opportunities for others to lead within her team, but teachers are reluctant. She invites teachers to share their best practices so others can learn from them. She asks teachers to extend their own learning by discussing applications of new strategies. She tries to engage teachers in sharing professional texts that could advance the team's learning. Despite all her efforts, teachers are disengaged. Instead of actively taking responsibility for their own and each others' learning, they wait for the team leader to lead. What might hold teachers back from being skillful contributors in the team?

Explore Possible Causes

Willing but overloaded. It is possible that teachers are reluctant to take on leadership within the team simply because they are overloaded with what they already have to do. Teachers may be more than willing to participate and do what the team leader asks but don't want to take on more responsibility.

Misleading leadership. Leaders are not the only ones who can lead. Yet this can be the thinking behind a teacher's decision to hold back in a team meeting. If roles are undefined or if expectations have never been communicated, teachers might expect the team leader, because she holds the leadership title, to do everything (particularly if she is getting something they are not such as a stipend or a reduced course load). Even if a member of the group, other than the team leader, wants to lead, he might hold back for fear of overstepping the team leader's role.

"Us and Them." How leadership roles are created is just as important as how they are defined. If a principal hand picks standout teachers to be leaders, she risks having them stand apart from others. This creates a polarizing culture between team leaders and team members. Even in schools where teachers apply for the role, the perception that one needs to be recognized as the leader in order to lead prevails. Consequently, teachers who are not appointed or recognized hold back. A greater divide emerges when team leaders are viewed as middle management, a pseudo-administrator, or, worse, the principal's pawn. Emotions of jealousy, resentment, or feeling overlooked can contribute to the "Us and Them" divide, causing teachers to retreat from being learning leaders in a team or derail a team leader's efforts to lead.

The expert/colleague paradox. When named team leader because of her expertise, a teacher is put in a paradoxical role—the peer expert (Mangin & Stoelings, 2011). According to one study, a teacher's expertise can actually decrease others' acceptability of her leadership (Timperley, 2005). In this snapshot, it is possible that Nadia's team views her role as being there to impart wisdom, and they are present to absorb it. Even when Nadia acknowledges the expertise of others, teachers are still reluctant to lead. She is challenged with fostering open communication and reciprocal learning in which everyone, herself included, is there to learn, regardless of labels.

Team leader reluctance. The skillful team leader asks a difficult question when considering why teachers in her team are reluctant to lead. Is it that teachers in the team are not willing or could it be the team leader is not ready to share responsibility? According to Wagner et al. (2006), a leader's actions, or inaction, may actually obstruct change (p. 55). A team leader might resist sharing the lead in an effort to maintain authority or control the function and impact of the team. A lack of confidence in her peers' leadership can cause her to withhold sharing leadership.

Respond

Proactive response: To prevent the team leader from being the only one leading the team's learning, the team leader can do the following:

Define leadership expectations and opportunities. Opportunities for nonappointed leaders to lead as skillful contributors must be defined within a team. "How leadership is defined will determine how people choose to participate" (Lambert, 2009, p. 13). Teachers need to know that they not only have permission to lead each other in learning but are expected to do so. Leading a team should not be analogous to a long road trip where one person drives while the others sleep. The skillful team leader might say on the first day, "No one person in this team can or should be the sole authority. I see my role as a representative of our team on the school instructional leadership team but not *the* decision maker. How does or doesn't this align with what you expect? What roles do we need so that we can share leadership?"

Once the team generates a short list, the team can determine details such as which roles, if any, should rotate, why, and how often. A sample list might include taking turns bringing in student work, hosting classroom observations, leading observation debriefs, finding professional texts to support team learning, taking notes for the team, monitoring the team's observance of group agreements, facilitating meetings, or communicating the team's needs to the principal.

Empower teachers. One of the greatest values of being a team is accessing the expertise and strengths of every member. The skillful team leader helps her colleagues tap into their ability to lead by saying, for example, "Each of us brings strengths to this work. Identify one way you can help lead our team. For example, I know Mrs. K is always knowledgable of the latest research on this topic. Mrs. K, your taking the lead on sharing relevant articles to our work could really move us forward. Mr. S, you always seem to get at critical questions that we don't always consider. Perhaps you would be comfortable doing this at each meeting to help lead our team into more analytical discussions?"

Redefine leading. Doing tasks such as facilitating a meeting or monitoring the team's observance of group agreements is only one way to share leadership.

Being a skillful contributor is just as critical to a team's learning and doesn't require a leadership title or official role. It involves strategic participation in which a team member asks provocative questions that challenge the team to think differently or voicing evidence-based observations and inferences that might launch a difficult conversation. Others might lead by modeling a lesson or support colleagues in the implementation of a new instructional strategy.

Norm for the unexpected. At times the need for leadership will unexpectedly pop up. For example, an upcoming conference requires one representative from the team to attend. Setting a group agreement to determine how a team will share unforeseen leadership needs can help prevent the team leader from being expected to take on everything all the time. For example, Nadia's team can agree to "take turns sharing the workload."

In-the-moment response: If teachers are reluctant to lead in a meeting, a team leader can do the following:

Reduce outside commitment. If reluctance to lead seems to be more caused by teacher overload than anything else, the skillful team leader minimizes the burden through open conversations about sharing the workload equitably and discussing ways to manage time. In this snapshot, Nadia might suggest, "What if we try on some roles for the next two meetings? I am happy to search for a reading while two other folks share a strategy that they are implementing. We can reevaluate after the second meeting to see if this is too much responsibility." If too much responsibility falls on the team leader, she needs to remember to ask for help.

Connect as a learner. The skillful team leader's primary role is to facilitate reciprocal learning, where both leaders and participants learn from each other. Expertise is a great asset to a team, but it must be shared with care so as not to negatively impact the team. If teachers assume only those with expertise can lead, the skillful team leader emphasizes her role as a learner too, thus becoming more accessible to teachers in the team. For example, Nadia might say, "Yes, I have had success with my students, but it is with much failure that I was able to succeed. And I still struggle with x, y, and z. I'm hoping the work we do as a team can help each of us, myself included, learn more."

Find an entry point and invite leadership. Some teachers hold back when it is not their official turn to lead. The skillful team leader listens for leadership entry points, moments when someone expresses interest to lead, and responds. For example, if a teacher recommends a successful strategy to others, the team leader can press gently by asking, "Would you be willing to bring in the resource that gave you that strategy?"

Solicit a friend. If inviting others to take responsibility for leading the team in learning results in the sound of crickets, a skillful team leader might call on a friend in the team for support. For example, "Mr. H, would you mind starting us off with a strategy that you use in your class?" Sometimes all it takes is for one person to begin taking the lead for others to do so too.

Self-check. The skillful team leader looks within to ensure that she is not holding team members back from leading. Asking a colleague to observe her words and actions as she leads can illuminate if there is a gap between the team leader's beliefs in sharing leadership with others and what she actually does.

Follow-up response: To sustain shared leadership for learning in subsequent meetings, the team leader can do the following:

Check in. The skillful team leader periodically checks in with team members to gauge a person's comfort level with his leadership responsibilities. If necessary, the team reevaluates what roles exist and how they are shared. For example, they can ask, "Does this responsibility seem like too much for one person? Should we divide the role? Which roles are essential to our success as a team, which can we eliminate?"

Look to others. Teams may not be fully aware of any inequities in leading. By speaking to and observing other teams, they can learn how others share responsibility for team learning, assess themselves, and modify when needed.

School leadership team response: To facilitate shared leadership throughout teams and the school, team leaders, the principal, and administrators together can do the following:

Change the name. Some schools are comfortable with the title "team leader," but others are not. Changing it to "team facilitator" or "team guide" may debunk some of the misleading connections associated with the name. So long as the role is well defined, even if rotated, the name doesn't matter. Instead of changing the team leader title, schools can also consider calling team members something that defines their role as leaders of learning such as "skillful contributors" or "leadership partners."

Be consistent. With multiple teams in a school, it is important to have clearly defined and consistent roles across teams. It will only cause conflict if some teams have appointed a single leader who is responsible for all decisions and tasks, while another team views all members as insightful thought partners who share the workload.

On the Flip Side . . . How Do I Foster Shared Leadership When No One Is the Designated Leader?

Having one designated leader can discourage shared leadership within a team, but teams without any appointed leader face their own set of challenges. A teacher might shy away from stepping up because he is concerned that others in the group will resist with a "Who put you in charge?" response. Those who do step up run the risk of being perceived as *the* leader and end up being given more responsibility than others in the group, causing the teacher to resent taking the lead. At worst, teams with no system in place for sharing the lead end up with no one leading. The team flounders and is low functioning. The bottom line—whether a team leader is named or not—teams must collaborate on how they will share the lead and foster reciprocal learning so that the team can thrive.

Dilemma 2: How Do I Foster Shared Leadership When Some Members Are Ineffective at Moving the Team Forward?

What does a team leader do when teachers share the lead but some fall short of their responsibilities, causing the team to come face-to-face with a hurdle? When school and team leaders share leadership without considering how people are leading, teams are set up to fail. The team leader is faced with the challenge of supporting each team members' right to lead without sacrificing the performance of the team.

Consider the following snapshot of a team:

Minisha is trained over the summer to be the eighth-grade team leader. The principal instructs the team to rotate the facilitator role in order to foster shared leadership. Every teacher agrees, but not all succeed in the role. When one teacher leads, the team ends up straying from the agenda and nothing gets accomplished. Another teacher facilitates with such a laser focus on the team's checklist of tasks that there is rarely any time to process what or why the team members are doing what they are doing. A third teacher has good intentions but never comes prepared with materials or an agenda for the team, making their time together unproductive. Although Minisha does not want to take back the lead, she is concerned with the team's low function and the mounting levels of frustration among the members.

Identify the Hurdle

In this snapshot, sharing the lead is not the problem, doing it effectively is. Teachers equitably take turns facilitating, but the team quickly gets frustrated by some people's inability to move the team forward. Instead of reaping the benefits of shared leadership as named in the introduction of this chapter (i.e., creating ownership for learning, teachers' taking responsibility for the outcome of decisions, enhancing teacher morale, job satisfaction, and feelings of empowerment, etc.), Minisha's team is at risk of being low functioning, low impact. Minisha must learn why.

Explore Possible Causes

Lack of skill. Sharing the lead does not mean passing out leadership roles as if one was dealing cards. Yes, every person can and should lead, but leading a team in learning takes skill to be effective. It involves "developing skills in dialogue, inquiry, reflection, collaboration, facilitation, and conflict resolution" (Lambert, 2005, p. 39). In this snapshot, teachers are expected to lead with no training, consequently their skill at doing it well varies, and the team quickly experiences the negative impact of poor leadership.

One size fits all. Some teams possess a limited view of sharing the lead—every team member wears every hat at least once. It's possible that some teachers in Minisha's team know facilitation is not its strength and would prefer to lead team learning in other ways. The team members may feel pigeonholed into a role that doesn't fit, and one in which they have no desire to get better at. Consequently, the team's function and potential for impact suffers.

Respond

Proactive response: To prevent ineffective shared leadership in a team, a team leader can do the following:

Rotate strategically. Rotating leadership roles and tasks is a means to foster shared leadership but only if school and team leaders work to develop these leadership skills in all teachers. Teams that are successful are usually thoughtful in advance of how they plan to rotate roles. Teams do not need to rotate a role every meeting. For example, Minisha's team might decide that someone new takes the facilitator role in each new inquiry cycle. This gives each team member time to become skillful at the leadership role.

Share where it makes sense. Successful teams think about the unique ways that each teacher can lead and cater to his or her strengths. They do not fall into the trap that every teacher must take on every role, and they find multiple ways for team members to contribute to the team's learning (i.e., researching and demonstrating teaching strategies relevant to the team goals).

Prep the leader. If a team decides to rotate roles, the skillful team leader meets individually with the teacher taking the lead to support his effectiveness. In this snapshot, Minisha can meet with each facilitator in advance of a meeting to identify objectives, desired outcomes for each meeting, and leadership strategies to achieve them. Writing the agenda in the language of objectives can keep the facilitator focused and moving the team toward action. Similar to writing classroom objectives, avoid nonmeasurable language such as "discuss," "review," and "talk about." For example, an agenda item that says, "Discuss failing students," would be rewritten as "Name all failing students for Tier 2 intervention." The desired outcome for the meeting would be that the team would leave that meeting with a list of all failing students recommended for Tier 2 intervention. Having a tangible outcome keeps the team on track regardless of who is facilitating.

In-the-moment response: If teachers are leading ineffectively, a team leader can do the following:

Gradually release. The skillful team leader transitions leadership gradually to teachers instead of throwing people with little experience or training into a leadership role. For example, Minisha might say, "I can facilitate the new protocol we are using today, who would like to co-facilitate it with me the next time?" Once a team member is capable of leading independently, the skillful team leader releases full responsibility. Key point: When in the instructional/modeling phase of gradual release, a skillful team leader is transparent about decision making. For example, "As facilitator of this protocol, the first thing I want to do is a quick overview of the process." In this way, other members learn how to take on the role.

Model being a skillful contributor. When a team member falls short of the responsibilities of a leadership role such as facilitator, the skillful team leader interjects with whatever the team needs to move forward. For example, when a team leader notices a teacher facilitator is dominating the conversation, she might interject, "Thank you for your insight, [facilitator]. I'm wondering what other teachers do to address this student-learning challenge."

In this snapshot, Minisha notices one facilitator is hyperfocused on tasks that keep the conversation superficial. She might say, "Before we move on, I want to respond to an assumption I hear us making." She can then encourage others in the team to speak up as well, regardless of who is wearing the facilitator hat for that meeting.

Follow-up response: To sustain shared leadership within a team, a team leader can do the following:

Reflect on skills. At the end of each meeting or at intermittent points throughout a team's cycle, one person can lead the group in a debrief about their sharing of responsibility for each others' learning and identify the support they need. For example, a teacher might request a facilitation workshop if the team is having trouble moving toward its goal.

School leadership team response: To foster effective shared leadership in teams, a team leader, the principal, and administrators together can do the following:

Build capacity. Rather than invest all of a school's training resources into one team leader, the school leadership team can have multiple teachers within a team trained in the necessary skills of leadership. For instance, one teacher from each team, other than the team leader, could participate in how to lead a professional book group. They can recruit team members to attend specific leadership training opportunities.

Dilemma 3: How Do I Foster Shared Leadership When Individuals Are Willing to Lead Tasks but Not Learning?

Some teams are enthusiastic to share responsibility for leadership tasks and roles in a team (i.e., taking minutes for the team or reporting out at a school-wide professional development), but leading each other in learning, particularly when a colleague shows resistance, suddenly becomes a challenge no one wants to take on.

Consider the following snapshot of a team:

Janice's literacy team shares responsibility for various tasks in the group. They thoughtfully rotate the roles of facilitator, they take turns bringing in student work, they all search for professional texts that can inform their discussions, and each month someone new types the notes from the meeting. In one meeting, Janice asks teachers to report out on the strengths and challenges of implementing student-writing conferences. All report success except for one teacher who is known to have classroom management problems. She says, "It's a waste of time especially in my fourth-period class. The minute I try to confer with one student, all the others are out of their seats, loud, and off task. I just can't do it with them."

Another teacher offers a suggestion for the teacher to try but is shut down immediately.

"Thanks, but you don't teach my kids. I've tried it all—nothing works," the struggling teacher says.

> *No one else asks questions or offers other solutions. Instead, the next teacher says, "Well, it works for me."*
>
> *When the meeting ends, teachers gather in the hall to talk about the struggling teacher, "I feel bad, but if she isn't going to take our help, it's not my problem. If she can't keep her kids under control, an administrator needs to step in."*
>
> *Janice appreciates her team's willingness to take on leadership roles, but she wants them to lead each other in learning too.*

Identify the Hurdle

Shared leadership is more than sharing responsibility for tasks; it's about sharing responsibility for the learning of oneself, one's students, and one's colleagues. Teams that collaborate are expected to lead each other in learning, even when a colleague is unreceptive. Some teachers, such as the one in this snapshot, attempt to lead by offering teaching suggestions but release themselves from responsibility as soon as the colleague pushes back. Instead of sharing responsibility for a team member's problem, these teachers rationalize that "if she isn't going to take our help, that's not my problem." Why might a teacher take the lead on tasks that help the group function but shy away from leading colleagues in instruction? Why might a teacher be willing to work with students who show reluctance to learn but not adults?

Explore Possible Causes

Job expectations. A teacher might be reluctant to lead a colleague in learning if not officially appointed to do so (as a mentor, for example) because she views it as an invasion of her colleague's privacy. The teacher might be willing to share a few helpful tips along the way, but ultimately relinquishes any responsibility for what a colleague chooses to do with students. (Note: In rare cases, the teacher who shows reluctance to learn may have more serious challenges warranting administrative action. If action has yet to be taken, teachers in the team are not likely to get involved. Teachers look to the team leader or administrators to solve learning issues.)

Fixed mindset. A teacher who holds a fixed mindset about teaching (Ch. 2), rooted in the belief that some can teach and some can't, is likely to withdraw from leading a colleague in learning. She might be thinking, "I can't help this teacher excel because her ability to improve as a teacher is limited."

Path of least resistance. More often than not, teachers care very much about the learning of their colleagues. They want to become a community where learning is reciprocal. However, when a team member shows resistance, some teachers retreat in order to avoid conflict. It's easier to say, "That's not my problem," than to be the first to confront a colleague with an uncomfortable conversation about practice, beliefs, and values—particularly if that colleague is not open to listening.

Respond

Proactive response: To encourage teachers to share leadership for learning, a team leader can do the following:

Norm for learning. Teams are comfortable with setting group agreements about punctuality and confidentiality. Why not do the same for how a team will lead each other in learning? Before a team encounters difficult conversations, where one teacher is closed to learning and others are reluctant to press him or her, a team can set personalized learning agreements (Ch. 3) where individual members name one agreement they want others to hold them accountable to. For example, teachers in Janice's team might write, "I sometimes make assumptions about students and want people to 'point out my assumptions.' I sometimes make instructional decisions without being fully aware of their impact on students, so I want the team to 'query my instructional decisions.' I sometimes get caught up in the same old groove of teaching and want the team to 'nudge me out of my comfort zone.' I sometimes have good intentions, but don't implement them, and I want the team to 'keep me accountable to what we agree on.'"

Members can write their own personalized learning agreement on a folded card tent placed in front of them at each meeting as a reminder to themselves and the team. Teachers are more likely to lead each other in learning if they have an invitation to do so.

In-the-moment response: If teachers are reluctant to lead others in learning, a team leader can do the following:

Be curious. It's virtually impossible for a team leader to confront the teachers who say, "That's not my problem," without coming across as either abrasive, "Well, yes, she teaches the kids at our school, so it is our problem," or polyanna-esque, "We must own each other's problems. When you have a problem, we'll all help you too." Either response is likely to turn teachers in the team away. Instead, the skillful team leader does less talking and more listening. In this snapshot, Janice might privately and respectfully inquire, "Why do you think someone outside of our team should work with her [the reluctant teacher] instead of us?" Sometimes, openly talking about it permits teachers to hear their own comments aloud. It causes them to find empathy or creative solutions and to rethink their statements.

Summon courage. Leading requires courage—courage to question a colleague's choices and suggest solutions that might be shot down. The skillful team leader fosters rigorous discourse (Ch. 6) in which team members don't shy away from dialogue that pushes each other's thinking, beliefs, values, and practices.

Empower the teacher. Instead of only working with the team to take responsibility for the issues of a struggling teacher, the skillful team leader encourages the struggling teacher to invite help and actively listen. Janice might approach her privately and say, "I appreciate you sharing what is not working in your classes. I know teachers in the team have had mixed results with implementation. Would you be willing at our next meeting to lead the discussion on getting everyone to share what is working and why?" This depersonalizes the issue, and she might be more open to listening. Using a protocol such as the Consultancy can help frame the conversation (see Resource 4.1: Adapted Consultancy Protocol).

Shift focus from teacher to students positively. As is further discussed in Chapter 7, a teacher who seems reluctant to learn in the team likely has concerns about the practice she is implementing. She is vulnerable and is more likely to act defensively against any suggestion a colleague offers, interpreting their help as judgment that she is not doing enough. In this snapshot, the teacher's defense is to blame the students. The skillful team leader helps the team step back from overloading the vulnerable teacher with solutions and instead shifts focus onto the students in a positive way. For instance, Janice might say, "So it sounds like your primary concern is managing the class while conferring with other students. This is a common challenge when students in your class are used to one routine and now must learn a new one. How have students in our other classes adapted to the routine of conferring, and has anyone else worked through the problem of one or more students not adjusting well? If so, what did you do and how long did the transition take?"

Put the ball in their court. When a team seems to retreat from leading a colleague in learning, taking on a "that's not my problem" stance, and the struggling teacher resists help, the skillful team leader puts out the truth of the dilemma before the team, clearly and without judgment, and let's them decide what to do. For example, Janice might say, "One of our team members has shared that writing conferences are not working in her class. I want to playback what I hear from our team. Most of us, including the teacher who shared this dilemma, feel we can't help. Yet on day one, we shared the common belief that we are responsible for all students' learning, whether in our classes or not. So now it seems our beliefs and the real work of what we do are head to head. Are we still committed to that shared belief? Can we as a team succeed if we are not? So what do we do now?"

Follow-up response: To sustain shared leadership for learning in a team, a team leader can do the following:

Check the balance. Learning within a team should be reciprocal. If everyone on the team continuously focuses on one teacher's dilemmas, so that it almost feels like teachers are training one person in the group, conflict can result. The skillful team leader fosters conditions where all teachers are learning from each other, and if learning seems imbalanced, she looks at alternatives to help teachers who need more help such as assigning a mentor.

School leadership team response: To foster shared leadership for learning, team leaders, the principal, and administrators together can do the following:

Acknowledge the challenges and offer encouragement. By offering support and praise for teams that take responsibility for each other's learning even when challenging, a school leadership team encourages teachers to continue leading. For instance, after observing a team who holds each other accountable to their personalized learning agreements, a member of the school leadership team might write a note of genuine praise. Sample note: "I noticed you improved the function of your team through personal learning agreements. It is evident by the team's rich discussion of the shared student work that these agreements have helped the team members be more respectful of one another, enabling them to challenge instructional decisions without conflict."

Dilemma 4: How Do I Foster Shared Leadership When No One in the Team Has Authority to Make Decisions (Including Me)?

Some teams embrace shared leadership where every teacher craves responsibility, and they learn the skills needed to lead effectively. The only thing holding them back from making significant shifts in the status quo is their apparent lack of authority to do so. Lambert (2005) suggests there are three stages of leadership capacity: low, moderate, and high. Low-leadership capacity operates mostly under traditional leadership in which the principal is an autocratic leader. Moderate-leadership capacity emphasizes pockets of shared leadership but no real sense of common shared purpose. High-leadership capacity demonstrates how the principal and teachers share responsibility for teacher and student learning. How can shared leadership flourish in a team when it doesn't seem to exist at high capacity in the school?

Consider the following snapshot of a team:

When analyzing student work, Dave and his Grades 3–5 math team discover that students struggle with the common core's mathematical practice to "construct viable arguments and critique the reasoning of others." They identify a strategy they would like to collectively try, but it is time-consuming; if implemented, they are unlikely to keep with their pacing guide. Dave suggests that teachers stray from the pacing guide for one week in order to get more comfortable with the strategy and then pick up the pace once some mastery is gained.

An uncomfortable silence is broken by a teacher saying, "I do think that is what we need, Dave. But no offense, you are not the principal, and she won't let us do that."

Frustrated, Dave says, "Well someone could go to the principal and at least ask?" No one volunteers.

Finally, another teacher says, "Let's just stay on pace and do what we can . . . even if it is less than what we had hoped."

Dave wishes he and the team had more authority to lead.

Identify the Hurdle

In this snapshot, Dave's team identifies a student need and collaboratively determines what actions can solve it. They share responsibility for the problem, and they want to learn how to remedy it, but don't. Why? Dave must examine how shared leadership is embodied within the school to understand what is holding teachers back in the team.

Explore Possible Causes

The leadership hierarchy. The term *leader* brings up images of the boss or the authority, the one who "authors" decisions (Senge et al., 1994, p. 72).

It conjures the belief that only individuals appointed to an authoritative position, such as the principal or department head, can make decisions about teaching and learning. The hierarchical structure of schools contributes to this misperception of who can lead and who can't. Consequently, teachers such as the ones in the snapshot, pass up opportunities to make decisions because they don't see themselves as having the authority.

Leaders who don't share. In some schools, needing authority to lead is more than a perception, it is reality. Schools that operate under low-leadership capacity, where administrators control all decisions, send a clear message to teams: those who have authority lead, and those who don't follow. In this snapshot, it seems by the mere fact that the school has teacher teams led by teachers that the school is at high-leadership capacity; however, the team members' timidity to make decisions about their own professional and student learning indicates the school is likely at moderate or possibly even low-leadership capacity. It might look like collaboration is valued, but team members know who the decision maker is, and it's not them.

Negative consequences. Low-leadership capacity discourages teachers from proposing ideas. Some teams, such as the one in the snapshot, reject their ideas before even approaching a formal leader. Perhaps the fear of negative consequences holds them back. They resign to a "why bother" attitude—knowing that the proposal to act on a belief or practice, even when aligned to the school vision, will be rejected. When school leaders respond openly and positively to decisions made by teachers, teams are more likely to lead. When leaders micromanage team decisions, or undo their work, teachers are reluctant to step up.

Nonbelievers. One who has authority in a school can tell teams that leadership can come from anywhere within an organization, but teachers need to believe it. A school leader may make efforts to foster high-leadership capacity (i.e., form teams, train teachers as team leaders), and yet teacher teams don't believe they have the power to make decisions, causing them to withdraw from leadership. Perhaps experience in the past with current or former leadership causes them to be tentative. Until teachers see and believe their decisions are welcomed and encouraged by those with official power, they are likely to act as if they have little voice.

Respond

Proactive response: To foster shared leadership when no one on the team has formal authority, a team leader can do the following:

Norm a response to obstacles. The skillful team leader anticipates that the team will encounter moments when a solution lies outside of his or her authority. Before that moment comes, a team sets a group agreement for how it will move forward. For example, Dave can propose that his team "consider all solutions within and beyond our locus of control."

Meet in advance with decision makers. Once a team sets a student-learning goal the team informs the principal or other decision maker and gains clarity on the authority they have. Open communication about which decisions are shared up front will prevent teams from wondering if they can or can't act and help them work within their locus of control.

In-the-moment response: If team members shy away from leadership because they lack authority, a team leader can do the following:

Recognize, restrategize, reempower. When team members are reluctant to lead because they don't trust that they have the authority to lead, a team leader can be sure he has come across a "non-discussable"—a term coined by Richard DuFour and Robert Eaker (1998) implying something significant that no one is comfortable talking about. The skillful team leader points it out and empowers the team to move forward.

In this snapshot, Dave might recognize that the team has come across the non-discussable: "It sounds like we would rather alter our action plan then speak with the principal? Why?" He should then restrategize: "If asking the principal to stray from our pacing guide won't work, what might?" And finally, he should empower the team: "We make instructional decisions that we know are important for our students even when we don't have full support of those with more authority than us (provided they align with school mission, vision, and goals). In what specific ways can we as a team continue to do this?" Ideas might include communicating to others as to how the team's decision connects to the school vision and goals or sharing the dilemma with the authority figure to foster understanding of the team's action steps.

Keep brainstorming. Sometimes the first solution is not the best. It's fine to brainstorm the "if only someone else would . . . then everything would work out" solutions, but often the better solution emerges once the team has had time to mull over many options. Dave can ask his team to brainstorm the first solutions that come to mind on sticky notes. He can then draw a large circle on chart paper and have teachers place their sticky notes inside the circle, if it is within the team's locus of control, or on the outside, if they are beyond the team's authority. Once all sticky notes are placed, they can eliminate ideas. Teams often discover that solutions not requiring another's intervention are more desirable. If team members do determine that the only effective solution requires outside authority, then they can proceed with confidence that they have thoughtfully discussed why and that they can come up with a plan on how to communicate the need to someone with the power to make it happen.

Seek the go-ahead. In schools with low- or moderate-leadership capacity, the skillful team leader can volunteer, if no one else does, to ask permission to move forward with the team's desired changes. If the school is working toward high-leadership capacity in which decision making for learning is shared, the team members might invite the authority figure to join them in collaborating on a solution to the problem.

Let it out. Daniel Goleman (2002) recommends negative feelings be brought out into the open in a constructive way. When the skillful team leader senses team members have strong emotions tied to lack of shared leadership, he finds positive ways that people can not only voice their concerns but actually have an impact. In this snapshot, Dave might suggest that the team, or members who are willing, bring their concerns to the school leadership team. Chances are that if their team is struggling to advance learning because they lack authority to do so, other teams are as well.

Distinguish leader from leadership. "Leadership and leader are not the same" (Lambert, 2009, pp. 12–13). One does not need to be named a leader to show leadership. Ronald Heifetz, in an interview with Riggio (2008), reminds organizations that "leadership is sometimes practiced by people of authority, sometimes people in the middle, sometimes from people outside, and sometimes from people who don't have any authority at all."

In this snapshot, Dave might promote leadership by saying, "We don't have the authority to change the pacing guide, but we can take the lead on communicating with other math teams in the school to find out what they are doing about this student-learning problem. Once we gain some data we can bring this to the principal."

Be the authority. While it is always better to work with school leadership than around them, on rare occasions a team leader may find success by following the "easier to ask forgiveness than permission" adage. Although a bit of a stick-your-neck-out-there move, if confident that the decision is aligned with the school's vision and goals, and all other options have been considered and disregarded, a team leader can instruct the team to move forward, while he agrees to take the heat if questioned. In the best-case scenario, the decision is well received by the principal, and the team gains respect and more authority to make other instructional decisions. In the worst-case scenario, the team leader is reprimanded for acting with authority he does not have, but the team gains respect for its leader and is more willing to share responsibility for team decisions. (Note: If the authority figure values shared leadership, she might commend the team for their creative solutions.)

Follow-up response: To sustain shared leadership, a team leader can do the following:

Win the war, not the battle. The skillful team leader helps teachers see themselves as empowered, knowledgable problem solvers who share a vision with administrators for improving student learning. A team may lose a battle, but ultimately, they and the school's leadership team are looking to win the same war. If Dave's team does not win permission to stray from the pacing guide, he can connect teachers to administrators in strategizing alternative solutions to improve students' ability to construct viable arguments and critique the reasoning of others.

School leadership team response: To foster shared leadership schoolwide, the team leader, the principal, and administrators together can do the following:

Redefine the leadership hierarchy. While the hierarchical structure of schools is unlikely to change, leadership within the hierarchy can be redefined.

"Leadership capacity will be enhanced when the principal supports the leadership experience of others" (Lambert, 2003, p. 50). The principal still remains the boss over many decisions; however, she and her teachers are leading each other in learning. Learning is the great equalizer. Schools can adopt a new logic, "All bosses are leaders, but all leaders do not have to be the boss." When those with authority are willing to redistribute power, call on others to lead, and be clear about which decisions are shared and which are not, teachers will want to lead.

School leaders can use Lambert's (2000) Z-C-I chart in which decisions needed to be made by an authority figure are listed under "Z," decisions that those with authority only need to be consulted on are listed under "C," and those decisions that authority figures only need to be informed of are listed under "I." Not only will a Z-C-I chart promote clear communication between administrators and teams about which decisions are shared and which are not, but it will also draw attention to any imbalance of power. If all instructional decisions are in the "Z" column, it is evident that leadership is not shared.

Build trust with a shared vision. For a school to achieve high-leadership capacity, "Each participant shares the vision, understands how the school is moving toward the vision, and understands how he or she contributes to that journey" (Lambert, 2005, p. 40). If the teachers and administrators have a clear, common vision for the direction of instructional learning, then all can begin to lead ideas and actions toward that consistent vision.

Define agreements and protocols for decision making. A team leader can initiate an up-front conversation with the principal, teachers, and administrators as to how much authority the team has in making decisions for their instruction and their students. Determining parameters for decision making, such as ensuring all decisions are evidence based, also helps set clear expectations for shared leadership. Filtering decisions through the question, "Is this action or behavior consistent with our vision and values?" (DuFour & Eaker, 1998, p. 187) can keep teams focused and help a principal trust teachers to make mission-aligned learning decisions.

Clarify "loose/tight." The principal can be "tight" and directive on the vision and values that teams must hold fast to but can be "loose" and open to how teachers will uphold them (DuFour & Eaker, 1998). Clarifying which decisions are loose and which are tight improve communication between teams and school leaders.

Involve the principal as a collaborator. Having the principal or other

Suggested expectations for administrative participation in a team include the following:

- The administrator acts as a skillful contributor and not as the team leader.
- The administrator and the team are all learners.
- The administrator does not evaluate team members.
- Team members resist Q&A of the administrator (where a team dumps problems on the administrator and expects him or her to solve them).

Sample agreements for administrators and teachers in a team include the following:

- Suspend judgment
- Share professional challenges honestly through a solutions-oriented lens
- Assess the team's dynamic regularly and constructively

administrator as either a regular team member or a frequently scheduled visiting team member allows them to share in decision making as opposed to acting as a gatekeeper, accepting or rejecting a team's ideas. When this strategy is implemented with clear expectations and norms (see the sidebar on p. 72), leadership shifts from the traditional hierarchy to a collaborative partnership. School leaders can make transparent which teams they will participate in, when, and most importantly why; they are not there to evaluate but are there as a learner and a collaborator.

If a team or administrator breaks one of the agreements, the team members need to determine, in advance, how they will address it. For instance, if teachers on the team look to the principal to provide all of the solutions to the challenges shared, the principal empowers teachers by asking, "What efforts have been made to solve this problem thus far? Let's figure this out together."

On the Flip Side . . . How Do I Foster Shared Leadership for Learning When I Have Authority, but It Works Against Me?

Occasionally, a person with evaluative power leads a team. While at first this may seem like the ideal circumstance reducing hurdles, it can actually create new ones. When one person is designated a leader, others are more likely to defer all decision making to him or her and refrain from taking responsibility for the team's learning. The skillful team leader finds a way to not only acknowledge authority but also encourage others to lead. Rather than try to hide the fact that he or she has evaluative powers (i.e., "Act like I'm not the department head"), a skillful team leader might say, "As department head, I am empowered to make certain decisions that teachers are not able to make. However, I don't have all of the answers, and I don't expect to make all the decisions regarding the learning of this team or meeting the needs of our students. I hope we can collaboratively take ownership for the challenges we all face and problem solve together."

Additionally, a team leader with formal authority may have a more difficult time fostering reciprocal learning. Teachers might be reluctant to show vulnerability and expose failure, a necessary component of being a learner, and may refrain from offering the team leader feedback needed for their own learning.

The skillful team leader who holds evaluative power acknowledges both his position of authority and his role as a learner. For example, he might say, "Being department head means that I do evaluate teachers when I step into the classroom; however, just as when I evaluate, I understand that in order for each of us to get better we need to experiment, learn, and fail. I want to encourage learning in this team, and to do so, I will put myself out there as a learner too. I will ask questions to which I don't know the answer, I will lead lessons that may or may not be effective for all students, and I will likely make assumptions about learning for which I want someone to challenge my thinking. I need to learn with you so that we can collaboratively get better." Then the team leader needs to follow through.

CONSIDER SCHOOL CULTURE: SHIFTING FROM A CULTURE OF DEPENDENCY TO A CULTURE OF SHARED DECISION MAKING

A team's reluctance to share leadership for learning may go deeper than the possible causes explored thus far. The skillful team leader examines the role school culture plays for it is possible that teachers have settled into a "culture of dependency," where they become reliant on others to lead. "Dependency causes people to ask permission, abdicate responsibilities, and blame decision makers" (Lambert, 2005, p. 40). Instead of acting as partners in learning, school leaders govern and teachers follow. The traditional top-down approach to professional learning (where those with authority determine what, when, and why teachers learn) prevails, and the only thing shared between school leaders and teachers are feelings of frustration.

Recognize the Signs of a Culture of Dependency

A team affected by the culture of dependency can look high functioning on the surface, but signs of an unhealthy culture may exist:

- Teams have agendas that they follow, but rarely do teachers other than the team leader take responsibility for creating it and keeping the team accountable to it. Teachers might be heard asking the team leader, "What are we doing in today's team meeting?"
- Teachers passively expect someone else to make team and schoolwide learning experiences valuable to them. If it does not meet their needs, they disengage from learning and complain instead of taking action to improve the learning experience.
- Teachers in a team wait for permission to lead or assume they can't and don't even try.
- Administrators appear to be open to team learning decisions, but then they move forward with their own agenda.
- Team leaders are responsible for logistical aspects of a team, but school leaders are still puppeteering the strings when learning decisions are made.

Where Does the Culture of Dependency Come From?

Until recently, teacher professional development has rarely exemplified shared leadership for learning. For some schools, it was (and sometimes still is) not that uncommon to mandate teachers to attend a few isolated days for professional development throughout the year, where they have little to no voice in the topic, agenda, or design of the day. They are expected to show up and be "present." When teams did meet, it often resembled a designated leader rattling off housekeeping details, with an occasional "instructional focus" such as setting a midterm schedule to a group of teachers. Professional development, absent of shared professional learning, has in some schools fostered a gap between believing in the value of sharing leadership and actually doing it in matters impacting teaching and learning. This gap creates a culture of dependency where it is OK to be a passive learner, reliant on others to lead. Teachers grow to expect others to lead their learning and shy away from taking responsibility.

In other circumstances, past professional development is not to blame for teachers' dependency on others to lead learning—current leadership is. When school leaders give authority to teams to make learning decisions but then withdraw it, teachers quickly learn that they are not empowered. They might wonder, "Are they taking our input only to do whatever they had planned in the first place?" or "Are we really able to lead or will our decisions be undone?" It only takes one mistake on a school or team leader's part for a teacher to perceive that shared leadership is not really shared.

A closer look reveals that beneath a culture of dependency lies mutual mistrust: formal school leaders who don't trust teachers to make instructional decisions and teachers who don't trust them. Schools who struggle with trust likely harbor harmful beliefs about teachers and school leaders (i.e., teachers think school leaders are out of touch with what teachers and students need and are incapable of making good instructional decisions; school leaders think teachers lack the knowledge and perspective to make sound decisions). These and other negative beliefs inform how much or how little a school embraces shared leadership. School leaders give teachers less responsibility for decision making and micromanage those that they are given. Teachers, not having the trust of their leaders, refrain from stepping up to take the lead for fear of being reprimanded, shot down, blamed, or ignored. Simultaneously, teachers don't trust the decision making of their school leaders and therefore share no responsibility for poor decisions. Mistrust abounds and teams can't authentically practice shared leadership for learning.

Regaining trust is possible but difficult. Beginning with beliefs, individuals at all levels of the organization need to foster a culture of shared leadership where they believe that the best decisions for improved teaching and student learning are made together. In leading each other, they learn from one another. Schools operating at high-leadership capacity can feel like winning a three-legged race, where two partners, bound together at the ankles, swiftly stride in sync toward the finish line. At first, it feels awkward, and the team may even take a tumble, but once they begin to share the lead they are unstoppable. They know where they're headed, they give and take to maintain a steady pace toward their goal, maneuver obstacles in the field together, and charge forward together, ultimately taking shared responsibility for their win or loss.

An effort to shift the culture of dependency to a culture of shared leadership for learning has come about as more schools become PLCs. The *Standards for Professional Learning* (Learning Forward, 2012) holds the bar high, recommending schools "develop collective responsibility" where "peer accountability" for learning is at the heart of teams (see www.learning forward.org/standards/learning-communities#.UM0t3Hdr2ew for more details). The standard carries the belief that "the more one educator's learning is shared and supported by others, the more quickly the culture of continuous improvement, collective responsibility, and high expectations for students and educators grows." Changes in school culture can take awhile to catch up to changes in standards. When a culture of dependency holds teams back from fully embracing shared leadership for learning, a team leader can together with other school members do the following:

Get on the same page. When schools clarify school mission, vision, values, goals, and what decisions teachers have authority to make, all members of the school have a compass by which to guide their decisions. Those with formal authority avoid circumstances in which they need to undo teacher-led learning decisions. Those with authority are not perceived as "pulling the carpet from under a decision that teachers thought they had the authority to make" (Lambert, 1998, p. 7). Teachers learn that they do have power over decisions about teaching and learning and are not helpless. In fact, they are essential to the learning community and are expected to lead.

Be transparent. Even when school leaders articulate or even cocreate mission, vision, values, and goals with the faculty, things happen that can cause a leader or team to change course. When everyone is transparent in decision making, people are more willing to embrace change.

Unite the "Us" and the "Them." When a school struggles with shared leadership for learning it can often become a power struggle between those with authority and those without, particularly when those involved have a self-authoring mind (Ch. 2) in which they believe very strongly in their point of view. Instead of different stakeholders advocating their own interests, they can shift to common ground about what is in the best interest of students. The skillful team leader listens for statements like "As principal I want . . . " or "As a teacher I want . . . " and suggests language that unites stakeholders, such as "As a principal (or teacher) I see that students need . . . "

Assess the school's leadership capacity. A school can discuss the three levels of leadership capacity—low, moderate, and high—and assess where they put themselves and how to shift to higher capacity (see Resource 4.2). Lambert (2003) also has a leadership capacity survey in her book *Leadership Capacity for Lasting School Improvement* that schools may want to take.

Ask courageously. Teachers and leaders can initiate courageous, reflective conversations about leadership. Some thought-provoking questions include the following:

- What school conditions support teachers to take the lead on learning? What conditions make it difficult? What can we do about it?
- Does the principal trust others to make learning decisions? Do administrators/team leaders trust teachers to make learning decisions? Do teachers/team leaders trust administrators and the principal to make learning decisions? If yes, how does he or she show it? If no, why not?
- In what ways do those with authority contribute to teachers' reluctance to lead?
- In what ways have authority figures been responsible for teams making decisions that stray from our school vision, values, and goals? Have we set clear norms for decision making? Have we set clear expectations?
- What does it mean to be responsible for another's learning?

Foster a culture of reciprocal learning. Leading is not hierarchical. Good ideas can come from anywhere in a school. The principal, administrators, team leaders, teachers, and students are equal partners in taking responsibility for each others' learning. The principal, administrators, team leaders, teachers, and students can regularly reflect on the question, "How do I contribute to the learning of others and how do others contribute to my learning?" (Lambert, 2003, p. 2).

Redefine success. The school can recognize and celebrate teachers who collaborate and share responsibility for each others' learning and that of all students. A principal might bring the faculty together through the reminder that a school cannot achieve its mission when some individuals succeed while others fail.

Give it a chance. Teachers who have taught in schools with low-leadership capacity in the past can learn to accept shared leadership. They need to trust and give leadership a chance. To facilitate this trust, school leaders can be transparent about their learning, their successes, and their failures. They need to co-construct learning with teachers rather than view them as "empty vessels" waiting to be filled with knowledge (similar to Vygotsky's theory about student learning). They need to share mission-aligned teaching and learning decisions with teachers in order for teams to trust that they have a voice that matters.

APPLICATION TO YOUR WORK: CONNECT, OBSERVE, EXPLORE, ACT

Think and write independently. Then, discuss with colleagues.

Connect	Observe
Remember a time as a leader or participant when you experienced shared leadership for learning. What did it look and sound like?	What does shared leadership currently look like in your school? In your team?
Explore	**Act**
What hurdles prevent your team from sharing leadership for learning? What have you done to overcome them? What have you not tried yet?	What will you and your colleagues do to foster shared leadership for learning in your team? In your school? Name next steps and support needed.

Seemingly SMART 5

Overcoming Hurdles to Set and Attain Impactful Goals

FOUNDATIONAL VALUE: GOAL SETTING AND ATTAINMENT

Schools value goal setting and attainment as a means to achieve professional learning for student achievement, but how can a team uphold that value when investment in goals is low and accountability is high? Building upon Anne Conzemius and Jan O'Neill's work around SMART goals, this chapter applies a skillful approach to dilemmas encountered when setting and advancing toward long-term goals and small student-learning targets. It offers team leaders strategies to engage a team in a process for goal setting to maximize impact on teacher practice and student learning. It explores the challenges of goal setting in schools where a "scapegoat culture" exists, and it suggests actions team leaders can take to shift to a "culture of mutual accountability."

WHAT ARE SMART GOALS, AND WHY ARE THEY IMPORTANT?

With the onset of professional learning communities (PLC), teacher teams (many for the first time) are empowered to set learning goals that meet their students' needs, monitor their progress, and make instructional decisions based on their findings. Research shows goals are more likely to yield improved performance when they are written with clarity, challenge, commitment, feedback, and task complexity (Locke & Latham, 1990). This translates into SMART goals for teacher teams. While loading the teaching vernacular with another acronym can be off-putting and bring out skeptics, what it stands for should not be dismissed.

SMART goals (Conzemius & O'Neill, 2002) are defined as specific, measurable, attainable, results oriented, and time-bound. Applied to teams, each criterion is defined as follows:

In support of team goal setting:

- "Abundant research and school evidence suggest that setting such goals (high-leverage annual improvement goals) may be the most significant act in the entire school improvement process, greatly increasing the odds of success" (Schmoker, 2003, p. 23).
- When everyone participates in goal setting, ownership builds. One study found ownership of a goal increases if individuals craft the goal; another found that even when the goal is imposed by someone else, so long as those achieving the goal have an understanding for the rationale, they can be motivated to accomplish the goal. Both studies found that when people have a say in how they are going to attain a goal (an action plan), ownership increases (Locke & Latham, 1990).
- Self-directed teams must "consistently focus on the issues that are most significant in improving student achievement, and set specific measurable goals to monitor improvement" (DuFour & Eaker, 1998).
- "Specific goals provide a clear direction for behavior and a clear indication of desired performance, and as such they serve as motivators" (Marzano, 2009, p. 6).

Specific. Team goals focus on priorities linked to the larger vision of success for the school and focus on the specific needs of students. A team has clarity as to who the goal is for, what change is expected to happen, and so forth.

Measurable. Growth from pre- and postassessment(s) indicate a team's achievement of its goals. Teams use interim assessments to monitor progress as they implement actions to reach desired outcomes.

Attainable. Team goals are challenging but will likely be accomplished given the time and resources available.

Results oriented. Team goals yield specific, desired, observable outcomes.

Time-bound. Team goals are achieved within a particular timeframe.

HURDLES TO SETTING AND ATTAINING IMPACTFUL SMART GOALS

The process for goal setting could not be more straightforward: determine where students are now, decide where they need to be, and plan how the team will get them there. But bringing a team together to come to consensus on decisions needed to advance goals can be complex. From the start, teachers uncomfortable with or lacking knowledge of SMART goals can show reluctance to a team leader's efforts. Teams with great momentum during the goal setting process can lose steam during implementation of a long-term goal, never achieving their desired outcomes. Even if a team leader is able to navigate around these challenges, she may find herself struggling to keep her team afloat in a scapegoat culture, where measurable goals and action plans are only used to find fault with teachers and deliver negative consequences.

Goal setting, which has the potential to truly transform teaching and learning and to solve problems that have plagued a school for years, can instead become a "going through the motions" process yielding little change.

A team leader might wonder, How do I advance our team toward achieving an impactful goal when

1. individuals resist the SMART goal process,

2. our goal is SMART but has little impact on learning, or

3. team members want to change course?

Dilemma 1: How Do I Advance Our Team Toward Achieving an Impactful Goal When Individuals Resist the SMART Goal Process?

Goals are intended to help a team focus on priorities and obtain measurable results. They are a tool to achieve greater performance for teachers and students. With them, a school has the ability to truly effect change at a deep level, where teachers shift what, why, and how they teach so that every student learns. But some teams get can't get past the particulars of goal setting. Time is wasted, frustration levels rise, and the team can't move forward.

Consider the following snapshot of a team:

> The principal requests all teams set annual SMART goals. Teachers in Ben's middle school Sheltered English Immersion team express that they want students "to improve their understanding of academic vocabulary." Ben follows up, asking, "That's good; now let's make it SMART." Teachers shift in their chairs, visibly perturbed.
>
> One teacher says, "The principal asked us to set a goal. We did. Does it matter if it fits the latest educational jargon?"
>
> Another says, "We've worked together before; I don't think we need to take up everyone's time to spell out each criterion."
>
> Someone else responds, "This isn't for us; it's for the administration. Let's just get it done."
>
> Ben does not want to waste the team's time with wording a goal, but he knows that overlooking important decision making about the goal can set the team up for failure.

Identify the Hurdle

Ben is challenged with getting his team to craft a SMART goal and a collective approach to achieving it. Although the team sets an initial goal of "improving students understanding of academic vocabulary," unanswered questions remain such as which students does the goal target? What does the team mean by "understanding"? What will teachers use to measure that understanding? What is the desired outcome and how long does the team have to reach it? What will evidence of learning look like? While Ben could simply go with the team's initial goal and lack of action plan, he knows his team can be more successful if their goal is SMART. Before he responds, he needs to consider the possible reasons behind teachers' apparent reluctance to the goal-setting process.

Explore Possible Causes

Need to learn "how to." It is possible that teachers are reluctant to write a SMART goal simply because they don't know how. For example, they may be unfamiliar with selecting measurements to monitor progress, or they don't know how to determine an attainable percentage for student improvement. Once teachers gain comfort with the process, they are more likely to go with it.

Don't know what they don't know. Teachers, who for the first time are setting team goals and seem adverse to the SMART acronym, may not be aware of the potential challenges that can come from overlooking each criterion. For example, if a goal is not *specific* (i.e., the target audience is too broad), students who most need the help can get overlooked. If the team does not determine measurements to indicate where students are starting from (i.e., a baseline assessment), teachers can misdiagnose a problem and waste time implementing strategies that don't yield change. A team with no interim measurements for progress can miss learning opportunities that inform their course of action only to discover, too late, that they cannot reach their goal. If the goal is *unattainable* (i.e., too challenging given the resources they have available), a team is likely to lose momentum and investment in seeing the goal to the end. A team that does not specify desired *results* risks doing a lot of work with nothing to show for it. If the goal is not *time-bound*, team members have no urgency to reach their goal and no clear sense of benchmarks they should be hitting to achieve the goal. Taking time to thoughtfully use the SMART acronym can help a team avoid a number of these hurdles, but if teachers aren't aware of the potential problems out there, they may not see the value in going through the time-consuming process.

Acronym reflux. There is no shortage of acronyms in education. For some, the thought of being told by school leaders to adopt another sets off an adverse reaction. Teachers immediately categorize the acronym as more educational jargon and don't give the meaning behind what each letter stands for a chance.

Paperwork overload. Teams thrive when there is a clear purpose for everything they are required to do. When a school places more emphasis on the tasks of goal setting (i.e., completing forms describing the action plan they will do) rather than time for the work (i.e., using meeting time to do the actions and reach the goal), teacher teams risk getting distracted from their purpose—to set and implement meaningful goals that will impact their practice and ensure students achieve. While writing down a goal and action plan keeps a team focused, accountable, and communicates the goal to others, it is critical that the process does not overwhelm the work.

Doubt. Developing a teacher team goal is empowering but not when it is already set by someone else. Some teachers may seem reluctant to move through the time-consuming process of setting a SMART goal and plan of action if administrators dictate to the team what they must work on in advance or permit the team to craft a goal and plan only to dismiss it later. Administrators need to be clear about the authority teams have to make these decisions, and teachers need to trust those who give it won't take it away (Ch 4).

Even if teacher teams have and believe they have the authority to set their own goals, any prior negative experience can discourage them from moving forward. When each September, teachers are asked to analyze data, write observations on lots of chart paper, and set goals, only to get to the end of the year without following up to see if the goals set have been accomplished (let alone checking throughout the year), people get disheartened. Worse yet, they are asked to go through the same process year after year. Teachers are left wondering, "Wait, what happened to that goal?"

Similarly, when schools have too many goals on which teachers are expected to focus, teams might question the value of goal setting.

Respond

Proactive response: To diminish the likelihood of teacher resistance to setting a SMART goal and action plan, a team leader can do the following:

Offer professional development. The skillful team leader first considers his team's familiarity with the process before assuming that they are resistant to it. Teachers are less likely to resist the SMART goal process if they understand in advance what it requires, why teams are doing them, and learn how to recognize when a goal is SMART, when it isn't, and how to change it (see Resource 5.1: Making the Shift From Seemingly SMART). Whether it is a formal schoolwide workshop or simply an initial team discussion, a team leader can build prior knowledge around SMART goals to answer teachers' questions and concerns before they need to move through the process and be accountable to them. (Important note: Schools should be cautious not to spend too much time prepping teachers on how to write SMART goals. It is better to take the approach one would with learning a new board game: Get the basics and then learn as you go.)

Create the need. Discussed more thoroughly in Chapter 6, teams that engage in evidence-based rigorous discourse in which they collaboratively analyze various forms of data that show what students do not know, can be the spark needed to get the team goal setting.

In-the-moment response: If teachers show reluctance to set a SMART goal, a team leader can do the following:

Toss the jargon; pose the questions. If teachers bristle at the thought of another acronym, the team can toss the letters but keep the content. The skillful team leader prompts the team members with questions that will aid them in ensuring that they have considered all essential components of a goal without needing to call it SMART (see Resource 5.2: SMA-H-RT Guiding Questions).

Unpack the meaning. Acronyms are intended to be an easy way to communicate a complex idea. If school and team leaders and teachers agree to use the acronym, SMART, they must foster a shared understanding of what each letter stands for and why it is important. The skillful team leader might say, "We've been instructed to set SMART goals. Let's think about what each of these letters really mean to our work and how they can help us set a meaningful goal that we can achieve. Let's also consider the challenges we might face if we don't ensure our goal is SMART." Then he can provide some examples from personal experience or ask the team, "Have you ever worked with a group who doesn't set a timeline for their school goal? What was that like?"

Follow-up response: To sustain teachers' openness to set SMART goals, a team leader can do the following:

Revisit and adjust. Like mission statements or group agreements, a SMART goal can't only live on paper. Ensuring the goal set is relevant requires a team to revisit and tweak its plans to reach it.

School leadership team response: To encourage teams to embrace SMART goals and action plans, a team leader, the principal, and administrators together can do the following:

Take the paperwork pledge. No longer is it acceptable to subject students to meaningless worksheets; why should teachers be subject to the same? Leaders must commit to purpose-driven paperwork. District, school, and team leaders pledge to only do written tasks that move teams toward their schoolwide vision, mission, and goals. Whenever possible, leadership teams should include teachers in selecting and generating the important tools that make the team's work meaningful and reject tasks that take time away from what is trying to be accomplished. At a minimum, the purpose of forms and worksheets must be clearly communicated to teams, and teachers must be given the time to do them meaningfully. Teachers should learn what comes about as a result of their written labor, but they should actually benefit from it. For example, if teams are completing action plans, they should reflect the real work teams are doing, and teams should have access to view other team's plans to gain resource ideas and collaborate on solutions to common challenges.

Trust teacher teams. As discussed in Chapter 4, the principal and administrators need to share leadership with teacher teams. By making the school mission, vision, values, and goals clear, they are more able to trust teacher teams to set their own SMART goals and action plans that align to them. Only when teacher teams believe they are trusted can they begin to trust the process.

Dilemma 2: How Do I Advance Our Team Toward Achieving an Impactful Goal When Our Goal Is SMART but Has Little Impact on Learning?

The SMART acronym is intended to help teams stay focused and achieve what they set out to do. However, crafting a SMART goal is deceptively simple. It is possible for a team to craft a goal that technically meets each criterion yet has little to no impact on teacher practice or student learning.

Consider the following snapshot of a team:

Pedro's history team sets the goal: By the end of the semester, every teacher in the eleventh grade will hold ten teacher–student writing conferences per week. We will measure progress toward our goal with a weekly conferring log. We will produce a binder full of conferring resources. The conversation leading up to their goal sounds like the following:
  Pedro: "Our school wants all content areas to improve literacy."
  One teacher says, "My students struggle with free response to document-based questions [DBQs]."

Another adds, "Yes, especially those taking the AP exam. They can't write a clear and persuasive essay responding to the prompt using the given documents and outside information."

A third teacher shares, "The English teacher across the hall from me tells me she holds writing conferences with her students, and it has really helped. I always intend to do them but then run out of time; there's just so much to cover."

A suggestion is made: "OK, so why don't we set a goal to increase the number of writing conferences that we do with our students. Since there is not enough time during class, we could try offering time slots before and after school and during our lunch. I'm not keen on doing that for the whole year, but I'd try it for a few weeks."

Pedro interjects. "How many conferences should we aim for in a week?"

A teacher comments, "I think we need to be realistic here. How about two a day, totaling ten students a week? This way we can be sure to achieve it. I also think we should give ourselves the full semester to reach the goal because our meetings get canceled so frequently, and that could get in the way of reaching our goal."

Pedro asks, "OK, how will we measure progress?"

A teacher responds, "What if we each keep a log of the writing conferences we hold with kids? This way, we have a record of how often we don't reach our goal. We can also use the AP exam students take in the spring to see if kids improve."

One teacher hesitates. "I'm OK with this goal, but I am not really sure what to do in a conference."

"I've got lots of resources for you to use," offers another. "I've generated a list of questions that I ask when I confer."

Pedro concludes, saying, "OK, so let's collect all of these resources, and our end result could be a reference binder that we can share with other teachers."

By the end of the semester, each teacher reports that they have met the goal of ten conferences a week. The team members are pleased that they have a thick resource binder to use when conferring; however, they are frustrated that despite the more frequent conferences students are continuing to struggle with DBQ essays.

Identify the Hurdle

Pedro's team should be high functioning, high impact. Not only do they work well together, but they have agreed to a goal that meets each of the SMART criterion: The goal *specifically* targets eleventh-grade history students. The teachers specify that they want to accomplish ten writing conferences a week. They use a log to *measure* their weekly quota for conferring. They have a plan to *attain* the goal by meeting with students before and after class, during teacher lunch, and during class time. They determine that the team's work will *result* in a resource binder of questions for teachers to use when conferring. They set out to accomplish this goal by the end of the semester, thereby making it *time-bound*. So why aren't they able to achieve measurable gains for students? Most likely it is because their goal is *Seemingly* SMART.

Seemingly SMART goals are technically SMART, they meet each criterion in the acronym (e.g., specific, measurable, etc.), but the decision making behind one or more of the criterion is poorly informed or underdeveloped. The goals look good on paper but don't impact student learning.

A Seemingly SMART goal is

- specific but specifies an activity, not a student-learning outcome;
- measurable, but the measures don't give a team the information it needs when it needs it;
- attainable but only with unsustainable strategies;
- results oriented, but results are resources or plans, not learning outcomes; and
- time-bound, but bound by constraints.

Each element is described further in the following:

Specific but specifies an activity, not a student-learning outcome. Who, what, where, when? Every SMART goal lays out answers to these questions, but the Seemingly SMART goal falls short in that it fails to specify a learning outcome for students. Instead of specifying what understanding, knowledge, or skill students will master, the goal centers on a teaching strategy or something students must do.

In this snapshot, Pedro's team SMART goal, to hold ten student–teacher writing conferences per week, is a teaching strategy that does not specify what students will be able to know or do as a result of this increase in conferences. When a teaching strategy is named as a goal, focus is on what *teachers* are doing and not what *students* are learning. Consequently, Pedro's team achieves their goal of doing ten conferences per week, yet students don't get better at DBQ essays.

Having a goal that specifies outcomes for students instead of methods for teaching is a good start; however, it can still end up Seemingly SMART. Goals that focus on student-learning activities (e.g., Students will be able to discuss . . . Students will be able to complete chapter questions . . .) fall short of specifying the understanding, knowledge, or skill that students will be able to demonstrate when the goal is achieved. Marzano (2009) explains the distinction between student activity and student-learning outcome with a clear example. He writes that

> Students will understand that matter is made up of atoms and that atoms, in turn, are made up of subatomic particles. This is a learning goal. There is a clear outcome regarding what students should know about atoms. [versus] Students will write a paper describing the relationships among atoms and subatomic particles. This is an activity. The statement calls for something to be done (a paper to be written) and specifies a topic (the relationships among atoms and subatomic particles) but does not make clear the desired outcome regarding student understanding or skill. (p. 98)

It is important for teams to name specific teaching strategies or student-learning activities in an action plan, but the skillful team leader is careful that those actions are viewed as a means to the goal and are not the goal itself.

Measurable, but the measures don't give a team information it needs when it needs it. Tools to measure goals are intended to give a team timely information about progress and achievement of goals. Seemingly SMART goals use tools that don't give teams information they need when they need it. For instance, summative assessment tools such as the AP exam used in this snapshot, measure student learning, but they do not provide the team with timely information that will guide them as they work toward their goal. Once the team learns how students performed on the exam it is too late to adjust their instruction.

Simply using ongoing assessments to measure a goal does not meet the M in SMART. What a team measures matters. The Seemingly SMART goal often uses tools to measure implementation of a strategy instead of the desired learning outcome. In this snapshot, Pedro's team uses a log to monitor the number of conferences teachers hold each week. Teachers are able to track their implementation but not the impact of those conferences on students' DBQ essays.

Attainable with unsustainable strategies. The results of a Seemingly SMART goal are attainable, but they are likely not replicable because of the approach the team is using. Pedro's team members opt to achieve their goal by holding student-writing conferences before and after school and during teachers' lunchtime. While this approach will enable them to attain their goal of conferring with ten students a week, it is unlikely they can sustain this practice for long without burning out. In time, the problem will crop up again either with these or other students. The team that sets a SMART goal selects goals that can be attained and sustained.

(Note: A win is a win. Some will argue that attaining a goal is worthwhile even if results or the strategy used to get there are unsustainable. This approach can work, but teams should make these decisions strategically, knowing that if the goal is intending to solve an adaptive challenge, defined by Heifetz and Linsky, 2002, as one that requires people to adapt their beliefs and habits, one that has not been solved before, the problem is likely to reemerge with unsustainable strategies used to accomplish it.)

Results oriented, but results are resources or plans, not learning outcomes. SMART goals are not intended to yield just any result, but a result in student learning. A team that produces a thick, beautiful binder full of teaching strategies, lesson plans, and blank templates but never measures the impact of those resources on student learning has likely set a Seemingly SMART goal. While achieving the production of a binder of resources for conferring is useful for Pedro's team, it is not sufficient. The result of their goal must show how the resources they create and collect advance students' ability to write DBQ essays. Teams that make student learning the outcome of their goal don't just put ideas in a binder, they put them into practice.

Time-bound, but bound by constraints. People are more likely to reach a goal when there is a clear time frame for achievement. In schools where team meeting time is sacred—no interruptions, no canceled meetings, all members are present at each meeting, no unrelated last-minute agenda items—SMART goals work. Time is protected for teachers to achieve their goals. However, if teachers are accustomed to disruptions to team time on a regular basis, they learn to adjust their time line. Suddenly, instead of a goal being driven by the urgency of student needs, it is driven by school constraints, thus making it Seemingly SMART.

In the given snapshot, Pedro's team extends its time line for achieving the goal because of frequently canceled meetings. Of course, team members need to take into account outside factors when setting a time line, but the first response should be to minimize time disruptions, not compromise the time line of a goal.

To sum up, a close look at Pedro's team goal reveals that it is Seemingly SMART on every level. But it only takes one of these underdeveloped SMART criterion to derail a team. For instance, team members might craft a time frame for their goal that is based on the needs of students, but they select a measurement tool that does not give them information they need when they need it, thus keeping them from making adjustments necessary to meet their goal in the time allotted. Whether a team goal is lacking in some or all elements of a SMART goal, the skillful team leader considers why his team is settling for Seemingly SMART.

Explore Possible Causes

Missed diagnosis. Why is it so common for a team to select an activity as a goal instead of a student-learning outcome? Most teams have a strong desire to do something about a problem, and there can be such a momentous dash to act that they skip the diagnosis or misdiagnose the problem. In this snapshot, Pedro's team pinpoints that students struggle with DBQ essays but never gets at the underlying causes. Instead, the team members jump to a strategy that they hope will fix the problem, and they make implementation of that strategy their goal. Even if the team accomplishes their goal of ten conferences per week, they are unlikely to see a significant change in students' writing because they never uncovered why students struggle with DBQ essays.

Fear of not measuring up. A teacher reluctant to measure a goal, or one who selects a measure that doesn't provide information that the team needs when it needs it, might be anticipating failure. Intentionally or not, she guards herself with a tool that measures her effort rather than the impact she has on student learning. The unspoken sentiment in Pedro's team might be "I'm comfortable sharing my weekly conferring log which reveals how hard I am working at holding ten conferences a week, but please don't ask me to regularly share the student DBQ essays that result from my conferences." Using student work as the measurement tool instead requires the team to have vulnerability-based trust (Lencioni, 2003) where they must expose to their colleagues their level of effectiveness with students.

"Shotgun" goal. Pressure can cause a team to set a Seemingly SMART goal that can only be attained with unsustainable strategies. Like some shotgun weddings, these teams make it to the altar, but they can't sustain the marriage. Perhaps administration has offered to reward a team (or has threatened them) to reach a goal, and so the team members are willing to do whatever it takes to achieve it, even if only for a short while. Pressure can come from within a team too, where members are so committed to attaining their goal that they are willing to take on unsustainable measures to achieve it.

A simple plan. A goal that results in a teaching plan is worthwhile. Curriculum should be aligned, and a teacher team that achieves this is on the right path. However, a bound curriculum cannot be the only result of a team's collaboration. Known as the "'bookends' of learning" (Allison et al., 2010) curriculum and assessment both play critical roles in a team's inquiry cycle. But the team with the Seemingly SMART goal stops at the curriculum plan. One reason for this is that high-functioning teams are and want to continue to be productive. Producing a binder of lesson plans is a result they can efficiently accomplish. Analyzing assessments to find out that their lesson plans didn't work and that they need to revise and reteach slows down momentum and increases the chances of conflict where the team members have different opinions on how to proceed. Even teams that don't fear becoming low functioning, may come short on student-learning results because they assume teachers know how to teach and adapt the curriculum they generate. This is not necessarily the case. Pedro's team can craft a binder full of conferring resources for teachers to use, but teachers may have varying success with using them, consequently producing little to no change in student learning. The skillful team leader ensures the team goal results in measured gains in student learning, not just a plan to get them there.

Fear. Research shows there is a negative side to goal setting; it can generate tremendous anxiety. "Goals are tied to accomplishment, therefore not achieving a goal indicates failure" (Williams, 2011). Teams that fear failure would rather set a Seemingly SMART goal to reduce anxiety and avoid negative consequences (from administrators, colleagues, parents, and even themselves) if they don't achieve it.

Fear of success can also pressure a team to select a Seemingly SMART goal—particularly when the reward for doing good work in schools tends to be more work. When fear governs a team, its goal is likely one in which members have little investment and little to lose. Typically, teachers can accomplish this type of goal without significant changes to their practice or thinking, thus resulting in a going-through-the-motions process leading to more of the same. Although perhaps not the intention of Pedro's team, setting a goal where teachers must hold ten student-writing conferences per week is safe. No one is required to change how he or she teaches.

Inadequate action plan. In some cases, an underdeveloped goal reveals holes in an action plan. For example, a team can craft a goal that is SMART by specifying sustainable strategies to attain a goal, but if team members have tried them in the past with no success, they can't expect to get different results. If teachers on Pedro's team have used conferring in the past with no success, they need to either change the strategy or improve upon it to see improvement in student DBQ essays. Unless the team members commit to an approach beyond what they have already been doing, the team risks a goal and plan that looks good on paper but not in practice.

Respond

Proactive response: To avoid a Seemingly SMART goal teams can do the following:

Get beyond semantics. The difference between SMART and Seemingly SMART is well beyond the wording of a goal. It is about the process of arriving at a goal. Teams who go beyond Seemingly SMART have thoughtful conversations about desired student-learning outcomes. They identify the best tools to measure learning and reject goals that can only be met through unsustainable means. They resist using team time to generate teaching resources without looking at the impact of those resources on their desired outcome for student learning, and they improve the system within which they work instead of allowing dysfunctional aspects of the school, such as interrupted schedules, to impact their goal. When disruptions to team meeting time are constant, team members work with others to ensure they have the time they need to achieve their goal.

Start with data. The skillful team leader uses data to inform a team's SMART goals. Whether creating long-term goals or "incremental learning targets" (Allison et al., 2010) to reach those goals, the Leadership and Learning Center (2012) recommends first collecting and charting data, then analyzing data (evidence of strengths and obstacles) and prioritizing needs. In this snapshot, Pedro's team might look at sample DBQs to determine what students are and are not doing well with respect to specific standards or subskills. Then they create a visual representation of the data such as a scatter plot of students' names and performance on specific DBQ skills, a bar graph comparing groups of students, or a chart with columns—exemplary, proficient, approaching, emerging, no evidence (Ainsworth et al., 2007)—that shows individual student performance in a particular skill. Knowing what students should be mastering and seeing visually where they are can aid the team in setting SMART goals and small learning targets to get there.

In-the-moment response: If a team sets a Seemingly SMART goal, a team leader can do the following:

Add on. No need to abandon a Seemingly SMART goal that focuses on an action. Jenny Miller, coach and consultant, recommends teams simply add the language "so that student(s) will learn . . ." to the end of their process goal to identify the student-learning outcome. Additionally, adding the words "as measured by student performance on . . ." to the outcome commits the team to measure the learning outcome and not the implementation of a strategy. Apply both phrases to Pedro's team and their goal now reads: *By the end of the semester, every teacher in the eleventh grade will hold ten teacher–student writing conferences per week so that students will learn how to write persuasive evidence-based DBQ essays. Progress will be measured by student performance on monthly DBQs from prior AP exams using the AP scoring rubric.*

Balance strategies in an action plan. Teams can avoid committing to unsustainable strategies by varying the intensity of strategies over the year. For instance, instead of team members committing to using their lunchtime for a semester to provide extra help to students, they can do it for a few weeks and craft a plan to gradually release to more long-term sustainable strategies.

Refocus the goal on learning. If a team is keen on using its time to produce a teaching resource, the skillful team leader helps teachers see that this is not the result they are after but rather a means to achieve their student-learning outcome. Pedro might ask, "What student learning do we expect to result from this teaching resource binder? Let's name that learning as our goal."

Additionally, throughout the team's work together, he can encourage teachers to share the student work that results from implementation of the resources in the binder.

Determine urgency first. When setting the timeframe within which a goal must be achieved, a team should prioritize the urgency of students needing to reach that goal. The skillful team leader uses data and backward planning to inform the timeline for a goal. If team meetings are canceled frequently, the team members need to come up with an alternative plan to continue advancing toward the goal despite their inability to meet regularly. For instance, teachers will analyze assessments independent of the team and use meeting time to only share specific findings and problem solve. Simultaneously, the team leader works with the school leadership team to diminish the external factors taking meeting time away.

Follow-up response: To sustain a team's commitment to stay SMART, not just Seemingly so, the team leader can do the following:

Ask questions. Throughout the team's implementation of their action plan to achieve their goal, teachers can revisit the guiding questions for generating SMART goals (see Resource 5.2: SMA-H-RT Guiding Questions).

School leadership team response: To discourage a team from setting Seemingly SMART goals, a team leader, the principal, and the administration together can do the following:

Offer professional development. Teams that learn the distinction between SMART and Seemingly SMART goals gain an understanding of the thoughtful decision making that must go into each criterion (see Resource 5.1: Making the Shift: From Seemingly SMART to SMART). A school leadership team emphasizes also the risk that Seemingly SMART goals pose—technically SMART but little impact on teaching and learning.

Dilemma 3: How Do I Advance Our Team Toward Achieving an Impactful SMART Goal When Team Members Want to Change Course?

It is understandable how a team would want to give up on a goal imposed by someone else or revamp one that ends up being Seemingly SMART. But what if the team has full ownership of the goal-setting process and crafts a goal that is SMART, not just Seemingly SMART, yet once into implementation, team members cringe at the thought of spending another minute working toward this goal?

Consider the following snapshot of a team:

Kate is setting a long-term SMART goal with her Grades 9–12 foreign language team. The conversation leading up to their goal sounds like the following:

One teacher suggests, "What about improving students' subject–verb agreement? I'm haunted by that every year."

Another responds, "I'd rather work on improving their vocabulary; without that they can't read, write, or talk."

"We focused on vocabulary all last year. I could use a break. I think we should use this time to get students to appreciate the customs and traditions of different cultures instead of just learning how to order a hamburger," suggests a third.

Distinct opinions put the team at a standstill. Finally, someone says, "I know a lot of other teams are working to improve students' open response; maybe we should give prompts and aim to move every student up one score on the schoolwide rubric?"

Teachers agree. "It's a measurable student-learning outcome and will help our colleagues out too. Let's do it."

One teacher admits, "I don't have my kids do open responses, but I guess I could do a few to help out."

A teacher adds, "Hey, it's not my first pick either, but if it's what everybody wants, I'll take one for the team."

Teachers leave the meeting feeling productive, but weeks later, momentum for the goal is dwindling and frustration is mounting. Teachers voice their thoughts:

"This goal is taking time away from our 'real' teaching."

"How am I supposed to fit it all in?"

"If our periods were longer, we could reach this goal."

"How are students supposed to write strong open responses when they can't even read what we are giving them?"

The team wants to give up on the goal, and Kate feels like teachers' valuable time has been wasted.

Identify the Hurdle

Teachers in this team snapshot struggle to come to consensus on a team SMART goal, and not long after they do, they lose their drive to achieve it. This team has a SMART goal, not just Seemingly so, but is it the right one? SMART goals are intended to help schools keep focused on priorities and resist a "putting out fires" mode in which immediate needs take precedence over important ones (Schmoker, 1999). Staying focused on the priority can be a challenge, but for some teams the trouble starts in agreeing upon one. Kate must find out why a team that was given complete ownership over its own goal setting process crafted a goal that its members don't own.

Explore Possible Causes

Group decision making. Consensus for a team goal is challenging when people bring their own "distinct perspectives and values" (Schmoker, 1999, p. 25). These distinct viewpoints are each valuable and important and because of this can cause conflict or put a team, such as the one in the snapshot, at a standstill. It is not uncommon for individuals to want to resolve this conflict and decide on a goal too quickly (Garmston, 2004). Teachers that settle often do so with good intentions; they want to keep the team cohesive or want the team to move forward so they go along with the group. Unfortunately, those good intentions can still lead to a least-common-denominator goal with minimal relevancy to each person, minimal drive to achieve it.

Preference not priority based. Conzemius and O'Neil (2002) suggest that goal setting should be strategic. If teachers make deliberate decisions about the specifics of a goal based on data, the goal is more likely to make an impact on teacher practice and student learning. However, if specifics of a goal are indiscriminate, based on individual teacher preferences, likes and dislikes, arbitrary numbers, or assumptions about what students need, a team is unlikely to make the strides needed.

Kate's team starts out with teachers' preferences for goal setting (e.g., "We focused on vocabulary all last year. I could use a break") instead of looking at their own assessments (i.e., homework, quizzes, notebooks, etc.) to determine what students in their foreign language classes actually need. Without data, agreeing upon a priority is a challenge. Even when they do eventually agree on a priority, it is not based on their own student data. Consequently, it is not a pressing need.

The missing "H." The SMART goal model, even when used effectively, is essential to goal setting, but it is limited. It does not account for the role that personal commitment plays in the success or failure of a goal. Teachers aren't driven to reach a goal because it is measurable (or any of the other words in the SMART acronym); they are motivated by goals that are critically important to their work with students—heartfelt goals. Daniel Goleman (2002) writes that "The more personal the commitment to learning goals, the more likely you are to achieve them" (p. 147). No one wants to put in loads of time on a team goal that doesn't ultimately help with the current students and problems teachers face. A team goal should relate to the work teachers do in the classroom: just as teachers' work in the classroom should be driven by the team's SMART goals. When they are not connected or teachers don't see how they are interrelated, the goal is perceived as another thing teachers must do and can't wait to unload.

On the contrary, when each team member has a heartfelt personal commitment to the decided goal, thus making it SMA-H-RT, the goal takes priority over other needs. (Note: The added "H" in SMA-H-RT is for heartfelt, intended to be pronounced with a heavy Boston accent as a tribute to my native-born husband.) Every team member is genuinely invested in the goal; they cannot *not* work toward it—essentially, they do whatever it takes to achieve it.

Reasons for Kate's team choosing a goal to improve open response range from "other teams are doing it," to "it meets the SMART acronym criteria," to "if it's what everybody wants, I'll take one for the team." Their responses indicate that this is not a heartfelt goal to which they are committed to achieving.

WHEN "WHATEVER IT TAKES" CROSSES ETHICAL LINES

Some researchers say there are downsides to goal setting—specifically that it motivates unethical behavior. Individuals can be so focused on accomplishing the goal that they cross ethical lines, and they may not even be aware they are doing so (Larrick, Heath, & Wu, 2009; Ordóñez, Schweitzer, Galinsky, & Bazerman, 2009). A team so focused on getting results, particularly when those results are going to be publicized across a school and community, may be tempted to alter results, thus fostering a school culture of unethical behavior. The skillful team leader, together with the team and the principal, continuously works to foster ethical learning conditions that honor risk taking and welcome learning from failure.

Differentiating adaptive from technical work. Even if the team goal is based on data and is heartfelt, a team might still lose motivation to achieve their goal. The skillful team leader considers the type of problem the team members seek to solve and how they are solving it. Adaptive challenges require a team to forge into unknown territory, often looking for solutions they have never thought of, thus having difficult conversations about values and practices (Heifetz & Linsky, 2002). It requires experimentation and learning. SMART goals that attempt to tackle adaptive challenges are hard, and when a team is not advancing toward its goal, its members are likely to get discouraged. If conditions within the team and school are not there to support teachers through the challenge of adaptive work, or if teachers are only looking at solutions they have tried in the past, the team may not make progress, may lose its drive, and may see dropping the goal as the only way out.

For instance, if a team such as Kate's sets out to improve open-response scores by instituting a technical solution in which students at every grade level use a common schoolwide graphic organizer (e.g., AEE: answer, evidence, explain), yet never addresses the adaptive problem that the majority of students are reading below grade level, teachers will not see improvement in open-response scores. The following is another example that illustrates the distinction: If a grade-level math team discovers that 40% of students are repeating geometry class (causing the class size to be too large), adding another section of geometry is putting a technical solution on an adaptive problem—the problem being that too many students are failing geometry. The math team needs to set its goal on reducing the number of failing students, not just finding solutions to deal with the overflowing class size.

Too big they fail. Kate's team members are not making progress toward their goal. Frustration builds as does desire to abandon the goal. People get on board "when they begin to feel the magic of momentum/when they begin to see tangible results" (Collins, 2001, p. 178). Although Kate's long-term team goal specifies that teachers will move every student up one score on the schoolwide rubric, they need to define the high-leverage skills students need to master at each level. Without breaking down the goal into specific skills that groups of students must be able to do and without measuring student progress every few weeks, the team members have their eye on the big-picture goal but aren't making the incremental gains needed to get there. The lack of progress negatively impacts their motivation to achieve the goal.

Gravitational pull. Even when a team does select a goal that is a priority, things that "must be done by yesterday" or urgent upcoming needs can pressure teachers to forsake their goal. In the case of this snapshot, the pull teachers are feeling is not trivial; it is from challenges they are seeing in their classroom. Whatever the pull, a team is left making tough choices: to recommit to its goal or to stray from it.

It's emotional. Goal setting may seem like a simple numbers game. For example, "X% of students should be at this standard. Y% are not. Therefore, we will get Y% to reach standard by this date." But there are strong emotions attached, particularly when goals are not reached. After all, those numbers represent kids. Educators can be embarrassed and discouraged by failed goals.

They can feel defeated when strategies don't work and incompetent when they are out of solutions. Some teachers would rather abandon a goal than face the emotions brought on by failure. It's possible that teachers on Kate's team are not making progress with the open-response goal, and this is causing them to want to change course to something at which they can succeed.

Respond

Proactive response: To promote consensus in a team goal in which all members are invested, a team leader can do the following:

Lead with data. Priorities become clearer when teams look at multiple sources of data together. The skillful team leader facilitates discourse around a team's own assessments and that which informs school goals. Nancy Love's (2009) data-driven dialogue protocol is particularly valuable for teams to see trends and patterns as well as specific areas of need (see Resource 5.3: Data Analysis Protocol). Once a team begins to look at data together, priorities based on student needs and not teacher preferences emerge.

Ainsworth (2003) recommends data teams prioritize standards, also known as determining Power Standards. They advise teachers to prioritize using three criteria: endurance, leverage, and readiness. The skillful team leader asks the question, Will (achieving) this standard or indicator provide students with knowledge and skills that will be of value

- beyond the single test date,
- in multiple disciplines, or
- in preparing students for the next level of instruction?

Answers to these three questions focus a team on setting a small short-term learning target that will bring the team members closer to their long-term SMART goal.

Norm for decision making. The challenge for team members is to remain honest decision makers, ensuring that "no one's individual interest can dominate the proceedings" (Senge, Kleiner, Roberts, Ross, & Smith, 1994, p. 73). Knowing in advance that there are times when a team struggles to come to consensus, the skillful team leader cocreates a group agreement about how the team will make important decisions such as goal setting. For example, "Make decisions in the best interest of the students," or "Keep personal agendas separate from team goals."

Scrap consensus. In many instances, teams do well coming to consensus on a SMART goal—they are able to look at common assessments to determine needs for students and can take a more focused, coherent approach to instructional strategies. However, if team members struggle to come to consensus on one or more goals, it might be because their students have different needs. If this is the case, agreeing upon one common goal is not in the best interest of students. The skillful team leader helps teachers decipher when they need to come to consensus on SMART goals and when they need to set goals independent of one another.

Make it SMA-H-RT from the start. In a job where teachers can't help going home thinking about a particular struggling student, a lesson that flopped, or a concept that students just aren't grasping, why wouldn't a team set a goal that, if met, would help its members sleep at night? There are so many real student-learning issues common to teachers, which also align to school and district goals, that to choose one that is not heartfelt increases the risk of a team just going through the motions to achieve the goal superficially or, worse, abandoning the goal. While it is possible for some teams to gain commitment to a goal once they begin working toward it, naming a SMA-H-RT goal from the start lowers the likelihood of a team wanting to give up. To identify a heartfelt goal, the skillful team leader asks, "How critical is it to us that we achieve this goal? How would our work be different if we didn't work toward it? What are we willing to do to achieve this goal?"

Connect goals and "real" work. The "real" work of teachers is to promote learning for student achievement. The team goal and action plan should advance that work. The skillful team leader asks teachers one or more of the following questions: "Is this goal relevant and meaningful to our everyday work? When achieved, what impact will it have on student learning in our school? How will achieving this goal make us more successful as teachers?"

In-the-moment response: If team members' drive to accomplish their goal shifts, a team leader can do the following:

Prioritize priorities. Perhaps best said by Wagner et al. (2006), "The individual teacher, school or district with ten priorities has none" (p. 66). The same is true for teacher teams. In order to progress with clear purpose, a team must come to consensus on what is most pressing, urgent, and critical for their students. It's easy for a team to get distracted by multiple priorities. The skillful team leader poses the decision making to the team. Kate might respond to her team's low investment in pursuing the goal by saying, "A month ago we chose to improve student open responses. Was it a priority to us then? Is it still the priority now? What evidence do we have that our students need this? 'Is this something peripheral to our purpose that we need to resist, so we stay focused on our goal?'" (Wagner et al., 2006, p. 67). What evidence do we have of this?" If the team members answer "yes" to Wagner and Kegan's question, then they need to reevaluate their goal. If they answer "no," the team leader can respond, "Let's stay focused on what we set out to achieve." Teachers on Kate's team who voice that the open-response goal is taking away from their "real" teaching are a likely indication that they may not be focused on the right priority at the right time for their students.

Carpe commodum. "Seize the opportunity." Disagreement over priorities is an opportunity for rich discussion about instructional decisions. The skillful team leader encourages teachers to share their thinking about what they are seeing that urges them to push for a particular goal or desire to abandon one. Kate might say, "Please speak more as to why you think this should (or shouldn't) be our goal. What evidence do you have that the goal is needed (or no longer needed)?"

Think big, stay small. A long-term SMART goal is an essential first step for a team to define a specific endpoint for the team's work. All members have a clear vision of where they are headed and what must be accomplished by when. However, even when the goal is specific, it can still be broad by failing to name and measure exactly what skills each group of students needs to master to achieve that goal.

Based on the work of the Scaffolded Apprenticeship Model (SAM), the strategy of "getting small in order to go big," teams set small learning targets to achieve a big long-term goal (Scharff, Deidre, DeAngelis, & Talbert, 2010, p. 58). Just as individual teachers set learning targets for their daily lessons, which are described as a "lesson-sized chunk of information, skills, and reasoning processes that students will come to know deeply and thoroughly" (Moss & Brookhart, 2012), teams use data to identify a measurable, teachable, and assessable skill (Talbert, Scharff, & Lin, 2008). "The tight focus on a small group of students . . . shifts the conversation from generalities and assumptions about why struggling students can't learn to specific information about what they don't know and how teachers can help them learn it; and illuminates places where a small, strategic system-change can make a big difference" (Scharff et al., 2010, p. 2). Like stepping-stones across a river, each learning target brings specific groups of students that much closer to reaching the team's SMART goal.

Once used as an approach by teams who needed to reach underperforming students, setting small learning targets is now seen as an approach to help move all students. Hence, a team might have multiple learning targets for different groups of students within each inquiry cycle.

In this snapshot, Kate's team might target students who scored two where they cite no evidence from the text with the learning target "I (student) will identify up to three pieces of evidence in the text that answer the given prompt." Another group of students who scored 3 on the rubric, and who are skilled at identifying evidence from the text but not at analyzing that evidence might have the target "I (student) will explain how my evidence answers the prompt." As teachers move through the inquiry cycle, they determine how they will assess these targets and collaborate on minilessons that will target these specific skills.

Change the strategy. Before abandoning a goal, a team closely examines its action plan to reach it. Doing the same thing team members have always done in the past will not yield new results, and it can discourage teachers from wanting to continue. The skillful team leader can redirect the conversation to brainstorm alternate strategies and how the team might implement them. For example, Kate might say, "I hear people's frustration with our goal. Before we toss it, let's look at the strategies we have been using to attain it. How might we look at this problem differently? What better strategies exist? What have we not tried, even if it requires changing our habits or those of our school?"

Break up. Some teams have a better chance of being high functioning, high impact when they form smaller teams within a larger team, where groups focus on heartfelt goals specific to their students' needs rather than complying with goals that are not priorities to them or their students. Having one's own goal does not mean working alone. Time can be broken up so that miniteams meet separately from the larger group, but at other times, the larger group gets together to share progress, challenges, and give feedback on goals. Kate might suggest that her team break off into one group focused on improving students' vocabulary while another works to improve students' open response, provided those teachers have evidence that these goals are student priorities.

Even if the team keeps with the same long-term goal, they may opt for differentiated learning targets depending on their students' needs. That being said, teams in which teachers teach the same grade or content are highly likely to have students with the same needs, and therefore coming to consensus on learning targets can aid the group in valuable collaborative learning opportunities such as lesson study in which teachers demonstrate one common teaching strategy multiple times to improve instruction.

Follow-up response: To sustain investment in a SMART goal, a team leader can do the following:

Gauge drive. Teachers can set a goal to which they are personally committed and driven to reach, only to lose investment once they are into implementing the action plan. The skillful team leader recognizes the signs of motivation for achieving a goal or lack thereof. Signs of investment might include teachers who voluntarily bring related resources (e.g., readings, resources from workshops, etc.) to team meetings, who discuss the goal outside of team time, who offer to share student work even if they are not scheduled to, who initiate conversations about the goal and action plan with colleagues on other teams, or who yearn to showcase their successes and problem solve with others publicly.

Signs of dwindling motivation include teachers who superficially implement agreed upon strategies, make excuses for not giving assessments, come unprepared to meetings with no student work, or talk negatively outside of team meetings about how the team's goal and action plan is a burden that is taking away from their "real" teaching. The skillful team leader brings awareness to these signs and asks the team to recommit to the goal or find out why they don't want to.

Check in. Just as team members build in assessments for their students to monitor progress toward the goal, they can build in checkpoints to assess their motivation toward achieving a goal and reflect on how it is changing their instruction, their mindset, and their students. In a goal with a six-week time frame, a team might have three checkpoints (first day and then every two weeks) asking teachers to fill out three short-answer questions rating their commitment to the goal, what they have implemented to reach the goal, and concerns they have as they approach their goal's deadline. The skillful team leader also repeats the commitment questions she asked at the start of the team's work. For example, "How is this goal still relevant to your everyday work? If you were invested at the onset and are no longer, what has changed? What do we need to do to ensure this goal is not an add-on but is instead a critical component toward achieving our school's mission, vision, and goals?"

School leadership team response: To prevent teams from giving up on goals, team leaders, the principal, and administrators together can do the following:

Provide a lens. Teams are better able to identify high-priority student needs once the school has done so. A school leadership team can share data from state, district, and schoolwide assessments in a digestible, visual so teacher teams can clearly see student needs and school priorities. Additionally, having a principal who articulates school goals and priorities clearly, and who is transparent about how she or he arrived at them, guides teams to align their goals to them and focus on strategies to attain them.

Create conditions for progress. The research of Teresa Amabile and Steven Kramer (2010, 2011) indicates a connection between progress and motivation: Small wins are more frequently associated with high motivation. The researchers advise leaders to ensure meaningful goals and to provide resources and encouragement individuals need to succeed. They stress that changing goals, bogging people down with demands that are distractions, or withholding resources negatively impact people's drive to achieve goals. Teams are more apt to stay motivated for their own goals if conditions in the school support their ability to make progress toward them.

Dare to be adaptive. School leaders can encourage teams to set goals around the adaptive challenges of the school. They can help teams move beyond technical solutions and create conditions that support teams in sticking with problems that require them to learn collaboratively, fail, and shift the status quo. The principal can show support by explicitly stating that teams will not be penalized for choosing to find solutions to adaptive challenges when solutions require the school to do things differently.

Look for the "H." Schools can conduct learning walks in which teams look for evidence of others working toward their SMA-H-RT goals. If heartfelt personal commitment is there, evidence of teachers working toward their goals will be everywhere, not just in a discussion at a team meeting or on a piece of paper hanging in the teachers' lounge.

CONSIDER SCHOOL CULTURE: SHIFTING FROM A SCAPEGOAT CULTURE TO A CULTURE OF MUTUAL ACCOUNTABILITY

When teachers show reluctance to setting and attaining impactful goals, the skillful team leader considers the possible existence of a scapegoat culture, where the school values goal setting as a powerful tool for advancement yet uses it as a "gotcha" technique to designate blame. Instead of teachers and district school leaders together taking responsibility for poor performance on student assessments and unattained goals, they resort to finger pointing. Today's focus on rigorous accountability from the No Child Left Behind Act and Obama's "Blueprint for Reform" keeps schools accountable to the goal of college and career readiness for all. Failing students can no longer go unnoticed—neither can teachers or principals.

This heightened accountability has some people concerned. Although the word *accountability* simply means to hold someone responsible for the results of decisions and practice, when said within a scapegoat culture, it takes on a negative connotation. Here, school leaders use accountability measures to find fault with others in order to deliver consequences to them. Those who don't accomplish goals are penalized. Instead of being mutually accountable, individuals fault others. Even when school leaders are not pointing fingers, in a scapegoat culture, teachers assume they are and act defensively. Fear is the undercurrent, and the opportunity to grow and impact student learning is often missed.

Recognize the Signs of a Scapegoat Culture

- Teams set easily attainable goals that do not work to solve high-priority needs. A teacher might say, "I don't want to be penalized for a goal I can't reach."
- Teams relinquish responsibility for students' lack of knowledge or skill. "This isn't our problem. They should have taught this last year."
- Teachers keep problems to themselves. They don't bring in student work that shows students' struggling. When asked how they are doing, especially by an administrator, teacher answers, "Great!" regardless of challenges.
- Principals and teachers with poor test results are admonished, demoted, transferred, or fired without specific feedback to grow or the opportunity to learn and improve.

Where Does the Scapegoat Culture Come From?

One doesn't have to look too far outside of education to see that scapegoating is embedded in our culture. When the 2010 BP oil spill occurred in the Gulf of Mexico, blame shifted for months between Halliburton, Transocean, Cameron, and BP's management. In sports, Red Sox first baseman Bill Buckner was deemed responsible for the 1986 World Series loss. Blaming an individual for direct harm that he or she caused is accepted by most, but blaming whole groups of people collectively for harm brought about by a few members raises morality questions. Marion Smiley (2005), professor of philosophy at Brandeis University, questions if "particular groups in history can legitimately be considered morally responsible for the suffering that group members have brought about through their faulty actions" such as holding all Germans responsible for the victims of the Holocaust. She highlights the notion that people who are not responsible for harm are "blameworthy" simply because of their association with a group (para. 5). The U.S. education system is most certainly struggling with moral questions about who is responsible for failing schools, and regardless of where one stands on the issue, the need to hold groups accountable can quickly slip into a scapegoat culture, where teachers are a primary target.

Blame seems to creep up when stakes are high. There is tremendous pressure on schools to perform, and when they don't perform well, they need to determine a root cause. As teachers in particular come under scrutiny in today's educational debate, it is difficult to break from the habit of blame.

Fear drives the scapegoat culture. Not knowing the cause of a problem or having to face one's shortcomings as a contributing cause to the problem is frightening. It's more comforting, even when it is not true, to hold the assumption that if I find the person or group responsible for the problem and penalize or get rid of them, I eradicate the problem. Additionally, teachers who fear becoming the scapegoat are wary of measured goals and avoid risk. Even in schools where school leaders are not pointing fingers, teachers may still carry the belief that they are.

Tackling any gap in school culture is hard, but this one seems particularly so. School leaders and teachers need to foster trust and shift the blame associated with accountability to a culture that reflects, learns, and acts together. They need to adopt the belief that every stakeholder is a contributor to student success and failure (from the superintendent to the custodian).

To initiate a shift from a scapegoat culture to a culture of mutual accountability, team leaders together with other school members can do the following:

Reward responsibility. "Great teams do not wait for the leader to remind members when they are not pulling their weight" (Lencioni, 2003, para. 26). Teams are more likely to set loftier goals if they know that they are going to be treated as professionals, and that they will be given the opportunity to reflect and learn from failure rather than have someone else put them "in a corner." Schools can foster a safe environment for an individual or team to initiate responsibility for failure by having faculty "debriefs," where teams openly share failures and what they have learned from them.

Reflect, don't deflect. When failure to reach a goal is viewed as an opportunity to learn, grow, and change—not blame—teams continue to take risks. To foster this, school leaders and faculty can continuously ask

- what part did I play in this outcome,
- where do we need to be, and
- what do I do with others to get us there?

Summoning the village. Hillary Rodham Clinton (1996) said, "It takes a village" to provide for children. When schools are able to adopt this belief, they begin to focus on solutions that don't ask only one stakeholder to make a change (which assumes that stakeholder is to blame for the problem). Instead, they look at what each stakeholder can do. By taking collective responsibility for the solution, they are taking collective responsibility for the problem.

APPLICATION TO YOUR WORK: CONNECT, OBSERVE, EXPLORE, ACT

Think and write independently. Then, discuss with colleagues.

Connect	Observe
Remember a time as a leader or participant when your team set an impactful SMA-H-RT goal in which everyone was invested. What did team meetings look and sound like?	How invested is your team in setting a SMART goal or implementing the goal you have? What evidence do you have that your team goal is not Seemingly SMART? If your team has set a Seemingly SMART goal, what impact is it having on the school? on your team? on students? Is your team "staying small to get big"? What evidence do you have that your team is accomplishing its learning targets and advancing toward your SMART goal(s)?
Explore	**Act**
What hurdles prevent your team from setting and attaining an impactful SMA-H-RT goal? What have you done to prevent your team from having a Seemingly SMART goal? Why are your learning targets advancing (or not advancing) small groups of students toward your team's long-term SMART goal? What have you not tried yet? Why?	What will you and your colleagues do to shift from Seemingly SMART to SMA-H-RT? Name next steps and support needed.

Off-Course Discourse 6

Overcoming Hurdles to Lead a Team in Rigorous Discourse

FOUNDATIONAL VALUE: RIGOROUS DISCOURSE

Professional learning requires teams to engage in rigorous discourse, but what if discourse is just talk? This chapter applies a skillful approach to overcoming hurdles brought about by challenging conversations about data sometimes laden with blame, excuses, and assumptions. It offers strategies to team leaders to facilitate discourse that is evidence based, dialogic, culturally proficient, reflective, and actionable, even in schools where the "culture of nice" keeps talk superficial.

WHAT IS RIGOROUS DISCOURSE, AND WHY IS IT IMPORTANT?

For high-functioning teams to have a high impact on student learning, teams must do more than talk. They must engage in rigorous discourse. Rigorous discourse draws on the models of collegial inquiry (Drago-Severson, 2004), data-driven dialogue (Love, 2009), and collective inquiry (DuFour & Eaker, 1998). A sign that a team is engaging in rigorous discourse looks similar to Jim Knight's (2007) example of a principle of praxis: "When teachers . . . really consider how they teach, really learn a new approach, and then reconsider their teaching practices, and reshape the new approach, if necessary, until it can work in their classroom" (p. 49). It's not just studying theory, or sharing ideas, or swapping lesson plans; it's about the real application of what is learned in the team and implemented in the classroom to obtain measurable growth for students.

Rigor is achieved when discourse is evidence based, dialogic, culturally proficient, reflective, and actionable. Together these five criteria elevate learning and a team's ability to achieve their goal. All team discourse does not need to be rigorous, but team discourse without rigor is just talk.

Rigorous Discourse Is Evidence Based

Teams engaged in rigorous discourse ground conversations in evidence. They strategically work with a diverse pool of assessments (i.e., district standardized assessments, student work, observational data from a classroom lesson, teacher–student conference notes, etc.), moving discourse through phases such as Nancy Love's (2009) data-driven dialogue: *Predict* what the data will show, *go visual* with a means to see patterns and trends, *observe* without judgment based on the data, and *infer* causes for the results to inform next steps. Throughout the inquiry process, they use not only their own assessments as evidence to inform their action steps, but they read research-based practices and professional texts to gain new ideas and strategies to achieve their goal.

Rigorous discourse using student data might sound like the following: "I notice students were stronger at determining the author's purpose in the passage on the last assessment than on this assessment. When we specifically compare questions, I notice . . . I'm wondering if this is because the second passage requires students to infer . . ."

Rigorous discourse using an article might sound like the following: "I connected with the second line in Paragraph 2 [reads the line] because . . ." "The author's point seems to be . . . but I'm unsure how that would work with my students." "This text makes me think of the demonstration lesson Mrs. J. did last week." "The results from this research article align with my own findings . . ."

Rigorous Discourse Is Dialogic

Discourse by its very name indicates written or verbal communication between two or more people, but not all communication in a team is rigorous. Monologic discourse in which fixed ideas are transferred and no new insight is gained is void of rigor (i.e., a team leader teaching other members how to fill out an action plan). Dialogic discourse, on the other hand, "connotes social relationships of equal status, intellectual openness, and possibilities for critique and creative thought" (O'Connor & Michaels, 2007). This type of talk is rigorous because it fosters learning and change. Within a team, there is room for both types of discourse, but to be considered rigorous, it must be dialogic.

Rigorous discourse when dialogic might sound like the following: "I hear your point about implementing the strategy of . . . but in looking over the evidence again, namely, here . . . I'm thinking that this strategy might not resolve the problem. I'd like to gain ideas on how to adapt it or learn about others."

Rigorous Discourse Is Culturally Proficient

Teams of teachers talking while huddled over spreadsheets, state test reports, photocopies of student work, and school data, looks like professional learning but isn't, unless it is brazenly honest about culture-bound assumptions inviting multiple perspectives to the conversation. This means teams hold culturally proficient conversations where teachers do not let unsettling remarks settle. They actively listen for culture-bound assumptions such as

"Student X comes from a family of very nice, hardworking, blue-collar workers; he'll do well as a store clerk, but there is no way he'll make it in college." They respectfully question each others' beliefs, values, and teaching decisions about cultural[1] groups and apply what they have learned. They act with a moral responsibility to meet the social and cognitive needs of all children, particularly those most often underserved (Lindsey, Jungwirth, Pahl, & Lindsey, 2009, p. 37). They engage in difficult conversations from a stance of curiosity without attacking colleagues, while simultaneously advocating for equity.

Rigorous discourse when culturally proficient might sound like the following: One teacher says, "'What good will it do to talk about student achievement when we know these kids are doing the best they can for who they are?' Another responds, 'What might be some things that can support our conversations about how all demographic groups are being served by us'" (Lindsey et al., 2009, p. 68)?

Rigorous Discourse Is Reflective

Discourse without rigor can resemble a group of people mindlessly going through the motions on a morning commute. They make decisions without thoughtful reflection. For example, in week one of a team's inquiry cycle, the team might notice twenty-four students don't know how to write a topic sentence. Team members commit to teaching students how to write topic sentences explicitly. Two weeks later they reassess, and twenty students still can't write a topic sentence. They conclude that they need to reteach topic sentences. There is no discourse about how they are teaching it or for what purpose. No one discusses why the reteaching worked for four students but not for the other twenty. No one publicly considers how they will change their instructional practice in order to meet the different needs of their students or how their beliefs about teaching students to be better writers might need to evolve in order to get different results.

Rigorous discourse plunges people into consciousness. They have a heightened awareness of self and practice. They wrestle with what they believe to know as true and what evidence shows to be true. Covey (2004) believes people come face-to-face with a "paradigm shift," where initial ways of thinking, traditional behaviors, and perceptions shift our thinking and actions

Rigorous discourse when reflective might sound like the following: "I'm thrown off when I see this data because I truly thought X was working."

Rigorous Discourse Is Actionable

Team members who have an exhilarating, dialogic conversation about what they read in a professional text or see in their data, who are brazenly honest about what they see and hear, who are fully conscious of their own assumptions and contributions to problems, yet who never transform any newly acquired learning into actionable steps for teachers and students, fall short of rigorous discourse. Information gained through talk on its own holds little value until it becomes actionable knowledge, where educators are capable of applying their learning to their practice (Argyris, 1993). Conversations yielding "aha" moments of awareness

---

[1]As authors Lindsey et al. (2009) point out, culture in this context is defined not only as ethnicity but also includes "race, age, gender, sexual orientation and identity, faith, spirituality, language, ableness, geography, ancestry, language, history, occupation, and affiliations" (p. xiii).

In support of rigorous discourse:

- "When teachers get together to talk in concrete, precise language about instruction and student work, their teaching dramatically improves and student achievement rises" (White, 2010).
- In a 2003 study designed to assess the impact that collaborative inquiry using assessments had on teacher teams, researchers found that "teams began to see that when they control data they can shape the debate. They came to see that what they do in the classroom really does matter and that they can determine outcomes through their own action" (Huffman & Kalnin, 2003, p. 21). Using data for professional debates around teaching and learning connects teachers professionally, breaking through isolation (Huffman & Kalnin).
- "Innovations which include strengthening the practice of formative assessment produce significant, and often substantial, learning gains" (Black & Wiliam, 1998, p. 140).
- Rigorous discourse requires teachers to make evidence-based decisions using formative assessments, which when shared with students improves their performance. Formative assessments make students aware of learning goals, give them multiple opportunities to demonstrate understanding, and teach them what to specifically continue doing and where to improve (Emberger & McTighe, 2006; Stiggins, 2002).
- "When a value for diversity exists, managing issues that arise from cultural differences are surfaced, explored, and resolved as part of ongoing communication, problem-solving processes, and collaboration" (Lindsey et al., 2009, p. 89).

and knowledge are only valuable if they also result in teachers and students changing what they do or deliberately recommitting to what they already do with newfound purpose, heightened awareness, vigor, and fidelity. (Chapter 6 explores how to overcome the hurdle of moving from knowledge to action).

Rigorous discourse, when actionable, might sound like the following: "So we have identified a problem of focus and some specific causes, and potential strategies that could work. Now, let's set a time line naming when we will implement the strategies and when we will assess if they are advancing our goal."

In short, anytime team members look at evidence and suddenly become visibly aware of their own shortcomings; anytime someone panics that he or she has been teaching the "wrong way" his or her whole career; anytime someone squirms at hearing a negative assumption about students and is compelled to speak; anytime a team looks at assessment data and says, "What the heck do we do now?" and anytime team talk translates into actionable knowledge, that team is likely engaging in rigorous discourse.

HURDLES TO LEADING A TEAM IN RIGOROUS DISCOURSE

Most literature will say that working in a team requires teachers to step out of their comfort zones. Rigorous discourse goes a step further. It requires people to be vulnerable. They become conscious of teaching decisions and the impact, positive or negative, that those decisions have on students, and they do so publicly in front of their colleagues. Stepping out of one's comfort zone doesn't begin to cover it. Rigorous discourse can drudge up feelings of self-doubt, uncertainty, defensiveness, and even panic. Consequently, some teams avoid it.

A team might encounter any number of hurdles in trying to engage in rigorous discourse: teacher reluctance to use evidence as the basis for dialogue, censored dialogue about data, or dialogue laden with blame and excuses. Even high-functioning teams who look at evidence regularly and take responsibility for problems can end up with little impact on student learning because of the limitations of their own culture-bound assumptions.

In trying to overcome these hurdles a team leader might wonder, How do I lead our team in rigorous discourse when

1. individuals show reluctance toward assessments,

2. we can't move beyond superficial talk,

3. blame and excuses dominate talk, or

4. unsettling remarks settle?

Dilemma 1: How Do I Lead Our Team in Rigorous Discourse When Individuals Show Reluctance Toward Assessments?

Teams that don't ground conversations in evidence can't expect to reach a level of rigor that fosters learning because there's little substance to talk about. Data from assessments prompt teachers to identify student-learning needs, deeply reflect on their instruction, question practice and thinking, and make critical decisions for student learning. Rigorous discourse without data is like trying to get a weightlifter's body without weights. There might be a modest benefit, but no one should expect transformation.

Utilizing assessments is a critical part of the inquiry cycle. They can provide baseline information for team goal setting, track teacher and student progress toward the goal, and inform next steps. They are a means to communicate areas of strength and weakness to students so that they may take an active role in achieving the goal. Despite the benefits, some teachers are reluctant to use them.

Consider the following snapshot of multiple teams in a department meeting:

> *Teams in Chung's history department have been given annual goals for their students. Chung announces that they will now need to determine pre-, interim, and postassessments to monitor progress throughout their inquiry cycle. Teachers respond, "We don't need to do a baseline assessment: we already know what the problems are. These kids are over tested. Why do we need to contribute? I don't want to take any more time away from instruction. It'll be obvious if they improve." Based on teachers' reactions, Chung wants to skip the assessments altogether, but he knows to do so would mean the teams would be missing out on important information to influence their actions for achieving their goals.*

Identify the Hurdle

The teachers in this snapshot raise valid concerns. Kids are tested a lot. Time used for test taking in class is time when the teacher is not able to instruct. Although these objections are raised with the best intentions for students, they are not actually in the best interest of teacher learning. Assessments provide critical information to teachers about their own practice. Teams learn from assessments, and this helps students. So why would some teachers in a team be reluctant to use them?

Explore Possible Causes

Preposition confusion. Teachers with the notion that all assessments are evaluative are likely to be wary of them, but not all assessments serve the same purpose. Stiggins (2002) differentiates between assessments *for* learning and assessments *of* learning (see Sidebar). Teachers who are less familiar with assessments *for* learning are more likely to have a knee-jerk reaction to using them.

Stiggins (2002) defines assessments "of" learning versus assessments "for" learning:

Assessments *of* learning are evaluative and typically summative. Examples can include the following: a state test determining if a student graduates high school with a diploma, a final exam determining if a student grasped all of the material necessary to move forward to the next grade, or a graded final unit exam to determine what learning the students mastered for a permanent mark in the grade book.

Assessments *for* learning are often formative, administered more than once to find out what students know and can do so that teachers can adjust their instruction or set up interventions and enrichments to meet students' needs. Examples might include the following: quizzes, student notebook entries, writing prompts, or exit tickets. Summative assessments can also be used *for* learning, for example, a team looks at state test results from the spring to identify annual goals for their incoming students. Assessments *for* learning, whether formative or summative, provide specific data that can help both teachers and students pinpoint areas of strengths and areas for growth.

Loss of independence. A teacher might be comfortable with assessments *for* learning but less confident in creating and using them with a team. Anxious that she will need to alter or abandon assessments she already gives can cause a teacher to voice concern.

Assessments with no data-driven dialogue. Teams who have administered assessments in the past but never got to analyze them in a way that informs their next steps are likely to see them as a waste of time.

The trusted gut. Reticence to using assessments as a team may come from a lack of clarity or consensus on *what* to use. Some goals are easily measured (e.g., a team uses attendance records to monitor an attendance goal), but other more subjective goals challenge teams to find a suitable assessment tool (e.g., a team wants to improve students' critical-thinking skills, but has no rubric to measure them). Rather than spend time engaging in a difficult conversation to define what improvement looks like, teachers may resort to following their gut: "We'll just know when the kids can do it." Even when the unscientific gut is right on, it does not provide specific information needed to advance individual students. When teachers do not have a clear sense of how to measure their students' performance and growth, some resist doing so altogether.

Concern for what might be learned. Data expose problems. Some teams fear opening up a Pandora's box and are concerned that they won't know how to solve the problems inside. Others might worry that the problems revealed by data paint an insufficient picture of students' strengths and needs, thereby imposing them to make instructional changes based on limited or misguided data.

Limited understanding of the cycle. Ask any teacher if he or she wants to achieve continuous improvement for students and the answer is likely "yes." However, teachers new to the inquiry cycle may not have a grasp on how data play a leading role in making that desire a reality. Instead they view pre-, interim, and postassessments as an add-on to the team's work, instead of as an integral part in achieving growth in student learning.

Respond

Proactive response: To encourage rigorous discourse that utilizes assessments for learning, a team leader can do the following:

Distinguish prepositions. Understanding the difference between assessments *of* learning and *for* learning (Stiggins, 2002) and actually using them for the purpose for which they are designed can help teachers embrace their use in a team. Chung might share a short reading from Stiggins (or the previous sidebar) to help team members understand the distinction and identify what information they need when they need it.

Connect to inquiry. Assessments for learning are a key component of professional learning, not an add-on. The skillful team leader points out the lead role that data play in the inquiry cycle. In this snapshot, Chung's teachers might be more ammenable to giving a baseline assessment when they see it is the first step in a larger process for achieving continuous improvement. To help the team see the big picture, Chung might share the inquiry cycle referenced in Chapter 3.

Putting assessments in their place. "We are still the designers, deliverers, and assessors of learning experiences," remind the authors of the book *Data Teams: The Big Picture: Looking at Data Through a Collaborative Lens* (Allison et al., 2010, pp. 362–363). The skillful team leader not only ensures members see how data are essential to inquiry, but also reminds teachers how they are essential to data. Preassessments identify needs, but teachers decide big goals and small targets. Interim assessments provide feedback, but teachers use feedback to adapt teaching. Postassessments measure growth, but teachers determine next steps.

Include the little "d." John D'Auria (personal communication, February 16, 2012) cautions teacher teams to not be threatened or too enchanted with what he calls "Big D" data (i.e., state tests, district assessments, etc.). Some of the most informative evidence comes from "little d" data—observational data made by teachers, school leaders, students, or parents, teacher–student interviews and conferences, walk-through data, and teacher created assessments, and so forth. To paint a full picture of students' strengths and needs, teachers are more likely to embrace the use of assessments in a team to inform their instructional decisions when the evidence chosen is both "Big D" and "little d" data.

In-the-moment response: If a team is reluctant to engage in rigorous discourse that uses assessments for learning, a team leader can do the following:

Suggest time-preserving assessments. Not every assessment used to see where students are at with respect to the team goal needs to take up an entire class period to administer. Teachers can utilize time already set aside in the class to assess understanding and bring that data to their team. For instance, data from a do-now prompt or from answers to questions on an exit ticket can provide teachers with the information they need to assess learning. Collaboratively generating assessments for learning that can be built into the routine of what teachers and students already do reduces teachers' reluctance to giving them (and students' reluctance to taking them).

Lead with the gut; then name it. Although instinct can't be measured, it should not be dismissed. In his book *Complications*, Atul Gwande (2003) shares how although evidence pointed to one diagnosis, his gut pointed to another. In the end, listening to his gut saved a woman's life. Gut assessments typically come from learning experiences. When teachers respond to the request for giving an assessment by saying, "We'll know when they know," the skillful team leader defines with his or her gut. In this snapshot, Chung might probe, saying "So we have a gut feeling that students are reaching our goal. Have you had this gut feeling before? If so, what did you see or hear from students?"

Foster choice. Common assessments make comparing and drawing conclusions easier during the observation and inference phases, but they don't have to come at the cost of one's independent decision making. So long as a team agrees on what they are intending to measure, several options exist: Teachers can share assessments they already give as a starting point for creating common team assessments; teachers can agree to common benchmarks throughout an inquiry cycle, but vary daily formative assessments; individual teachers can adopt the new team common assessment but continue to supplement with their own.

Follow-up response: To sustain rigorous discourse using assessments for learning, a team leader can do the following:

Press onward. Nothing sustains a team's momentum like progress, and assessments keep track. Teachers are likely to get on board with using them once they see they are learning how to meet their students' needs more effectively because of them.

School leadership team response: To facilitate rigorous discourse where teams use assessments for learning, team leaders, the principal, and administrators together can do the following:

Support the process. By providing time and resources for teams to create and analyze assessments for learning, a school leadership team recognizes them as important for rigorous discourse. Examples of support might include the following: relieving teachers of duties or setting aside time on a professional development day for teachers to create common assessments, providing question stems or an online question bank for teams to draw from when crafting assessments, partnering with outside organizations that make formative assessments aligned to course standards for teachers to use and do the initial legwork of providing disaggregated student data for teachers to analyze, or providing more time in meetings for analysis and action planning.

Model. The leadership team is not exempt from using evidence from assessments, and, in fact, must use it regularly as a team to set school goals and guide their decision making. In this way, they model the value of using assessments *for* learning.

Dilemma 2: How Do I Lead Our Team in Rigorous Discourse When We Can't Move Beyond Superficial Talk?

Giving assessments as a team is a first step; talking about them in a way that fosters learning for improvement is another. How is it a team leader who has followed all the recommended steps to ensure a high-functioning, high-impact team still encounters superficial levels of discourse that never reach the level of rigor needed for learning and change?

Consider the following snapshot of a team:

> *Pat leads a team of teachers that has set a goal to improve student writing. The team meets twice a month, has discussed articles about literacy and implemented literacy strategies, and is for the first time looking at student work. Pat uses a protocol to guide the discussion and asks his team, "What do you notice?"*
>
> *One teacher responds, "I notice that the presenting teacher is a really good teacher." Others agree and share more compliments, asking if they can borrow the teacher's lesson. Pat appreciates that teachers are open to looking at student work together, but he does not know how to facilitate discourse that will yield changes to instruction and impact learning.*

Identify the Hurdle

Teachers in this team talk about evidence, but it is not rigorous. No one voices observations about student-learning problems in the student work, no one questions the teacher's instructional decisions, no one shares individual challenges in teaching writing, and no one voices thinking or beliefs about the student work or his or her own practice. The team is sharing, but the team is not engaged in learning. Pat must find out why his team takes a significant amount of time to look at assessment data collaboratively yet keeps the conversation superficial?

Explore Possible Causes

It's a phase. When teams are looking at student work for the first time, it's as if they are reentering Tuckman's (1965) forming phase of team development (Ch. 3), where teachers are in an initial stage of "hesitant participation . . . in which members test the group (and leader) to discover how they will respond to various statements" (n.p.). This phase of testing the waters can cause teachers to hold back from saying what they are actually thinking, which might be why teachers in this snapshot only offer praise to the presenting teacher.

Assessment doesn't measure up. Even if everyone is on board with giving assessments as a team and the purpose of the data meeting is clear, the wrong assessment can stifle discourse (Timperley, 2005). Team members need to be deliberate in the assessments they choose to ensure the data will help them monitor their goal.

Learning environment. People need to feel safe in order to engage in rigorous discourse. If they are concerned that what they say will be received negatively, they are less apt to share honest observations about data or make insightful inferences.

Considerations for selecting assessments:

- Number of data sources: Multiple assessments testing the same thing, triangulate with at least three sources (i.e., quiz, notebook, student interview) whenever possible to "illuminate, confirm, or dispute what you learned through your initial analysis" (Parker-Boudett, City, & Murnane, 2006, p. 90).
- Type of assessments: Nancy Love (2009) states that the most successful teams "put in place benchmark common assessments and engage teachers in regular analysis of item-level data and student work to identify and address learning problems" (p. 13). She presents The Data Pyramid (see Figure 6.1), which names and defines the types of data teams can use and how often teams should use them. Determining which type of assessment to use with which students and when depends on what information teams are seeking.

Figure 6.1 The Data Pyramid

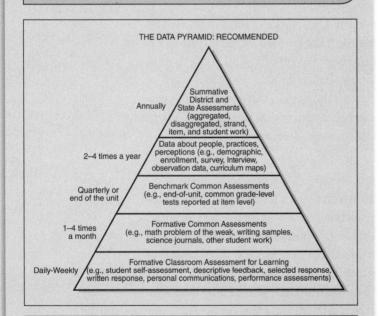

Source: Love, N., Stiles, K. E., Mundry, S., & DiRanna, K. (2008). *The Data Coach's Guide to Improving Learning for All Students: Unleashing the Power of Collaborative Inquiry.* Thousand Oaks, CA: Corwin. Reprinted with permission.

(Continued)

Respond

Proactive response: To facilitate an honest learning environment for rigorous discourse, a team leader can do the following:

Be selective. If choosing the wrong assessment can stifle data dialogue, choosing the right one can bring rigor to a team's discourse. Although not a fully comprehensive list, the following considerations should be made when a team is selecting assessments: number of sources used as evidence, type of assessments, resources needed to administer the assessment, validity, reliability, and timeliness (see sidebar on pages 112–113). Selecting evidence for a team to analyze that meet these criteria does not guarantee rigorous discourse; however, it certainly raises the likelihood.

Norm for rigor. Before team members engage in rigorous discourse, they set up group agreements that call awareness to moments when the discussion lacks rigor, and they design ways the team can go deeper. Examples include

- inviting others to question your assumptions, beliefs, and actions;
- going beyond the surface;
- respectfully challenging viewpoints;
- agreeing to disagree without being disagreeable; or
- zooming in to the real issue.

Group agreements that live on a piece of paper in a drawer do not move a team into rigorous discourse. The skillful team leader asks the team to use them at each meeting and evaluate its own ability to uphold them.

Share responsibility. Teachers are more apt to speak honestly about a lesson or assessment they had a hand in creating rather than if one of their colleagues does it alone. Sharing in the decision making diminishes the natural instinct for an individual teacher to defend his or her choices when he or she gets poor results, and it promotes collective responsibility for the outcome. Whenever possible, the skillful team leader cocreates an assessment or lesson with the team.

Go first. If a team is taking turns presenting data, the team leader can offer to share his students' low-

(Continued)

- Resources needed to administer the assessment: Teams consider the time it takes to administer an assessment and the personnel and other needed resources and weigh those considerations against the value of the information they will gain from administering it (Parker-Boudett et al., 2006).
- Validity: Assessment questions measure what is intended to be measured and has been taught. Time spent on teaching content or skill should be reflected in the number of questions asked (Reeves, 2002, as cited in Allison et al., 2010). For instance, if 30% of an assessment measures a particular skill, it is because teachers have spent one-third of instruction teaching that skill.
- Reliability: If the assessment were administered again to a similar group of students at the same proficiency level, it would yield the same results (Allison et al., 2010).
- Timeliness: Consideration is given as to when the material is taught and when students are assessed in order to provide timely feedback to students.

performing work for team feedback first. If colleagues such as the ones in this snapshot are offering mostly praise, the team leader can invite more specific, constructive observations about his own data. Before having others share, Pat might bring in his own student work and say, "Thank you for your positive comments. I'm concerned about this student's response here [indicate in data]. Why do you think this is occurring, and what do you think I might do differently?"

In-the-moment response: If a team's discourse is superficial, a team leader can do the following:

Drill down. In order to foster rigorous discourse, teams need to be able to draw out as much information as possible from the assessment(s) selected. Love (2009) uses a process called "drilling down," in which a team looks at multiple sources of data over time, searches for patterns or trends and looks for common problems across data, accesses strand data, does item analysis, and analyzes disaggregated data to gain insight into individual groups and specific students' strengths and weaknesses. When teachers are able to compare data in these ways, insightful observations, connections, and inferences drive the conversation. One way Pat could facilitate drilling down with student work is by having the presenting teacher share student writing from the same students over time.

Follow the team's lead and go deeper. Although sharing successes and praise is not the ideal end result, it does put people at ease and can be a good launching point for a team leader. As people voice positive feedback, the skillful team leader probes them to think more critically about specifics by posing questions. For instance, Pat might ask any of the following: "What do you mean by 'good'? Where in the student work do you see an example of this?" or "What specifically worked? How do we know?

Why do we think it worked?" or "How can we replicate success with this student? How can we help other students in all of our classes achieve similar success?"

Focus on the dilemma, not the teacher. Many protocols ask the presenting teacher to set forth a dilemma for the team to discuss, thereby creating a non-threatening lens through which teachers can look. If the presenting teacher does not identify a concern, it could be because he or she is concerned that others will judge his or her teaching. To overcome this, the skillful team leader gently probes, saying, "Why did you choose to share this student's work with us? or "What concerns do you have about this student's work?" By writing the presenting teacher's dilemma on chart paper or repeating it for the team, the teacher leader can revert to the teacher's question, focusing the team to discuss the dilemma and not the teacher. For example, in this snapshot, Pat might say, "Can you find places in this student's work that confirm the presenting teacher's dilemma?" Using a protocol such as the Adapted Consultancy Protocol found in Resource 4.1 can help.

Focus on students. To invite rigorous discourse in a team that is unaccustomed to it, the skillful team leader focuses the discussion on student learning instead of instruction. For example, instead of asking, "What could the teacher do differently?" the team leader might ask, "What does this student need instructionally? What strengths and needs do we see in this student's work? What evidence in the student work demonstrates student understanding or confusion? What patterns of strength and need do we see across the student work? What do students need to know and do better?" Focusing the discussion on students reduces any concerns of blame or judgment and encourages the team to look more analytically, discuss more openly, and problem solve collaboratively.

Model curiosity, observation, and honesty. Whenever individuals have a difficult conversation, it is best to begin from a stance of curiosity (Stone, Patton, & Heen, 1999). The skillful team leader models wonder, data-based observations, and honest feedback so that other team members have unspoken permission to do the same. For example, if the team in this snapshot has been working on descriptive writing and sees some successful uses in the student work, Pat can comb through the work looking for places that raise questions. He might say, "I notice the student has a lot of descriptive language throughout her writing. She uses it effectively in paragraph two, but it seems repetitive in paragraph three. I wonder if this student knows when to include detail and when to go without." The wondering brings the discussion to a safe but more critical level, allowing for others to build on the teacher leader's observation or feel comfortable expressing their own observations.

Redirect. If all efforts to move the conversation into rigorous discourse fail, a team leader may opt to redirect. For example, Pat might say, "I've heard a lot of positives about the student work and teacher's instruction. With the time remaining, let's look to see if there are specific areas in which the students can improve. For example, I notice in paragraph two of the student essay [state positive], but then [identify problem]. Does anyone else notice places where the students have this or other specific areas of need?"

Follow-up response: To sustain rigorous discourse that is brazenly honest, a team leader can do the following:

Debrief. At the end of each meeting, the skillful team leader asks for teachers to do a quick "fist-to-five" in which team members raise up to five fingers indicating their assessment of the level of rigorous discourse achieved (the team should define each level first). For example, a person would hold up his or her fist if he or she felt the team never engaged in rigorous discourse, one finger if there was an attempt, two fingers if it was somewhat achieved, and so forth. If major discrepancies in numbers occur, the team leader can briefly invite people to voice their reasons and set a goal to improve at the next meeting. If someone voices a significant comment that could affect the team's future dynamics—for instance, if someone voices that he or she felt personally attacked—then the team leader can mention that "this issue may need more time than we have allotted" and ask permission of the team to schedule time for a deeper debrief at the next meeting.

Give exit tickets. The skillful team leader assesses the impact of rigorous discourse on the team. Three useful questions teachers can answer on a half page of paper as they leave are (1) "What new thinking do you have?" (2) "How might you apply it?" and (3) "How can the team support you?" He then collects the slips and, at the start of the next meeting, hands them back to individuals on the team and asks people to share an update.

Approach individually. The skillful team leader follows up with one-on-one conversations to assess teachers' responses to the team's rigorous discourse. He might ask, "How comfortable are you with the conflict generated by that assessment? What moments were you able to speak honestly? What, if anything, held you back? In what ways did our team's discourse today help you think differently about your own beliefs and practice? What actionable steps did you set, and how can the team and I support you in implementation?"

School leadership team response: To facilitate rigorous discourse that is brazenly honest at the team level, team leaders, the principal, and administrators together can do the following:

Fishbowl best practice. Teams can model the process live in a fishbowl, where observers sit encircling the team, recording moments when teachers on the team showed evidence of the criteria of rigorous discourse. If live observation is not possible, videotaping is a good alternative with time to debrief.

Dilemma 3: How Do I Lead Our Team in Rigorous Discourse When Blame and Excuses Dominate Talk?

Some teams successfully engage in rigorous discourse about evidence, boldly and honestly stating what they see, but when inferring causes, they can't move past blame and excuses. "The most successful Using Data schools . . . stop blaming students and their circumstances for failure, and, instead, use research and data about their instructional practice to generate solutions to identified gaps in student learning" (Love, 2009, p. 14). When blame and excuses dominate data conversations, team learning hits a wall and rigorous discourse can't be achieved.

Consider the following snapshot of a team:

> *Maryann is a math team leader in a Grade 6 team. Together, teachers are analyzing the results from a district student assessment they were required to give students. Maryann's students scored much higher than the other classes. As teachers look at results, she hears comments such as "They asked questions about concepts we did three months ago. I didn't have time to go over it with my kids," "Question 8 uses vocabulary my kids have never seen," "I have a really tough group this year," "My group of kids just aren't good at test taking," "They should have learned this stuff in fifth grade." "Well, I must stink as a teacher because my kids bombed," and "Maryann's kids did well—what are you bribing them with?"*
>
> *Maryann feels bad about teachers' reactions to the results, and she wishes her team could use the data as a learning opportunity instead of a blamefest.*

Identify the Hurdle

Teachers in this team look at the low-performing student data and begin to blame the test, the students, the teachers in the grade levels before, and even themselves. When they see success in Maryann's class, more excuses follow. The conversation is never able to break free of excuses and blame. Even if the team members point to causes outside of themselves that are partly responsible for students' low performance, they can't achieve a level of rigor that will yield learning and action.

While it would be easy for Maryann to dismiss teachers' excuses as complaints and plunge forward with an action plan based on the causes she sees, or equally tempting to allow the conversation to linger in blame and excuses so teachers can vent, neither approach brings about learning. The skillful team leader uncovers teachers' reasons for responding to the evidence in this way and initiates a shift from blame and excuses to rigorous discourse where reflective learning emerges.

Explore Possible Causes

Just a phase. It is not uncommon for teachers new to looking collaboratively at ongoing assessments, particularly those not crafted by the team, to start out with blame and excuses for the data. A 2005 article describes how a school in Georgia noticed its teams moved through several stages, beginning with feeling confused and overloaded by the data and unsure of what to make of it to feeling inadequate by the results and distrustful of the test to blaming test items for students' poor performance. Eventually, they were able to look objectively at the data, infer causes, generate solutions, and finally were able to use the data to modify instruction (Trimble, Gay, & Matthews, 2005).

It's not personal, but it is. Data might seem dry, but make no mistake about it—interpreting them can be emotionally charged. On their own, assessment data have no judgment, no feelings—this is what people bring to them. When individual teachers privately examine assessments that reveal minimal to no growth for their students, they can feel emotions such as inadequacy, guilt, anger, frustration, or confusion. Although uncomfortable, they are able to manage these emotions in private and take action as they see fit. However, when a team monitors progress using assessments, suddenly data become public to colleagues, administrators, and even parents and students. Teacher successes and failures are exposed and expectations of what a teacher must do are raised. Knowing the data are public heightens emotions of defensiveness, and some team members may resort to blame.

Defense mechanism. Several studies show that a person is more likely to resist a change when they project (unconsciously) their own "unacceptable feelings, impulses and thoughts to another person . . . Essentially, the psyche tricks itself into believing that the cause of the anxiety is located in somebody else" (Bovey & Hede, 2001, p. 11). In this snapshot, teachers may struggle in dealing with the feelings of not providing students with what they need to succeed, and consequently, they may project those feeling on others through blame.

Groupthink. "When in Rome . . ." If some teachers are in a place of blame and excuses, it is easy for others to join in. The phenomenon known as *groupthink,* a phrase coined by Irving Janis (1972), describes how people sacrifice their own views to achieve group unanimity, a feature often present in teams. This occurs particularly when one or more team members have a socializing mindset (Ch. 2), where although a teacher may see contributions to a problem that a team fails to name, they hold back to conform and fit in.

Respond

Proactive response: To prevent team discourse from getting stuck in blame and excuses, a team leader can do the following:

Establish a clear outcome. Having a clear purpose for looking at data elevates the level of rigor (Timperley, 2005). For example, if Maryann's team has a shared purpose for designing an intervention, it will spend less time blaming and more time problem solving. The common desired outcome focuses the team and unites its members toward a goal.

Norm for responsibility. Because analyzing data from assessments can generate emotionally charged conversations, a team can agree to take responsibility and shift to solutions whenever possible. For example, team members might adopt the agreement, "Look externally and internally for causes" or "focus on what we can do."

Play out "what if?" For teams who are quick to blame and make excuses, team members can play out potential scenarios of concern before they look at the data. "What if our students 'bomb' our assessment? What if only one teacher's class 'bombs' while the others' do well? What if colleagues, parents, and administrators judge us by the results of these assessments? What if we are blamed for student failure?" Honest discussions up front about these potential negative conversations can relieve pressure and help manage emotional responses to data. When teams bring the conversation back to the purpose of these assessments—for learning—then teams can answer these "what-if" questions with "then we learn, and we make changes." Teachers are less likely to bring up blame and excuses when they play out the scenarios in advance, and they are reminded that the point of talking about the data as a team is to learn.

In-the-moment response: If team discourse is stuck in blame and excuses, a team leader can do the following:

Move the team to the "balcony." When problems revealed in data are close to home, it is easy for teams to get caught up in who to blame. The skillful team leader helps her team minimize emotional reactions and gain some distance from the problem in order to acquire new perspectives and insight. Heifetz and Linsky (2002) refer to this as moving from the dance floor to "get on the balcony" (p. 51). While they recommend leaders do this, it can be very valuable as a team exercise. In this snapshot, Maryann might do this by saying, "Right now we are reacting to the results seen on these math assessments as they relate to us. Let's for a moment, get on the balcony to see the data from an elevated perspective. What patterns and trends are we seeing across the data? How has our teaching and our school already attempted to improve these areas? What evidence from other assessments support that this is an area of need?"

Re-see the problem. "If you start to think the problem is 'out there,' stop yourself. That is the problem" (Covey, 2004, p. 44). The skillful team leader aids the team in shifting focus from blaming other people and circumstances for problems, and instead she shifts focus to the members' own contributions as individuals and a team. Maryann can model reflective thinking by asking, "When I see the students who did not perform well in our data, I need to see in a deeper, more fundamental way how I have contributed to the problem, and more importantly, I need to see what I can do with others to change the results."

Assess. The skillful team leader prepares her team for the expected phases that a team might move through when collaboratively looking at data. Together they assess where they are at, where they need to go, and how they will get there. The Achievement Network has modified the phases shared in the article by Trimble et al. (2005) into a usable tool for teams to assess where they are in the process (see Resource 6.1: Six Phases of Adopting Data-Driven Instruction).

Validate and verify. Blame and excuses can paralyze a team. The skillful team leader is able to validate loaded emotions that naturally surface when looking at data but then shift the conversation to test out causes. Love (2009) emphasizes that successful teams "make sure that the causes that are to be acted upon are in fact supported in research and focused on policies, practices, and beliefs that are within educators' control to act upon, not focused on blaming students or their circumstances" (p. 65). Teams should generate multiple possible causes for the student-learning problem (this may surface some blame), but then test those theories in the classroom with students to verify the causes and adapt before setting a course of action. Key questions adapted from Love for teams to consider include "Where are we placing blame?" "What else could be a contributing factor?" and "What will we do to verify these causes?" (p. 67).

Exercise locus of control. Sometimes blame and excuses are justified. Yes, students probably should have learned these math concepts in fifth grade, but this is beyond the team members' control—they can't go back in time. The skillful team leader asks, "Which of these causes are within our control to act upon and can have a great impact on student learning? What interventions can we create to help students who should have but didn't learn these essential concepts last year?"

Normalize blame. Looking for someone to blame is a normal human response when goals don't look like they are going to be reached. This is particularly true when teachers and formal leaders are feeling emotions such as embarrassment, discouragement, incompetence, and so forth. Instead of stifling the defensive mechanism to blame, the skillful team leader decides when it is OK to go with it. Maryann might allot no more than five minutes for team members to silently write out every person/event/organization they feel the need to blame for the failure. Chances are, even if some individuals name themselves responsible for the failure, they will still trace their failure back to the fault of someone else. For example, "I should be able to help this student graduate, but his parents don't make him come to school." After noticing a lot of scribbling the skillful team leader responds, "It seems that many people/events/organizations have contributed to the results we are seeing in this assessment. Regardless of their contributions, if in fact we are ultimately accountable, whether that is fair or not, we need to do what we can now to accomplish it. So without naming aloud anyone from your paper, let's identify some causes we can begin to problem solve. For example, instead of saying, "Mrs. K from fifth grade," we might say, "Former teachers failed to teach students these concepts." The team leader then skillfully flips the response to something her team can address, "So because of that, these students lack the know-how" and she scribes on chart paper "students lack know-how." Once people who are blamed are converted into causes that the team can address, she can shift the team to action. "We have our list; let's tackle a few. For example, how can we provide students with the know-how they need?" (Note: This exercise is meant to clear the air, but if it is done verbally or goes on for too long, it can cloud the air, weighing the conversation down and making teachers feel helpless and possibly angry. Keep it short and silent.)

Follow-up response: To sustain rigorous discourse that moves beyond blame and excuses, a team leader can do the following:

Approach individually. If blame and excuses become a pattern for a particular individual on the team, the skillful team leader speaks privately to help heighten her awareness and mobilize her to take action. Maryann might begin the conversation with one of the teachers in the snapshot by saying, "I know you were frustrated with the test results again and expressed that the test was much at fault. I'm wondering if there was any nugget of value from this assessment that might inform your next instructional steps with your students. If not, let's think about what assessments you use in your class that can better inform your instruction for specific students. Would you mind bringing one in for the team to take a look at?"

School leadership team response: To facilitate rigorous discourse void of blame and excuses, team leaders, the principal, and administrators together can do the following:

Model. If the leadership team does not use data to blame, teachers are less likely to do so. Instead of pointing fingers and using data from assessments as a hammer coming down on selective groups/individuals, the school leaders can focus discourse on actively exploring multiple causes of a problem (including reflecting on their own contributions) and focus on developing an action plan to address them.

Reward responsibility and action. Leadership teams can find ways to praise teams who get beyond blame and excuses for student-learning problems. Having a team of teachers share out their processes for arriving at their action plan—specifically how some considered blaming students but then discovered through verifying causes that their actions were actually causing students to respond in the way they were—can influence other teams to take a second look at who they are blaming.

Dilemma 4: How Do I Lead Our Team in Rigorous Discourse When Unsettling Remarks Settle?

The skillful team leader builds the foundation for teams to feel safe by having open, honest conversations—culturally proficient discourse about evidence. But what does a team leader do when discourse reveals assumptions about cultural groups that no one notices (or if anyone does, no one knows how to address them)?

Consider the following snapshot of a team:

> *Gary is a team leader in a high-achieving, public, suburban school district that recently adopted a program that accepts a small percentage of eligible low-income urban students to attend its schools. He and his team have just observed a live demonstration lesson of a respected colleague who was leading a reading conference with a student in the program. The demonstrating teacher first asks the student to explain what he likes in his book. The student enthusiastically responds. Then the teacher asks a higher order analytical question. The student does not answer for a long time and then unexpectedly cries. The teacher ends the conference immediately.*
>
> *In the team debrief, the demonstrating teacher feels terrible, and she expresses her regret for pressing the student to think more critically about the book. "I should have stopped after the first question," she says.*
>
> *Another teacher replies, "Don't beat yourself up; that's all we can expect from students in that program."*
>
> *Another adds, "They just can't reach the level of rigor we expect here."*
>
> *Others agree. Gary hears the assumption made about the urban students from this program, but given the uncomfortable circumstances, he is concerned about speaking up.*

Identify the Hurdle

Rigorous discourse surfaces assumptions, beliefs, and values that are sometimes disturbing to hear and calls for a culturally proficient mindset to examine them. The comment made about urban students from the program being incapable of higher order thinking about text is more than teachers blaming a student for poor performance on a test, as seen in the prior dilemma. This snapshot digs up harmful assumptions that bring forth an equity issue, an issue that no one either sees, wants to address, or knows how to address.

Teams that foster rigorous discourse do not let unsettling remarks settle. Instead, they view themselves as morally responsible to meet the social and cognitive needs of all children, particularly those most often underserved (Lindsey et al., 2009, p. 37). They replace assumptions with evidence, knowing that it is the only way to understand student-learning problems (Parker-Boudett et al., 2006). The challenge for a team leader is to neither gloss over negative assumptions nor attack them head-on with judgment, but instead he must explore why they are made to stimulate rigorous discourse so learning can result.

Explore Possible Causes

Camaraderie. Perhaps the statement "That's all we can expect of students in that program" is only said to make the demonstrating teacher feel better about a conference gone wrong. No one feels good about pushing a student to the point where he or she cries, and no one wants to watch a respected colleague feel bad about it. Teachers, particularly those who have formed a bond in a team, want to support one another.

Overlooked. It takes skill to notice assumptions. Senge, Kleiner, Roberts, Ross, and Smith (1994) argue that others are often more aware than is the person stating an assumption. Teachers in this snapshot do not seem to be aware that making a statement about a student's ability based only on his or her socioeconomic background is an assumption.

Bound by beliefs. Assumptions come from beliefs and values which are extremely difficult to shift. The more bound people are to their initial perception of the way things should be, the more challenging it is to make a paradigm shift (Covey, 2004). Teachers in this snapshot may not believe that commuting low-income urban students into their district is "the way things should be." This belief underlies the negative assumptions that are voiced during the debrief of the conference.

Fixed mindset. Although not necessarily the case, there is a possibility that teachers in this snapshot have a fixed mindset about all low-income urban students, rooted in the belief that students from this socioeconomic background are only capable of low-order critical-thinking skills and don't have the capacity to learn and grow.

Respond

Proactive response: To prevent discourse that is not culturally proficient, a team leader can do the following:

Envision the team. This is a strategy I share in Chapter 3. Applied to this dilemma, the skillful team leader invites members early on to define their vision of the team. They must consciously commit to suspend their own and others' assumptions. Gary might ask, "Are we a group of educators who essentially 'yes' each other, shielding each other from responsibility of evident problems in our practice? Or do we act like critical colleagues asking provocative questions, examining multiple perspectives of a problem, and both supporting and challenging each other's beliefs and actions?" Discussion of the type of team they want to be can pave the way for future culturally proficient conversations.

Draw out assumptions. Love (2009) encourages teachers to bring assumptions forward during the prediction phase of a team's data-driven dialogue, to put them aside during the observation phase, and, last, to revisit them when inferring causes and generating solutions. Before his team views the conference, Gary might ask teachers to write down their predictions of how well the student from the program will be able to answer a higher order thinking question about his book. Next, team members can name assumptions they see that inform their predictions, then put them aside temporarily so they may objectively observe the lesson. In other words, if a teacher expects the student can't complete the learning task, she needs first to be aware of her assumption, and then to observe the conference, taking care not to exclude evidence that may call her assumption into question. Finally, in the debrief, Gary has the group revisit its initial assumptions to see if any have changed.

Norm for rigor. Suggested in an earlier dilemma in this chapter, norming for rigorous discourse in advance can, in this case, encourage a team to successfully engage in culturally proficient conversations. When team members expect their colleagues to question their assumptions people are more willing to speak up. At a minimum, a team leader can refer to this group agreement to kickoff the discussion. Gary might say, "In keeping with our norm, 'question each other's thinking and conclusions,' let's play devil's advocate and question the statements voiced here before we draw any conclusions."

In-the-moment response: If a team member makes a negative assumption, a team leader can do the following:

Suspend assumptions through paraphrasing or questioning. Teams cannot overlook assumptions, but instead they need to suspend them out in front of the team for everyone to discuss. Senge et al. (1994) recommend individuals bring them forward, make them explicit, give them considerable weight, and try to understand where they come from. The skillful team leader respectfully zooms in to the assumption through repetition, paraphrasing, or questioning for all to see and explore.

Repeating the assumption permits others to hear and reexamine it. For example, Gary might repeat, "So we are saying, 'That's all we can expect from students in that program. They [low-income urban students from that program] can't reach the level of rigor we expect here.'" Further thoughtful questions can help teachers see the implications of what they are saying. For example, Gary can ask, "Are we comfortable with only having this student write about the parts of the book he likes? Will only writing about the parts of the book he likes help this student reach our team goal of all students achieving higher order critical thinking about text? Are we saying that he will never be able to critically think about text because he is a low-income urban student from this program?"

Besides repeating and paraphrasing the stated assumption, the skillful team leader may opt to reframe it as a question that requires a team to look back at evidence (or lack thereof), thereby engaging members in thinking about the belief behind the statement. For example, Gary might ask, "What evidence do we have that this low-income urban student or others can't critically think about text?"

Shift from believing to seeing. Data can put assumptions to the test. What individuals believe to be true about students is challenged by what they see in students' work. Looking at student work can "surface and challenge many assumptions—assumptions about what students can and cannot do, about which students can do what, and about why students are or are not able to do something" (Parker-Boudett et al., 2006, p. 88).

While the team in this snapshot uses the teacher–student conference as one data point, Gary can next lead the team in looking at written responses from the struggling student in the conference and also the responses from other low-income students who come from the same urban program. Grounding the conversation in multiple data sources often puts assumptions to rest, but in some cases it raises more complex questions. As teachers grapple with their own beliefs and what the evidence shows, and what they will do with this information, the team leader can be assured that his team is engaging in rigorous discourse.

Shift mindset through inquiry. Raising awareness of harmful assumptions through data can be more powerful than talking about them. An evaluation of a program in New York showed that when team members moved through the cycle of inquiry, setting small learning targets that resulted in evidence of a shift in learning outcomes for students, their mindsets shifted too. Team members who held assumptions about student motivation or ability (who essentially had a fixed mindset) let go of assumptions and focused on the instruction they gave in specific, high-leverage skills (Talbert, Scharff, & Lin, 2008). In this snapshot, Gary can refocus the conversation to the learning targets they did or didn't set for these students and analyze the student work that resulted. Once he is able to gain traction with the team by teaching a specific skill the students need and can acquire improved learning results for those students, teachers mindsets are likely to begin to shift.

Suspend assumptions. Using data is a great entry point into shifting mindset, but in some cases teams need to be made aware of the assumption before they can change their beliefs. Gary can find out what the team knows, needs, and has learned after a culture bound assumption is suspended. Using a K-N-L (*k*now, *n*eed to know, have *l*earned) Suspending an Assumption Chart (see Figure 6.2; inspired from the well-known K-W-L chart: What I know, what I want to know, what I learned), the skillful team leader can frame the conversation.

Figure 6.2 K-N-L Suspending an Assumption Chart

K	N	L
What I think I know about . . .	What I need to see/hear in order to shift my understanding about . . .	What I have learned from rigorous discourse with my team about . . .
(e.g., low-income urban students' ability to think critically about text)	(e.g., low-income urban students' ability to think critically about text)	(e.g., low-income urban students' ability to think critically about text)

Learn; don't judge. Whatever approach a team leader uses to suspend assumptions, he must be mindful of tone and stance. If there is a hint of judgment or if he uses trigger words (words that might trigger others to think he is judging their beliefs), he will only escalate the problem. The skillful team leader does not make assumptions about any teacher who voices an unsettling comment. If Gary were to respond by saying, "How can you believe low-income urban students can't critically think about text!" he is not likely going to influence anyone to reflect on their beliefs. Although it can be hard for a team leader to keep his judgment in check, attacking people's beliefs or trying to convince others of his cultural viewpoint will stifle rigorous discourse.

Verify. Rigorous discourse does not stop at the first possible cause or conclusion. The team members look for holes in their thinking, examine their inference for harmful assumptions, and then verify the cause by looking at more evidence. In this snapshot, a teacher tries to hold a student to a high expectation. When the student can't meet the expectation, the team assumes the student is incapable and concludes that the teacher should lower her expectations. Gary can ask the team to search through other assessments beyond this one reading conference (e.g., student notebooks) to find supplemental evidence that proves or disproves its conclusion about the student's ability.

Keep an eye toward instruction. When verifying causes to test conclusions, the skillful team leader also has teachers reflect on their practice to see if instruction is to blame. Gary might remind teachers on the team, "With assessments, we get what we give. How we teach often elicits the response we get on an assessment. Here we may need to take a closer look at how we are preparing all students to critically think about text. What can we do differently in our instruction that might elicit a different student outcome for this student and others who struggle with higher order thinking about text?"

Praise honesty. The demonstrating teacher in this snapshot shows courage and vulnerability by sharing evidence of a student not learning in her class, and her colleagues are brave to voice what they believe deep down—exactly what a team wants in rigorous discourse. A "my thinking is right, yours is wrong" type of conflict instigated by the team leader is likely to close the group off from open, honest conversation in that moment and in the future. Instead, the skillful team leader expresses appreciation for teachers' courage to speak freely and works as a team to understand where the assumptions are coming from. This means examining teaching decisions, and the beliefs that inform them, with a growth mindset (Ch. 2).

Think aloud one's own assumptions. The skillful team leader is aware of his personal assumptions and can talk through his internal conflict about them to launch a learning discussion. By doing so, others may feel comfortable sharing their thinking too. For example, Gary might say, "When I saw this low-income urban student who didn't critically think about his text during the reading conference, I couldn't help but think for a moment that maybe it was because he isn't capable. I know I'm not supposed to say that because we believe that every kid can learn, but what if he just can't because of his socioeconomic status and because of where he comes from. But wait, am I saying that he will *never* be able to critically think about text? Not now, not ever? Why else might he not be able to do this now? Maybe he needs some different or additional instructional support (i.e., scaffolding, modeling an intervention)." (Note: It is important that the team leader share his thinking about a real assumption of his own from which he is struggling to learn; otherwise, he must refrain from this strategy as it will appear phony.)

Ask "breakthrough questions." Named in the book *Culturally Proficient Learning Communities: Confronting Inequities Through Collaborative Curiosity*, breakthrough questions have the following characteristics: (1) open ended, with no right or wrong answer; (2) use tentative language such as "how might you"; (3) use plural language such as "what are some ways"; (4) embed positive intention and possibility such as "given your desire for all students to be successful . . ." (Lindsey et al., 2009, p. 65); and (5) use first person "we" instead of second person "you" when possible. In this snapshot, Gary could ask the following breakthrough question, "What might be some ways that we can continue to teach to the standards of our subject areas and adapt to the learning styles of our students in special education?" (adapted from Lindsey et al., 2009, p. 72).

Create a safe learning environment. Rigorous discourse, where culturally proficient conversations thrive, can only happen when teams are honest, and the team is a safe place to put it all out there. When this is the case, the team has to decide what to do with it. Sample ways to do this as excerpted from Love (2009) include the following:

- Establish group norms for talking about race/ethnicity, class, and culture.
- "Examine disaggregated data" (p. 93).
- "Dialogue about assumptions that underlie causes generated" (p. 93).
- Ask, "do our strategies address student populations most in need of our attention?" (p. 93).
- "Collect interview, survey, and/or focus group data from students from different cultures to assess the impact of implementation on them" (p. 93).

Follow-up response: To sustain rigorous discourse in which teachers engage in culturally proficient conversations, a team leader can do the following:

Shift focus to problem solving. Once a team leader surfaces the beliefs underlying an assumption, the team can begin to problem solve. Gary might follow up a discussion suspending assumptions by saying, "Thank you. We now have a common understanding of what we expect of all students. Given where this student is performing now and where we need him to be, how do we get him and others like him there? What scaffolding can we provide this student to reach the goal?"

School leadership team response: If teachers are uncomfortable having culturally proficient conversations, team leaders, the principal, and administrators together can do the following:

Suspend schoolwide assumptions. Negative assumptions about teacher and student learning unfortunately exist in schools. Whether spoken or held as a compass for one's actions, harmful assumptions such as "Students with disabilities are not as motivated as students in honors classes," "Failing students are lazy," "Veteran teachers are unwilling to change their practices," and so forth impact what people say and do. It's not surprising that an individual teacher working in a school operating under assumptions would also have them. When a school leadership team brings forth assumptions in an attempt to understand where they come from, it can begin to shift them.

One way to do this is to collaborate on a school leadership team protocol each time anyone on the team hears or sees a negative assumption. For example, the team might have a protocol: First, get clarification from the person stating the assumption by asking, "What do you mean by that?" Second, bring it back to the team to determine if this is a schoolwide assumption that must be addressed. Third, action plan a schoolwide response such as holding a cultural proficiency professional development.

Highlight evidence. Often, seeing is believing. Using evidence should be common practice. For instance, school leaders at Gary's school can ask teams who are achieving success with low-income urban students to share their data and strategies for achieving strong results.

CONSIDER SCHOOL CULTURE: SHIFTING FROM A CULTURE OF NICE TO AN HONEST, UP-FRONT CULTURE

When a team avoids difficult conversations, it can be an indication of a greater problem, one in which educators are censored by the culture of nice—an underlying school culture of politeness that inhibits educators from learning. Instead of inviting and telling the truth, educators protect themselves and others from dialogue that might generate conflict. Consequently, negative assumptions and beliefs are untouched, and practice never really changes.

Schools operating in a culture of nice value those who "don't rock the boat." The feeling in the school might be pleasant and friendly, but fear is the undercurrent. Non-discussables are only discussed in hidden corners with a glance over the shoulder to make sure no one overhears (or at a local pub after hours). Those who want to speak candidly are concerned about the response they'll receive and decide it is better or less complicated to mind their own business.

Recognize the Signs of a Culture of Nice

- Teachers rarely question each other's or their own practices, assumptions, or beliefs. Instead, they may only compliment each other, without investigating areas where the student needs to improve and how the teacher can change instruction to meet those needs. If teachers always leave a team meeting only feeling confirmed in what they have been doing, the team has probably never reached rigorous discourse.

- Teachers only share successful student work to avoid judgment from peers. While a teacher leader can still facilitate rigorous discourse around successful work, educators stuck in the culture of nice rarely question what makes the work successful and how to elicit similar successes from students not meeting expectations.

- Teachers who share their unsuccessful student work, and those examining it, make excuses as to why the student underperformed. In a culture of nice, teachers are more likely to find blame with the assessment or the student rather than analyzing the instruction that may have affected the student's work. This approach can come from good intentions, such as not wanting to hurt a teacher's feelings, but ultimately it doesn't change instruction and can be harmful to students.

- Teachers recommend strategies for the presenting teacher to apply, but they don't critically reflect and apply them to their own instruction. Teams who are stuck in the culture of nice may not explore the broader implications of what they are discussing. Some teachers are comfortable analyzing a colleague's dilemma and offering recommendations, but the rigor stops before they recognize the changes that they may also need to make in their own classrooms. Teachers might be so narrowly focused on the presenting teacher's student work that they fail to recognize their own students have a similar problem. Others who notice the problem might resist the given strategies because they don't think they will work with their students, or they don't know how to implement them.

- Pockets of candid dialogue occur within the school, but it is not embedded in the everyday interactions of all people.

Where Does the Culture of Nice Come From?

"If you don't have something nice to say, don't say it at all." Grandmothers have embedded this message in the minds of young children for years, and although it would be unfair to make Grandma the root cause of the culture of nice, a look into learned behaviors can provide some clues.

People learn how to act from the circumstances and people around them. How one might speak, dress, and act at a dinner in Buckingham Palace is likely very different than at a dinner at an uncle's house. Teachers, too, look to the culture within their schools to see how forthcoming they can be. If rigorous discourse about issues, culture-bound assumptions, and beliefs are avoided at the school level, teacher teams are unlikely to engage in them either. If the principal doesn't address ineffective practice in classrooms, or if teachers keep quiet when policy change is harmful to students, teams learn being nice is the acceptable way of communication. When someone does dare to speak the truth, or suspend assumptions, or admit faults, or make plans to implement significant change that upsets the status quo, people watch to see if she is encouraged or hushed. If the latter, then it is not uncommon for teachers in a team to play it safe and keep discourse nice.

The culture of nice might also come from people's misperceptions of and discomfort with conflict and confrontation. The words themselves bring up images of war (e.g., the Korean conflict, the Middle East conflict, "confront the enemy"). It's no wonder teams might picture a toe-to-toe, in-your-face standoff, and avoid it. Unlike other professions, for instance a prosecuting attorney, a teacher is not one that attracts people who are looking to pick a fight. Many hold the belief that real team players go along with the group so as not to create disharmony and to keep the team productive, a socialized mind (Ch. 2). So long as teachers think rigorous discourse means stirring up the drama, some will choose to stay out of it.

Yet studies show that teams experiencing conflict, debate, dissent, confrontation, and even criticism produce more creative solutions to problems than do teams that politely get along by settling for the first "predictable" resolution (Lehrer, 2012). This is not conflict for the sake of fighting, but it is conflict for the sake of learning. By no means does every conversation in a school or team need to engage in conflict, but in the culture of nice, people avoid them at all costs, even when someone really should say something.

Missing from the culture of nice is what Patrick Lencioni (2002) names *vulnerability-based trust*, where people expose their struggles and failures and readily admit when they need help. The act of analyzing student assessments and discussing other sensitive topics such as race or student equity requires all members of a team to be vulnerable and all to tell the truth, even if that means engaging in conflict for learning. Schools that don't have an honest and up-front culture, and instead protect themselves and others within a culture of nice, might go through the motions of collaborative inquiry but have little to no impact on teachers' mindsets, beliefs, or actions.

To shift from a school censored by the culture of nice to a school where educators are honest, up-front, and vulnerable, a team leader together with other school members can do the following:

Change the image. Being brazenly honest can create conflict in a team, and some teachers are not comfortable with this. They anticipate a knock-down, drag-out fight. But it does not have to be. "Truth telling doesn't have to be confrontational, although it may confront. It can be handled with sharpness or softness, but it confronts the usual tacit acceptance of the [teacher's] explanations. Truth telling refuses to sidestep or overlook: it boldly points out when the emperor is not wearing clothes" (Whitworth, Kimsey-House, & Kimsey-House, 2007, p. 20). A school can openly discuss the importance of truth telling and the value of conflict for learning:

- Why do we need an honest, up-front culture?
- What do we mean by "conflict for learning," and why is it sometimes necessary? When is it necessary?
- How comfortable are you with "conflict for learning"? If you are not, what do(es) you/your team/your school need to grow?
- What does "conflict for learning" look like (i.e., two or more people assertively disagree over interpretations of data, or a quiet moment where an individual asks a curve ball question after the team has already come to consensus)?
- What risks do we face if we engage in conflict for learning with another teacher, team, or school leader? What risks do we face if we don't?
- What can we do as a school to make rigorous discourse a part of our culture?

Build self-awareness. Sometimes, building awareness about people's own perceptions about conflict can help them become more comfortable with it. Discussing people's comfort with confrontation in multiple aspects of their life can provide insight into their willingness to engage in conflict for learning with colleagues and administrators. A free conflict resolution questionnaire is available at http://academic.engr.arizona.edu/vjohnson/ConflictManagementQuestionnaire/ConflictManagementQuestionnaire.asp

Look inward. Truth telling is often thought of in terms of person A telling person B what he really thinks and the reverse. While this is of course one aspect of truth telling, being honest with oneself is just as important and just as difficult. Schools need to foster opportunities for reflection where teachers (and administrators) confront their own beliefs and actions. Creating safe opportunities for teachers to share moments where cognitive dissonance causes them to wrestle with their existing beliefs and new thinking can foster vulnerability-based trust with colleagues. Teams might have teachers write changes in their thinking on an exit slip and have a few people share out. A question stem might be, "I used to believe [insert belief], but now, I'm questioning [insert issue with belief]."

APPLICATION TO YOUR WORK: CONNECT, OBSERVE, EXPLORE, ACT

Think and write independently. Then, discuss with colleagues.

Connect	Observe
Remember a time as a leader or participant on a team when you engaged in rigorous discourse. What did it look and sound like?	How rigorous is your team's discourse? In which of the five criteria (evidence based, dialogic, culturally proficient, reflective, actionable) is your team adept? How do you know? In which of the five criteria of rigorous discourse does your team need to grow? How do you know?
Explore	**Act**
What holds your team back from engaging in all five criteria of rigorous discourse? What hurdles must the team overcome to achieve rigorous discourse? What have you tried? What have you not tried? Why?	What will you and your team do to elevate your discourse? Name next steps and support needed to enact them.

Portions of this chapter were first published in "When Nice Won't Suffice," by Elisa MacDonald, *Journal of Staff Development*, June 2012. Reprinted with permission of Learning Forward, www.learningforward.org. All rights reserved.

Inertia 7

Overcoming Hurdles to Lead an Action-Oriented Team for Continuous Improvement

FOUNDATIONAL VALUE: CONTINUOUS IMPROVEMENT

In professional learning, teams strive for continuous improvement, but how does a team do so when there is resistance to change? This chapter applies a skillful approach to hurdles put forth by internal and external obstacles to change. It offers strategies to transform team learning into actions that yield sustainable results for teachers and students, even when a school's culture seems acidic to change.

WHAT ARE ACTION-ORIENTED TEAMS, AND WHY ARE THEY IMPORTANT?

Planning for action and taking action are two different things. A football team doesn't win by simply analyzing video footage and designing its game plan. The team members have to get on the field and play. School teams, too, must be action oriented. They collaborate, share leadership for learning, set goals, and engage in rigorous discourse all so that they can get in the classroom and implement. Turning knowledge into action brings about new questions and dilemmas for teams to pursue, hence becoming the basis for continuous

> **In support of action-oriented teams for continuous improvement:**
>
> - "Knowledge . . . is only as good as its intelligent application" (Schmoker, 2006, p.117).
> - Talk is no substitute for action. Having a plan is not the same as implementing a plan (Pfeffer & Sutton, 2000).
> - "It's not about giving the assessments; it's about doing something about the results" (Marshall, 2006, p. 2).
> - "Members of PLCs are action oriented: They move quickly to turn aspirations into action and vision into reality. They understand that the most powerful learning always occurs in the context of taking action" (DuFour, DuFour, Eaker, & Many, 2006, p. 4).

learning. Teams that engage in mindset-shifting discourse, produce elaborate plans for change, and have the best intentions, but never get "on the field" are up against the biggest hurdle yet—inertia.

HURDLES TO LEADING AN ACTION-ORIENTED TEAM FOR CONTINUOUS IMPROVEMENT

Transforming learning into action is harder than it seems. Even the best collaborative talking and planning can fall short of doing. Some teams engage in rigorous discourse, gaining knowledge on how to solve problems, but they get stuck when it comes to actually implementing what they've learned. This is often referred to as the knowing-doing gap (DuFour & Eaker, 1998; Pfeffer & Sutton, 2000; Senge, Kleiner, Roberts, Ross, & Smith, 1994), and it is status-quo's best friend.

Taking action involves implementing something new and sometimes letting go of something one is already doing; this requires change, and nothing adds to the complexity of a team like people going through a change. A range of feelings such as loss, fear, panic, uncertainty, and anxiousness can impact teachers' openness to change and consequently, their behavior in a team. These feelings are augmented when the change is imposed. Even when individuals in a team desire and plan to implement change, levels of use might vary. And unfortunately, the challenges for a team do not end once everyone is implementing a change successfully—often, factors beyond the team's control such as new leadership or a reduction of resources can bring its actions and results from those actions to a halt.

These hurdles may leave a team leader to wonder, How do I lead an action-oriented team when

1. change is a mandate that no one wants,

2. intentions don't align with actions, or

3. external changes impact our ability to sustain implementation or results?

Dilemma 1: How Do I Lead an Action-Oriented Team When Change Is a Mandate That No One Wants?

One person hikes an arduous trail to get to the top of a mountain. He makes decisions along the way, critically thinks around obstacles, and reaches the summit. He wants others to share in the wonder, and so he sends down a helicopter to pick up the rest of the team. They fly up to the summit, and once there, all they want to do is get down.

This scenario describes how, all too often, initiatives are received by those that must implement them and how those who impose the mandate overlook what people need to embrace the change. How is it that a mandate calling for action can actually immobilize a team?

Consider the following snapshot of a team:

> *Lorraine has been asked to lead her department in the district's new writing initiative, which mandates that teachers give feedback in a particular way. For several meetings, her team has engaged in rigorous discourse about students' essays, identifying each student's area for growth and studying the new method for giving feedback. Many teachers bravely admit to their colleagues that they never knew how to do this well, but they are willing to try. As a team they collaboratively craft an action plan outlining the strategies they will implement in the next six weeks and the expected outcomes they hope to see. They reach a point where all are ready to implement, except one teacher who says, "I understand this is what the district is mandating us to do, and I appreciate Lorraine's efforts to help us learn this new approach, but with all due respect, I'm not about to change what's been working for my kids for the past fifteen years."*
>
> *Another teacher responds, "We all have to do this, and most of us want to. It's in our action plan. You really shouldn't hold our team and your students back."*
>
> *The teacher reacts, saying, "I want kids to be better writers just as much as you do, but this is just one more thing we have to do today that will be gone tomorrow. So put what you want on your action plan; I'm doing what I know works."*
>
> *Tension is high, and Lorraine needs the team to move beyond talk about implementation and actually implement the mandate in a way that will benefit students.*

Identify the Hurdle

The team in this snapshot is required to implement a change, yet not everyone does so. As teachers confront one another, albeit breaking through the culture of nice (Ch. 6), tension mounts, contributing to the group's standstill. Lorraine must explore the causes for one teacher's reluctance to implement the change in order to bring cohesion to the group and mobilize the team.

Explore Possible Causes

It's a stage. Whenever an individual is required to change, he is likely to have concerns. Shirley Hord, William Rutherford, Leslie Huling-Austin, and Gene Hall (1987) offer a framework called Concerns-Based Approach Model (C-BAM; see Figure 7.1) to help educators understand the change process and better respond to an individual's needs.

In this snapshot, the teacher's statement, "I'm not about to change what has been working for my kids for the past fifteen years," indicates a personal concern. He is aware of the change he needs to make, but he is concerned about how the change will impact his approach to giving feedback thus far and how his students will respond. His concern holds him back from action.

The subtext of a mandate. People often resist change that is imposed. Even when mandates are well thought out and made in the best interest of those they impact, they are not always well received. The word *mandate* from the Latin *mandatum* means order or decree. The word itself does not exactly conjure up images of shared leadership. In fact, it can actually imply an unspoken subtext: "You need to change because you are not good enough." Individuals

Figure 7.1 Stages of Concern/Expression of Concern

Stage of Concern	Expression of Concern
6. Refocusing	I have some ideas about something that would work even better.
5. Collaboration	How can I relate what I am doing to what others are doing?
4. Consequence	How is my use affecting learners? How can I refine it to have more impact?
3. Management	I seem to be spending all my time getting materials ready.
2. Personal	How will using it affect me?
1. Informational	I would like to know more about it.
0. Awareness	I am not concerned about it.

Source: Taking Charge of Change, by Shirley M. Hord, William L. Rutherford, Leslie Huling-Austin, and Gene E. Hall, Alexandria, VA: ASCD. © 1987 Southwest Educational Development Laboratory. Reprinted with permission. Learn more about ASCD at www.ascd.org.

are more likely to interpret the mandate in this way if they have no say in the change requested of them or if they are made to undo something that they have just learned how to do (likely from a prior mandate). Likewise, they may interpret a mandate as judgmental if it comes from decision makers who are not practitioners or if teams don't trust the source. Interpreting mandates in this way can cause individuals to protect their way of doing things and initially resist a change.

"If it ain't broke . . ." It is rare for an individual to not want to improve upon his practice; however, a team member's reluctance to change may be interpreted in this way. A teacher who already has a successful practice in place is less likely to want to replace it with something with which he has not had prior success. Doing so seems illogical and not in the best interest of students. If the teacher on Lorraine's team uses methods for giving feedback that work (or there is no indicator that the methods don't work), then he is unlikely to embrace change to his teaching methods.

"Yes" to the what, "no" to the how. Individuals on a team who are reluctant to take action might not be opposed to *what* is trying to be accomplished but instead *how* the team is trying to accomplish it. The teacher in this snapshot may very well see a need for students to improve as writers but doesn't see how changing his methods for giving feedback will yield the desired result. While his approach of continuing with what he has been doing may not be the best approach either, he is unwilling to implement something new without knowing it will accomplish the goal.

Underlying mindset. While each of the above factors might contribute to a teacher's reluctance to implement an imposed change, a team leader must consider a teacher's mindset. As referenced in Chapter 2, "We can learn and reflect as much as we want, but the changes we hope for, or that others need from us, will not happen because all the learning and reflecting will occur within our existing mindsets" (Kegan & Lahey, 2009, p. 5). For instance, the teacher showing reluctance in this snapshot is unlikely to embrace a change that contradicts his mindset if

- he learns about the new method for giving feedback, but all the while he does not think students are capable of getting better at writing no matter what he does;
- he doesn't think he is capable of succeeding at the change;
- he assumes it's solely the students' responsibility to take his feedback (in whatever form he gives), and if they don't improve it's because they chose not to take follow his direction; or
- he does not share the school vision that all students will be independent, skilled writers.

Respond

Proactive response: To discourage reluctance to change brought on by a mandate, a team leader can do the following:

Learn one's change response. Early on, the skillful team leader finds out how different people in the team respond to change. If a lot of people are in the group, a team leader can have them make a human continuum, where those who are eager to change stand on the left and those who are the last to embrace change stand on the right. Everyone else self-selects where to stand accordingly. (Note: It is important to do this exercise with no judgment. Truthfully, schools need people at all points on the continuum to balance the changes that schools adopt.) Heightening awareness of one's own and others' comfort with change can open the dialogue and increase tolerance for other's responses to change. For instance, a team member might jest, "As you know I'm the last one to jump on board a change, so bear with me and hear me out for a moment."

Norm for action. Teams can collectively set expectations for implementation and determine their response when someone does not meet the agreed-upon expectation. For example, Lorraine's team might decide, "Every teacher is expected to implement our action plan. If someone fails to act, the group will press him to explain why. That teacher will listen openly to ideas and suggestions." Although, the conversation may still be tense, a teacher might be more accepting of a group challenging his unwillingness to act if he expects it.

Encourage dissent. A team should critically think about how to adopt an innovation without abandoning what is proven to work. When team members know it's OK to voice disagreement, they are more likely to think purposefully about why they're implementing the change in the first place. Doing so increases ownership in the change and the likelihood of the team implementing actions it can sustain.

In-the-moment response: If resistance to change hinders team action, a team leader can do the following:

Distinguish the act of resistance from the person. The skillful team leader recognizes that a person showing resistance to a change is not a resistant person.

Resistance is not an attribute; it is a temporary state of being. Instead, the skillful team leader models growth mindset language by using phrases such as "a teacher reluctant to . . ." or "a teacher showing resistance to. . . ." or "a teacher not yet on board with . . ." While this may seem like inconsequential semantics, the language is important for three reasons: First, it shows that the team leader has a depth of understanding and respect for all teachers. There is no judgment on the person showing reluctance, no label. Second, it preserves respect for the teacher in front of his colleagues. They are less likely to pigeonhole someone into a negative label if the team leader doesn't. Third, it normalizes resistance. Every person shows reluctance about something at some point in his or her life. (I might resist kicking a cement block in karate class, but that does not make me a resistant person.) By doing this, the skillful team leader is able to begin to address the concerns behind a resistant response.

Embrace resistance. Lorraine's instinct may be to go to an administrator who can demand the teacher implement the mandated change, but at best, it would foster compliance rather than learning (not to mention, going directly to an evaluator strains the trust and relations with that teacher). Ignoring the teacher's stance is a mistake too. Not only because that teacher's students would miss out on the benefits of the change, but also because it would further divide the team.

The skillful team leader views resistance to change as an asset to her team, knowing much can be learned from those who hold back (Kegan & Lahey, 2009). The skillful team leader must "explore and embrace resistance" (Fullan & Rolheiser, 1997, p. 46). Instead of reporting or ignoring a team member's resistance, the skillful team leader uses it as an entry point into rigorous discourse, where teachers can critically think about not only what they are about to do, but also what they are already doing. Lorraine might say, "Let's use this point of disagreement to be more thoughtful and purposeful in the actions we take. How can these distinct perspectives influence how we move forward?"

Acknowledge feelings; defuse storming. Moving through the change process affects people in different ways. The skillful team leader picks up on emotional cues and provides opportunities for people to express them safely. The dialogue in this snapshot is emotionally charged, with teachers (perhaps unintentionally) attacking each other personally. Lorraine needs to intervene. She might say, "This change brings up strong feelings for each of us. I'd like us to take a few moments to individually write down concerns and what support you need to move forward." She can use Hord's Stages of Concerns (Figure 7.1) to help teachers identify their trepidation and strategize ways to shift as a group toward Stage 6, Refocusing. In this way, Lorraine is validating all concerns, cutting off personal attacks, and shifting the team toward a solutions-oriented dialogue.

Discover a solution, don't defend one. It is tempting for a team leader or member, particularly one with a self-authoring mindset (Ch. 2), who firmly believes implementing the given mandate is essential to students' success, to push her ideas on the teacher showing reluctance; however, in doing so she is missing a learning opportunity. The skillful team leader steers away from defending the mandated change and instead takes what Stone, Patton, and Heen (1999) call a *curious stance.* In this snapshot, instead of Lorraine advocating for her position by saying, "Providing students feedback in this way works better than anything you have done in the past" (which would likely put the teacher on the offensive), Lorraine can genuinely and respectfully take a curious stance by saying, "Can you help me better understand your position?" As the teacher speaks, Lorraine and others listen to learn. They do not sit quietly, building their case and waiting to state their rebuttal. Taking this curious stance promotes understanding and the team is able to reach better solutions together.

Capitalize on the mandate. "Effective change agents neither embrace nor ignore mandates. They use them as catalysts to re-examine what they are doing" (Fullan, 1993, pp. 19–41). In this snapshot, Lorraine might respond, "I agree. We should not accept this mandate blindly, and we should not change anything that is working. Instead, let's look critically at both the strategies the mandate suggests and the ones we have been doing. Let's go back to the student work and find evidence where and for whom each strategy works and does not work."

Find choice in a mandate. If a teacher's reluctance seems primarily attributed to the fact that the change is imposed, the team leader can find places where teachers have input and voice. For instance, Lorraine might say, "While it is mandated that we give specific, individualized feedback to students, we do have creative input into the type of assessments that we provide feedback on. Let's focus on that which we have control over."

Start with the willing. The skillful team leader invites those who are willing to test out the waters first by implementing the innovative practice and sharing evidence of their successes and challenges through student work. Sometimes seeing a student benefit from an implemented strategy is enough to get a seemingly resistant teacher to change. While this approach can be slower than most administrators would like to see, sometimes it can bring about a longer lasting change because teachers come to see value in the mandate on their own.

Follow-up response: To sustain an action-oriented team, a team leader can do the following:

Approach individually. Knowing why someone is reluctant to implement a change to their practice is complex. Sometimes, the most effective approach to shift someone up through the stages of concern is to respectfully and privately ask them at different points in implementation. Using humble inquiry, an approach developed by psychologist Edgar H. Schein (2009), the leader asks questions to find out concerns and address them. Lorraine can ask at various points in a team's cycle, "What are you most concerned with? How can our team support you?"

School leadership team response: To encourage action for continuous improvement, team leaders, the principal, and administrators together can do the following:

Give the "why" before the "how." This approach is suggested by Pfeffer and Sutton (2000). Not every journey up the mountain can be made with everyone. When school leaders "send the helicopter" to bring others to the summit, they must convey why. A leadership team can work with district and school leaders to ensure that the faculty has a "big-picture" understanding as to why the school is implementing the new innovation before giving them steps on what to do. To meet the concerns of individuals at Stage 0, Awareness, leaders can hold faculty meetings, informal breakfasts, hallway conversations, and team-level conversations to facilitate a shared understanding of why this change is happening at the given time. Sharing data will also aid in teams understanding the need for the mandate. Through this dialogue, those imposing the change must communicate the why, connect with each individual's values, and relate to what is important to each of them.

Change the subtext. When articulating why a team or school must implement a change, school leaders need to convey collective responsibility for the problem to which the mandate is addressing. The new subtext is that "*we* need to do better," not just "*you.*"

Provide clear expectations. School leaders need to be specific as to what is expected to be implemented and as to what is left for teams to have the power to decide. They further articulate the district or principal's mandate about what needs to be accomplished and whenever possible allow teams to have input on how they will achieve the desired results.

Push back. Fullan (1993) "Neither centralization or decentralization works. Both top-down and bottom-up strategies are necessary (p. 37). He continued, writing that "It is possible for individual schools to become highly collaborative despite their districts, but it is not possible for them to *stay* collaborative under these conditions" (p. 38). The leadership team must be willing to push back at the district if the change seems wrong: wrong timing, wrong approach, wrong solution, wrong audience, and so forth. Likewise, the district should push back at schools if sustaining a current initiative needs to change. At the center of the push back must be listening, where district leaders, school leaders, and teacher teams share the goal of implementing and sustaining changes that evolve with the needs of the current student population based on evidence.

Dilemma 2: How Do I Lead an Action-Oriented Team When Intentions Don't Align With Actions?

It is incredibly rewarding when someone experiences an "aha" moment during rigorous discourse in which a shift in an individual's thinking is practically tangible. While it is most definitely a sign of learning and a marker that the team is developing as part of a professional learning community (PLC), the skillful team leader knows it is not the end goal. How is it that an individual can gain knowledge, appear to be moved by it, and still not put it into action? When a teacher seems to say "yes" in a team meeting, but follow-through in the classroom implies "no," the team is face-to-face with a hurdle.

Consider the following snapshot of a team:

> *Brandon is leading a math team engaging in rigorous discourse about differentiated instruction. Teachers are excited about the strategies presented, and one teacher says, "This article makes so much sense, particularly the strategy suggested in paragraph four."*

Another says, "I can't wait to try this with my algebra class."

Brandon says, "Great. Let's all try this with one of our classes. I'll type up the details of our action plan and e-mail it out."

When Brandon and the team check in one month later, they discover implementation is weak at best. One teacher admits to implementing nothing, saying, "I just didn't have time, but I'll try next week." Another has incorporated the strategy, but only in her Do Now, and a third teacher embedded the strategies into her lessons for a few weeks, but then reverted to her previous teaching methods, claiming, "It seemed to be working, but I was up planning until ten o'clock every night. I just can't keep that up, so I had to scale back."

Identify the Hurdle

The hurdle facing this team is unique in that it doesn't show up until *after* the team meets. No one is outwardly reluctant to change. The team is not storming (Ch. 3). In fact, teachers embrace the change publicly, but when back in their classrooms their good intentions don't translate into sustainable actions. Determining to what degree each teacher is implementing the change can help Brandon uncover what is limiting individuals from taking further action.

Hord et al. (1987) discovered that whenever an innovation is introduced teachers implement with varying levels of use (see Figure 7.2). While this figure is designed to provide leaders with schoolwide information about the fidelity of implementation of an initiative, it can also be a valuable assessment to a team leader whose team is experiencing inertia, where individuals don't move to action.

Figure 7.2 Levels of Use/Behavioral Indicators of Level

Levels of Use	Behavioral Indicators of Level
VI. Renewal	The user is seeking more effective alternatives to the established use of the innovation.
V. Integration	The user is making deliberate efforts to coordinate with others in using the innovation.
IVB. Refinement	The user is making changes to increase outcomes.
IVA. Routine	The user is making few or no changes and has an established pattern of use.
III. Mechanical	The user is making changes to better organize use of the innovation.
II. Preparation	The user has definite plans to begin using the innovation.
0I. Orientation	The user is taking the initiative to learn more about the innovation.
0. Non-Use	The user has no interest, is taking no action.

Source: Taking Charge of Change, by Shirley M. Hord, William L. Rutherford, Leslie Huling-Austin, and Gene E. Hall, Alexandria, VA: ASCD. © 1987 Southwest Educational Development Laboratory. Reprinted with permission. Learn more about ASCD at www.ascd.org.

Using this table, Brandon can assess where his teachers are in implementation of the new strategies. The team demonstrates various levels of use. One teacher is at Level II: Preparation—intending to make changes to his practice but has not done so yet. Another teacher is at Level III: Mechanical Use—where she has begun to implement the change but only partially. The third teacher is on the verge of refinement, Level IVB, but when the change becomes too much, she drops her level of use down. To help his team advance, Brandon must consider why his team is not taking the action needed.

Explore Possible Causes

Resistance. Brandon's team is not demonstrating resistance to change as in the prior dilemma; however, their reluctance to change might still be a factor. Resistance can take the form of obvious opposition (overt) or more subtle behavior (covert) (see Figure 7.3). Both overt and covert resistance, as

Figure 7.3 Overt/Covert Resistant Responses to Change

	Overt Resistant Responses	*Covert Resistant Responses*
Verbal	**A reluctant response might sound like the following:** **Refusal**: "I'm not going to . . ." **Challenge**: "Who put you in charge?" **Blame**: "I would, but I can't because . . ." **Logic**: "The original way works, I don't need to change." **Disbelief**: "This data doesn't reflect what you are telling us . . ." **Pessimism**: "This change won't work. I'll do it, but you'll see."	**A reluctant response might sound like the following:** **Gossip**: "I'd like to see her do this change with my kids." **Complaining**: "Here we go again." **Sarcasm**: "My kids are going to be so excited that I'm changing things *again!*" **Diversion**: "I know this is off topic but . . ." **Humor**: "If I do this, my kids are going to think aliens took their real teacher away." **Self-deprecating comment**: "With my luck, I'll try this and get worse results." **Learned helplessness**: "I could do this if I didn't have so many students."
Nonverbal	**A reluctant response might look like the following:** **Departure**: A teacher gets up and leaves the meeting.	**A reluctant response might look like the following:** **Distraction**: A teacher grades papers, texts, engages in side conversations during discussion about implementation. **Ignoring:** Teacher agrees at a team meeting to implement but does not. **Procrastination**: Teacher puts other priorities ahead of change. **Perfectionism**: Teacher expresses intentions to change but holds out for the perfect timing. **Absentmindedness**: Teacher forgets to bring in student work to show evidence of implementation. **Superficial implementation:** Teacher takes minimal action and consequently does not achieve desired results.

they are sometimes referenced (Bovey & Hede, 2001; O'Connor, 1993; Sharma, 2007), can immobilize a team. The teachers in this snapshot have intentions to change, but reluctance to act in the classroom may indicate covert resistance.

First-time hiccups. It is expected for teachers beginning to implement a change, even if voluntary, to revert to prior practice. Fullan (2001) refers to this as an "implementation dip." Grappling with personal and management concerns, wrestling with a change in beliefs and behaviors is part of the change process and dips are to be expected.

Group pressure. Although a teacher's words can indicate support of a new practice, she might have reservations that she is not comfortable expressing. Inhibited by groupthink, where people go along with whatever the group wants (Ch. 6), one or more of the teachers in the snapshot may actually be reluctant to act, but may not have the confidence in her own reservations to speak out. This behavior is exacerbated if a teacher has a socializing mindset (Ch. 2), in which she has not yet fully formed her own convictions, is influenced by others' desires and beliefs, and says what others want to hear (Kegan & Lahey, 2009). If everyone on the team in this snapshot, for example, is enthusiastic about the agreed-upon action steps, the teacher with the socializing mindset, or one influenced by groupthink, goes along with the plan in order to be accepted by the team.

An inactionable plan. If response to a team's action plan is genuinely enthusiastic, but a teacher does not implement it, there might be a problem with the plan itself. Action plans are intended to be useful road maps for the team to implement what is learned, but if they are too lengthy or complex, a teacher can become overwhelmed and paralyzed, concerned with not being able to do all the action steps right. If a teacher does not have a hand in how the action plan is written, it can read like hieroglyphics, discouraging her from trying to figure out what she is supposed to do.

Seemingly SMART. As mentioned in Chapter 5, having an attainable goal with unsustainable strategies can cause some teachers to drop implementation of a new practice regardless of intention. It's possible that the teacher who implemented more than the others reverted back to her previous methods because she could not maintain the pressure and lifestyle change of staying up until ten o'clock planning every night.

Team leader's assumptions. It is easy to mistake enthusiasm for understanding. Brandon's team is demonstrably excited to take action, but some may not have the depth of understanding of the new practice to execute it effectively. Brandon assumes his team has knowledge of the innovation: *what* it is, *when* do we do it, *with whom* is it done, *how* is it done, and *why* do we do it.

Fixed mindset. The skillful team leader does not overlook the possible presence of a fixed mindset. One or more teachers on Brandon's team might doubt their ability to succeed at the new practice and either avoid attempting implementation at all or revert to what they are comfortable doing so as not to be seen as a failure by their colleagues or evaluators.

Negative feedback. Nothing can discourage a teacher more from implementing a new practice than getting negative, unconstructive feedback early on, particularly from an evaluator. Although this snapshot does not reveal that any of the teachers on the team are criticized for their implementation, it is possible that the teacher who has reverted back to her prior method may have been discouraged by comments from an outside observer.

Respond

Proactive response: To prevent inertia and foster an action-oriented team for continuous improvement, a team leader can do the following:

Norm for "the dip." The skillful team leader alerts the team to normal behavior when implementing a new practice such as slipping back to one's prior teaching methods due to fatigue or setbacks. It is important to anticipate the dips and set group agreements on how the team will recognize when a team member experiences one and how they will respond positively. A team agreement might be "We will ask for help when we sense a dip in our own implementation, and we will reach out when we see someone else struggling."

Create an actionable plan. What good is a brilliantly written action plan for a new practice if it doesn't get anyone to take action? The best plans commit the team to act and plan for hurdles that might get in the way. Involving the entire team in writing the plan fosters understanding and investment. If time does not allow for this, or if a team gets stuck in the wordsmithing trap where teachers spend too much time coming to consensus on the wording of goals and plans, a member can type an initial draft for others to revise in a subsequent meeting.

Codesign a lesson. Collaboratively creating a lesson plan can help teams stuck in low levels of use. Not only will each teacher have a greater understanding of how to implement the new strategy or practice because they are involved in the design of the lesson, but each will also have a shared responsibility for the success and mistakes of the lesson. The team members then hold each other accountable to put that lesson plan into action.

Model and debrief. Some teachers need to see a new strategy or practice in action before they feel confident to give it a go in their own classroom. The skillful team leader models the new practice or arranges for teachers to observe each other's implementation. If classroom coverage is a challenge, he turns to videotaping or setting up practice runs in the team, where teachers try the strategy out on each other. Regardless of how the new practice is modeled, the debrief of the lesson is most important. It enables a team to air out concerns or challenges that teachers anticipate before implementing the practice in their own classes.

Deflate the emotion. Saturday Night Live aired a sketch of a character named Debbie Downer®. Whenever a group was excited about something, she would interject with a cautious comment that would bring the energy of the group down in an instant. By all means, a team leader should keep enthusiasm for change high; however, if there is a hint of doubt that talk may not lead to action, he can, without completely deflating the energy in the team, say something such as "We've got great enthusiasm for this new practice. Is there anything that might stop us from trying this out, and if so what can we do to make sure that doesn't happen?"

Assess depth of knowledge. The skillful team leader checks for understanding before, during, and after the implementation of a new practice. Brandon and his team can explore the following questions:

- What is the new practice?
- When should we use it? When should we not use it?
- How do we implement it?
- Why are we making this change at this time?
- How is this new practice fundamentally different from what we already do?
- What do we need to know or get better at in order to implement it?

Don't take "yes" for an answer. The skillful team leader is careful not to mistake enthusiasm for commitment. One teacher's "can't wait" comment in this snapshot indicates that she has every intention of implementing the strategy. But good intentions don't change a school (DuFour & Eaker, 1998), just as many well-intentioned New Year's resolutions never make it past March. The skillful team leader helps teachers commit to their intentions. Brandon can respond to the teacher by saying, "Great! What has clicked for you? Let's brainstorm what we and you can do specifically in the classroom?"

In-the-moment response: When a team intends to take action, but does so at different levels of implementation, a team leader can do the following:

Assess levels of use. The skillful team leader leads his team in assessing where they stand in implementation. Using Hord, Rutherford, Huling-Austin, and Hall's Levels of Use (see Figure 7.2) can initiate the conversation about the actions they have taken thus far and what they need to implement more fully.

Build solidarity. The skillful team leader creates safe opportunities for his team to discuss their challenges with implementation, affirming that they are all learners, leader included. In this snapshot, Brandon might say, "So this really requires a teacher to think differently about lesson plans which can seem like more work. What can we do to begin implementation in a way that is manageable while keeping true to why we are implementing this change?"

Start with one success. If team members have success implementing a new practice, the skillful team leader encourages them to bring in student work. Those who have reservations about changing are often more willing to try when they see their colleagues welcome the change, take the risk, and show proof of success.

Follow-up response: To sustain a high level of implementation, a team leader can do the following:

Return to the huddle. The skillful team leader encourages collaboration during implementation. Back to the football analogy, a successful team huddles, makes a plan, goes out on to the field, executes the plan to the best of its ability, returns to the huddle to determine its next moves, and so on until the goal is met. One of the greatest benefits of teachers doing inquiry as a team is the learning that transpires from a talk–action loop, where together teachers learn a new practice, try it, observe it in action or look at student work that results from it, reflect on it, and adjust.

School leadership team response: If a team struggles to implement a change at a high level of use, team leaders, the principal, and administrators together can do the following:

Give specific encouraging feedback. Ongoing, specific feedback from colleagues and school leaders is not only motivation for a teacher to stick with a change that is challenging, but will also improve their ability to do so effectively. At the same time, leaders need to be cautious about giving discouraging feedback early on when teachers are first implementing changes to their practice. In this snapshot, a leader might give feedback to a teacher on Brandon's team by saying, "I noticed you are differentiating your Do Now assignments. This seems to really engage every student from the start of class. Now, how might you apply the same strategy to the word problems you gave during the lesson? Have you tried [provide suggestion]?"

Make it easy to change and difficult not to. School leaders can give needed resources, supplies, structures, time, and professional development to facilitate faster implementation. Additionally, stopping "crutch" resources that make it easy to hold onto past practices (i.e., don't order one-size-fits-all workbooks, arrange for peer observations about specific aspects of the change initiative) will make resistance to change that much harder. (Note: The latter should not be administered as a top down, threatening, "change or else" approach. Teachers and team leaders need to be involved in the discussion about which crutches exist, which should be taken away and in what order, and what additional supports should be provided to teachers to make the transition.)

Dilemma 3: How Do I Lead an Action-Oriented Team When External Changes Impact Our Ability to Sustain Implementation or Results?

A look at most of the educational literature on the market today and one would be hard pressed to not see the word *sustainability*. Teams strive to implement sustainable practices for sustainable results. It makes sense that a team might struggle to attain sustainable results if a team member doesn't take action because of unanswered concerns, similar to the first dilemma of this chapter, or struggles to execute a change as seen in the second dilemma. But what if the threat to continuous improvement does not come from within the team but from without? What if team members implement action steps with a high level of use and have evidence of impact, but their success is interrupted by an external factor? Action-oriented teams can quickly become inactive if they don't learn how to adapt to challenges posed by people and circumstances outside of the team.

Consider the following snapshot of a team:

> *Michelle's team volunteers to meet over the summer to create a new curriculum that aligns with the state standards. Over the first year of implementation, the team meets regularly to assess how students are responding to the new curriculum, work through problems, and adjust instruction as needed. By the end of the school year, team members notice that students have made considerable gains. Motivated by these results, they set out to implement the same curriculum for a second year, until news of the new common core standards stops them in their tracks. One teacher says, "We are going to have to realign this curriculum to these new standards, which is going to mean changing what we teach and how."*
>
> *Another teacher says, "I know, but we just revised our curriculum and are finally starting to see measured student improvement. I don't know if I'm ready to do this again. Maybe we should just forget what we've done and find an existing packaged curriculum that aligns with the common core state standards and follow that."*
>
> *A third teacher, who is usually optimistic, symbolically takes her binder of lessons and drops it in the trash. Michelle wants to help her team navigate through the change, yet she feels ready to throw in the towel too.*

Identify the Hurdle

This is a high-functioning, high-impact team on its way to sustainable results when it is suddenly immobilized by changes beyond its control. It is not uncommon for external factors to negatively impact a team's ability to act. New district leadership might replace assessments teams have been using with new ones. A principal might lose funding for resources that a team needs in order to sustain actions. Staff turnover can cause changes to the makeup of a team. Schedule changes can reduce a team's time to collaborate. Parents might block a team's ability to implement an intervention with fidelity by refusing to grant their child permission to participate. These scenarios are familiar to teacher teams, sometimes even expected, and yet instead of evolving with change, they are paralyzed by it. Michelle must find out why.

Explore Possible Causes

Strong convictions. Can a team sustain improvement when individuals outside of the team make decisions that impede a team's actions? Kegan and Lahey (2009) say that adults who have reached a self-transforming mindset in their development are able to evolve with change instead of being immobilized by it (Ch. 2). Those with a self-authoring mindset can be so strongly focused on their own agendas that they are not yet able to transform their thinking and approach. Teachers may hold so tightly to their own convictions that those convictions aren't able to develop and grow as changes in the school landscape occur. In this snapshot, teachers are so invested in the curriculum they created that they resist adapting it.

Bound by success. The team in this snapshot is both motivated and handicapped by their success. As change occurs, the ongoing learner with a growth mindset adapts. It's possible that the team members in this snapshot hold a fixed mindset about themselves as teachers, concerned that they won't be as successful with a revised curriculum.

Dysfunctional conditions for change. When team members demonstrate that they are ready to embrace and adapt to change, but external factors cause the team's actions to come to a standstill, the skillful team leader considers the professional learning conditions of the school or district. School conditions must be organized for teacher and student success (Fullan, 2007). If, for example, Michelle's team members are not provided with time to help them change course, they are likely to stop action instead of evolving with the change.

Respond

Proactive response: To prevent external changes from immobilizing a team's actions, a team leader can do the following:

Anticipate healthy change. Change is inevitable. Fostering a healthy response to change in team members before they even begin implementation of new practices will help them adapt to external factors that come their way. For instance, early in the team's work, Michelle might say, "Aligning what we do in the classroom to our state standards is critically important. Of course, we must anticipate that standards might evolve, requiring us to adapt. Let's design and implement these lessons for the students and standards we have now, knowing that we will likely need to adapt them in the future."

Anticipate unhealthy change. Not all changes are the right changes for the right people at the right time. If a team has the ability to select their own team goal and design their own action plan, it should be planned with the awareness that external changes might threaten their implementation and disrupt results for students. Preparing teachers and ensuring that commitment is strong enough to "weather the storm" and adapt as needed will increase the likelihood that the team will remain action oriented.

In-the-moment response: If external factors impede a team's ability to sustain actions, a team leader can do the following:

Develop the mind. Mindsets are not permanent. They can evolve (Ch. 2). The skillful team leader works to advance people from a self-authoring mind to a self-transforming mind, from a fixed mindset to a growth mindset. One way Michelle might initiate the shift is to say, "Let's not abandon the work we've done that has thus far proven to show results. Instead, how can the current changes brought on by these new standards shape what we already believe and do? What new perspectives or new learning does this bring for us and for our students? In what ways are we limiting our success if we do not adapt to the change? What if we make this change and we fail? How can we make this worth trying?"

Focus on core principles. When external changes threaten the sustainability of a team's actions and student results, the skillful team leader brings the team members back to why they are doing this work in the first place. In this snapshot, Michelle might ask, "We have been implementing units aligned to our state standards because we believe [insert concept]. While this change will impact *what* we do and in some ways *how* we do it, it does not have to impact *why* we do this work. Let's figure out how to adapt with this change while staying true to what we are trying to accomplish."

Take control. The skillful team leader uses the hurdle of an external change as an opportunity to assess the team's current effectiveness and improve upon it. In this snapshot, Michelle can share information about common core, collaborating with others on ways in which adopting them might improve the good student results they are already getting.

School leadership team response: If a team's actions are negatively impacted by external changes, team leaders, the principal, and administrators together can do the following:

Be aware and collaborate. A leadership team must be keenly aware of what teacher teams are already implementing and ensure external changes do not interfere with their ability to sustain effective results. Having an open dialogue with teams in advance of new changes can help teams evolve with the change and be an opportunity for school leaders to make conditions conducive for optimal change.

CONSIDER SCHOOL CULTURE: SHIFTING FROM A CULTURE ACIDIC TO CHANGE TO A CULTURE OF CONTINUOUS IMPROVEMENT

If one wonders why plants in her garden aren't thriving or perhaps why certain weeds seem to be taking over, it may be time to test the acidity of the soil. If one wonders why teams are not eager to implement new practices, it may be time to see if that school's culture is acidic to change. The gap between wanting continuous improvement and achieving it widens with each change initiative that fails to bloom. Over time, passion and commitment to the success of a given change quickly expire as stakeholders unintentionally obstruct actions that yield sustainable results.

Recognize the Signs of a Culture Acidic to Change

- There's no apparent basis for change. Neither school leaders nor teachers have any cause for change. If one stakeholder does have evidence of a need, it is poorly communicated to everyone else.
- Teachers make efforts to implement change with no feedback from colleagues or school leaders. If any feedback is given, it is typically negative. This discourages teams from risk taking and experimentation.
- Expectations for results are unreasonable. Schools can't provide teams with the resources they need to implement or sustain the actions necessary to bring forth the desired change. Consequently, all are set up to fail (sometimes even before they start).
- Top-down change is given higher priority than is bottom-up change. When teams discover the need for change, there is a lot of excitement and planning, but action is either short-lived or not taken at all.

- Reluctance to change is viewed as a bug that needs to be squashed. The school administration only wants to hear positive voices. As a result, there is no forum to share concerns publicly, so it can turn into venting and gossip behind closed doors.

Where Does a Culture Acidic to Change Come From?

A close look at a school's change habits provide a first clue. It takes a toll on a community when districts, in which schools have had to implement one initiative after another, don't see the desired results they set out to achieve. Historically, schools make several mistakes that lead to this "adopt and drop" behavior. They increase the initiatives without increasing the resources—leaving less time, money, and emotional energy to implement the change successfully. Reeves (2010) refers to this as the "Law of Initiative Fatigue." Schools take action without taking notice of the mindset shift needed to achieve sustainable results—what teachers believe they and students are capable of doing. They discard an initiative before assessing the levels of use teachers carried out (Hord et al., 1987). Consequently, they never realize the intended results for students, and they have "no clear understanding of the factors contributing to failure" (Sarason, 1971, p. 46). Thus, they repeat the mistakes of the past. New change efforts are plagued by these missteps, generating assumptions that "this too shall pass." Instead of mobilizing teams to action, the mere thought of implementing a change makes even the most enthusiastic and committed discouraged.

Underlying a culture acidic to change is fear. "Fear creates knowing-doing gaps because acting on one's knowledge requires that a person believes he or she will not be punished for doing so—that taking risks based on new information and insight will be rewarded, not punished" (Pfeffer & Sutton, 2000, p. 4). When fear is present, teachers are less likely to experiment and let go of existing practices.

The culture of continuous improvement nurtures change for implementation and sustainability. Educators are thoughtful and strategic about the change initiatives they adopt. School leaders say "no" to change initiatives that will deplete their existing resources. High expectations for results exist coupled with the resources to reach them and a constant hunt to acquire more. School leaders and teachers value learning risks and encourage it through modeling, positive feedback, and celebration. They value honest discourse and see resistors to change as offering an important, sometimes overlooked, perspective that needs to be heard in structured, productive conversations. They continuously act and assess, offering support to those implementing at low levels of use. They are driven by the urgency to see results, but they don't shortchange time needed to be successful.

When a school has a culture acidic to change, a team leader together with other school members can do the following:

Create a need with mission and vision. Schools, in which people are a part of what the school is trying to accomplish and what they envision seeing and hearing when they get there, are able to look at their current state and identify places for growth and change. Once everyone is able to see the same need for change, he or she is more apt to embrace it.

One approach is for a school to create vision videos or skits. Instead of asking people to wordsmith a vision statement, which can be dry and meaningless, ask teams to make a video or create a skit of what they want to see and hear. For example, a video or skit based on the statement "We envision students with the skills and knowledge necessary to think, read, write, and communicate independently" might resemble the following:

Mrs. B   John, you look like you are struggling with this math problem.

John (student)   I am, Mrs. B. But I'd love if you would give me a few more minutes so that I can look through my notes and talk with my partner to see if I can work it out on my own. If not, I'll call you over, and by then I'll have a clearer sense of where I'm confused.

By having team members create vision videos or skits, they can really identify what it is that students and teachers should be saying and doing. They formulate a clear mental image of the vision, and it sticks with them throughout the year; it can be a good faculty bonding experience. As a follow-up to this activity, the school sets SMA-H-RT goals and spells out needed resources.

Limit change priorities. As mentioned in Chapter 4, "The individual teacher, school, or district with ten priorities has none" (Wagner et al., 2006, p. 66). Reeves (2010) recommends schools limit priorities to six, and old common sense says, "Bite off what you can chew." Schools need to look at resources they have, examine the need, and focus on changing what is pressing and urgent, aligned to the vision.

Provide ongoing vertical and lateral feedback. As educators do implement changes, feedback is critical for skill and morale in order to see desired results. Vertical feedback (i.e., principal to teacher team, teacher team to principal) and horizontal feedback (i.e., team to team, teacher to teacher) are both valuable.

Go public with risk. Evaluators and teachers can come to a common understanding of what risks need to be taken in order for the end goal to be reached. Together they can discuss supports needed for this risk. Supports might be tangible—an extra set of hands for the first time the teacher implements a change—or emotional—a peer support group or a school group agreement such as "permission to be a beginner." Going public with the risk teachers are taking and voicing the supports they need to be successful, opens communication and builds trust.

Celebrate learning bumps. Teams who share their struggles, dilemmas, confusions, and risks taken in the classroom encourage other teams to do the same.

Ask courageous questions. School leaders can begin to mend a culture acidic to change by asking the following questions:

- What values do we hold?
- Under what conditions will continuous improvement happen? How do we change cultures (Fullan, 2006)?
- Are there aspects of our school which do not support your implementation and that you are concerned might hold you back from embracing this change?
- How committed are you to implementing this change? (This question can be asked on a survey at different points in the course of change, and someone can track growth on a large chart for all to see.)

Stick with it. It can take at least three years before seeing full results from a change initiative (Hord et al., 1987). Schools can use Hord's Levels of Use to evaluate if the initiative is being implemented at its fullest before discarding it for something else.

Focus on success. Schools can sketch on paper a historical timeline of the initiatives they have worked on in the past five years. They can discuss the impact that the successful change initiatives have had on teaching and learning, and then they can reflect on what made some succeed and others fail. They might ask, "In what ways have we successfully responded to initiatives in the past?" (Lindsey, Jungwirth, Pahl, & Lindsey, 2009, p. 115).

APPLICATION TO YOUR WORK: CONNECT, OBSERVE, EXPLORE, ACT

Think and write independently. Then, discuss with colleagues.

Connect	Observe
Remember a time as a leader or participant when your team was action oriented for continuous improvement? How did your team transform knowledge into action? How did you implement change and overcome inertia?	At what level of use are you and other team members implementing a new practice? How often do positive intentions turn to action? How does your team respond to external factors that impact your actions or results?
Explore	**Act**
What hurdles prevent your team from transforming knowledge into action? What hurdles keep implementation of a new practice at a low level of use? What concerns do you hear and see from your team members? What have you done to anticipate and meet these concerns? What have you not tried yet? Why?	What will you and your colleagues do to be action oriented, always striving for continuous improvement? Name next steps and support needed.

A Closing Note

I opened this book with a story about my entry into team leadership. I'd like to close with the top three reasons I stick with it.

REASON 3: LEARNING

With each hurdle I encounter, I better understand the complexity of leading. I learn how to anticipate and avoid; I learn how to effectively respond. I am reminded of the people who through their own skillful team leadership have shaped my values, mindset, intelligence, and skill. Their excellence and commitment inspire me to persist and continue to learn. I take with me learning from the following people:

A coach who led me and a team of literacy coaches from multiple schools. Our needs and our experience varied greatly, yet she managed to foster a collaborative culture where we were both high functioning as a learning team and high impact in our own schools.

An assistant principal who truly understood the inertia teams can encounter when a mandate is imposed. She taught me to always listen carefully to teachers' concerns, assume positive intentions, and work tirelessly with others to meet their needs as they grow with the change.

Teacher leaders who I had the privilege of coaching, who skillfully surfed the waves of resistance, always managing to foster deep ownership in the team's important work.

A superintendent in a district where I consulted who not only valued a culture of shared leadership for learning in her district but actually put it into practice. She led a team of already outstanding principals to become even better. She modeled learning as she met with teacher teams, listening to their ideas and empowering them to set impactful goals that would lead to greater student achievement.

Coaches and teacher leaders with whom I now work, who skillfully lead teams of teachers in schools where students are grade levels behind. They overcome seemingly insurmountable hurdles by skillfully engaging in rigorous discourse that leaves no room for excuses or blame and continue to set high-impact goals and achieve them.

Colleagues who unwaveringly believe in my abilities even when a fixed mindset about myself creeps back in. Those who remind me that no one is expecting perfection, that I am allowed to make mistakes and will do better if I share them with others as learning opportunities, and that the best leaders are learners.

And the teachers with whom I have worked, who trusted me to lead our teams and jumped each hurdle that came our way *with* me, which enabled us to learn together.

REASON 2: TEACHING

Cliché as it may sound, I love teaching. I get a thrill when I talk about it with colleagues, when I discover a more impactful way of reaching students, when a colleague suspends my assumptions and probes me to think deeply about my practice, when my words or actions have an impact on someone else's beliefs about him- or herself as a teacher, when I know I'm contributing to a professional learning culture, and, above all, when my colleagues and I motivate one another to continuously learn and change in order to be our best selves.

REASON 1: STUDENTS

Seeing the impact of my team's learning on students keeps me motivated to continue leading adult learners. When a teacher brings in before and after pieces of student writing, and I know that I had a hand in helping that student learn even if I am not his teacher. When a teacher runs into my office excitedly to share with me that a student who had never read a whole book on his or her own just did and loved it, and I know our team helped to make that happen. Knowing that every hurdle we overcome as a team impacts the life of a student makes it worthwhile.

Learning, teaching, and students drive me to run toward the hurdles and leap. My family and friends remind me that I can. But at the end of a long, challenging day, it is my own inner voice that reminds me that leading teams of adult learners can be hard no matter how many years of experience you have. It tells me to stay rooted in my values and growth mindset; to apply emotional intelligence and skill to each hurdle. And it reminds me of my favorite quote, "Courage doesn't always roar, sometimes it is the quiet voice at the end of the day that says, 'I will try again'" (Radmacher, n.d.).

I hope this book helps you and your team find the courage to keep leaping.

Resources

Resource 3.1

Function vs. Impact

Function vs. Impact

High Functioning	High Impact on Student Learning
We have a shared understanding of our purpose for collaboration. (E.g., we know and are invested in what we set out to accomplish.)	Our purpose for collaborating will improve student learning. (E.g., we are collaborating so that X students are able to do Y by Z.)
Our group agreements promote productive collaboration. We keep ourselves and others accountable to them. (E.g., we respectfully agree to start and end meetings on time.)	Our group agreements keep us accountable to implementing actions that yield gains for student learning. (E.g., we agree to implement X strategy with Y group of students.)
Through roles, we equitably share responsibility for tasks in the team that keep us productive and cohesive. (E.g., we rotate the role of facilitator so that no one person carries the workload.)	We take on roles that share responsibility for team learning. (E.g., we each take on the role of speaking up when culture-bound assumptions about teachers or students are made.)
We collectively choose and utilize meeting tools such as agendas and protocols so that our team is productive, efficient, and on task. (E.g., we cocreate agendas and follow them. We make joint decisions on when to adjust times within an agenda. We respectfully follow protocols when needed.)	Our meeting tools bring our team closer to our student-learning targets and long-term goals. (E.g., our agendas specify desired outcomes that are directly linked to our team goal. Our protocols structure conversations that result in achieving the learning-centered desired outcomes of the meeting. We adapt protocols when needed to foster rigorous discourse that result in action.)
The team collectively agrees upon long-term goals. (E.g., consensus is reached for an annual team goal.)	Goals are SMA-H-RT, not Seemingly SMART. Each is the right goal at the right time for the right students. (E.g., we use data to set incremental learning targets for groups of students.)
Team moves through each stage of the inquiry cycle within the decided timeline. They do not get stuck at any one stage. (E.g., we unanimously commit to a goal. Next, we will take turns sharing best practice strategies.)	The team moves through each stage of the inquiry cycle making strategic decisions that enable them to achieve their learning targets and ultimately their long-term goals. (E.g., we set learning targets for specific students. Next, we will identify which strategies are best for achieving this target in the given timeline.)
We have an agreed-upon process for making decisions. (E.g., we ensure all opinions are heard when making collective decisions.)	We have an agreed-upon process for making decisions about instruction and student learning. (E.g., we use student work to make decisions about what skills to target.)

Resource 3.2

Team Function, Impact
Matrix Indicators

Indicators of a High-Functioning, Low-Impact Team:	Indicators of a High-Functioning, High-Impact Team:
Team members work well together and gets things done, but what they get done produces little to no measured gains in student learning.	*Team members work well together and achieve measured gains in student learning.*

<table>
<tr><td>

☐ Shared purpose for collaboration, but purpose is not for improved student learning (e.g., all on board to plan school fundraiser).

☐ Highly efficient; productive collaboration; meeting time is sacred (i.e., never cancelled or upstaged); if unexpected interruption, team swiftly reschedules and keeps pace with work; accomplishes desired outcomes on agenda, but outcomes do not advance student learning (e.g., book fair logistics, respectful discussion about instruction, no instructional changes made). Upholds group agreements for function (e.g., start and end on time), but no agreements for impact (e.g., "We agree to implement strategy and bring findings each week") (Ch. 3).

☐ Shared leadership for tasks but not for each others' learning (e.g., rotate note taker, but no one leads a model lesson for colleagues) (Ch. 4).

☐ Goal may not align to school goals; "Seemingly SMART"; no small learning targets. Attains measurable growth in non-learning matters (e.g., students improve in organization of note-taking, but don't show measured improvement in understanding) (Ch. 5).

☐ Collectively look at data, but poor considerations for data selection and weak analysis (e.g., analyzing use of transition words on open response when team goal is to improve reading comprehension). No actionable knowledge gained (Ch. 6).

☐ Agreed-upon process for decision making, but decisions made do not impact instruction or student learning. Little conflict, but members withhold or easily back down from diverging opinions (Ch. 6).

☐ Collaboration results in no change to classroom instruction (Ch. 7).

☐ Members love working with this team and typically are unaware that there is a need to change course in order to have a greater impact on student learning.

</td><td>

☐ Shared purpose for collaboration yielding measured gains in student learning (e.g., all are present to actively participate in evidence-based inquiry to improve student learning).

☐ Highly efficient and productive; meeting time is sacred (i.e., never cancelled or upstaged); if unexpected interruption, team swiftly reschedules and keeps pace with work; accomplishes desired outcomes on agenda that advance team SMA-H-RT goals and learning targets. Upholds group agreements for both function (e.g., start and end on time) and impact (e.g., "We agree to bring one question about our own data to each meeting") (Ch. 3).

☐ Shared leadership for tasks and each others' learning (e.g., team rotates teacher who brings in student work based on inquiry action plan). Willingness to share best practices, failures, and take collective responsibility for other teachers and their students (Ch 4).

☐ Comes to consensus on SMA-H-RT goals (aligned to school goals) and small learning targets for common specific groups of students to achieve long-term goals. Achieves sustainable, measured gains.

☐ Strategic, thoughtful considerations made about data and how to analyze and act. Engages in rigorous discourse—dialogue that is evidence based, dialogic, culturally proficient, reflective, and actionable. Team regularly shares both best practices and challenges for the purpose of implementing solutions (Ch. 6).

☐ Agreed-upon process for decision making about instruction. Engages in "conflict for learning" where members pose diverging views in order to transform their own beliefs and actions (Ch. 6).

☐ Collaboration results in positive changes to classroom instruction (Ch. 7).

☐ Members love working with this team.

</td></tr>
</table>

Indicators of a Low Functioning, Low-Impact Team	Indicators of a Low Functioning, High-Impact Team
No one gets along, nothing gets done, and few to no gains for student learning are made.	*Team members grouped together but act alone. Some highly dependent on a few. Student-learning goals are achieved.*
☐ No shared understanding of purpose for collaboration, members don't recognize a need for collaborating as a team.	☐ No shared understanding of purpose; members don't recognize a need for collaborating as a team yet individual goals and learning targets are met.
☐ Inefficient, unproductive. Meetings canceled or upstaged by other events or people. None or poor execution of group agreements, roles, agendas, protocols. Agenda outcomes don't exist or are not connected to student-learning outcomes (Ch. 3).	☐ Group agreements, roles, agendas, time management, protocols, are inconsistently used or used regularly but poorly executed. Meetings canceled or upstaged by other events or people; people don't know what meeting is about (Ch. 3).
☐ Some individuals are burdened with roles and responsibility, others with none. Lack of shared responsibility for tasks and each other's learning (Ch. 4).	☐ Lack of shared leadership for tasks, nor each other's learning. Some individuals are burdened with roles and responsibility, others with none. Willingness to share best practices but unwilling to take collective responsibility for failure (Ch. 4).
☐ No SMA-H-RT goals or have Seemingly SMART goals. No measurable student-learning gains for anyone on team (Ch. 5).	☐ Common SMA-H-RT goals, but individuals are left on their own to achieve them; measurable growth for learning and/or achieves learning targets and long-term goals, but teachers don't learn, and practice does not change. Gains commonly made by a few individual team members ("superheroes"). Improvement is inconsistent across classrooms. Gains made in student learning are unsustainable—when "superhero" leaves so do results (Ch. 3).
☐ Discourse not based on data or poor considerations of data selection (Ch. 6).	☐ Strategic, thoughtful considerations made about data and how to act; however, analysis and strategizing is commonly done independently. When done as a team, teachers rarely share failure (Ch. 6).
☐ No collaborative decision-making process; conflict debilitates the team from consensus or action.	☐ No collaborative decision-making process. Conflict resolved by members doing their own thing. If diverging opinions are voiced, no one listens to be transformed. Beliefs and practice are not influenced by others.
☐ Collaboration results in no change to instruction (Ch. 7).	☐ Team is not cohesive. Many members dread working with this team. Some are exhausted trying to make group a team; others are apathetic. Most tolerate dysfunction because they are getting results for students.
☐ Members dread working with this team.	

Resource 3.3

Compass Points: An Exercise in Understanding Styles in Group Work

Purpose: This exercise increases individual's self-awareness of strengths and areas for growth when working in a group. It helps teams identify the strengths and weaknesses of their own styles for group work, the challenge of communication, and emphasizes the need for all styles in a team.

Time allotted: 20–30 minutes

Group format: Team (This can also be done with multiple teams at a schoolwide PD.)

Supplies: Four signs each labeled with one compass point (North, South, East, or West)

Roles: Facilitator (can be the team leader)

PROCEDURE

First, the team leader sets up one compass point sign per wall: North, South, East, and West.

Next, team members read the descriptions of each compass point (p. 163) independently and then self-designate to the compass point they most resemble when working in groups. Note: Many people lean in more than one direction.

People should stand where they see themselves most of the time when collaborating with a team. If someone isn't certain, the team leader can assist by asking, "What frustrates you the most—being on a team that doesn't get to the big picture [East], doesn't name the details [West], doesn't produce [North], or doesn't hear everyone's feelings and viewpoints [South]?"

Next, those standing together at a specific compass point (e.g., North) answer the following:

- In one or two adjectives what is the strength of our style?
- In one or two adjectives what are the limitations of our style?
- What style do we find the most difficult to work with and why?
- What do other people need to know about us so that we can work together more effectively?
- Toward which compass point do we need to grow? (I.e., someone who is North may be so focused on a product that he or she needs to become more East to step back and see the big picture.)

Next, the group standing at each compass point reports out the answers to their questions with an emphasis on growth and need for communication.

Lastly, the team leader processes the exercise:

- It is natural for conflict to occur with opposite compass points, for example, East and West—East focused on big picture; West focused on details. When team members can respectfully listen to varying perspectives, the team does better than if everyone fits into the same compass point.
- All directions have profound strengths and potential weaknesses, and all are necessary for a successful organization or team.
- Every person is seen as capable of growing in each direction. Through work, effort, and practice, every person can develop the strengths of each compass point.

COMPASS POINTS

When working in a team to which direction do you relate most?

EAST	WEST
Vision, Big Picture	**Attention to Details**
"I need to look at the big picture and the possibilities before acting."	*"I need to know the small details before acting."*
• Visionary who sees the big picture • Very idea oriented, focus on future thought • Insight into mission and purpose • Looks for overarching themes, ideas • Likes to experiment, explore • Appreciates generating a lot of information	• Seen as practical, dependable, and thorough in task situation • Likes lists, charts, tables, organizing ideas, and tasks • Moves carefully and follows procedures and guidelines • Uses data analysis and logic to make decision • Weighs all sides of an issue, balanced • Introspective, analytical
NORTH	**SOUTH**
Results and Product Driven	**Attention to Relationships**
"I need to act now and come out with a product."	*"I need to ensure everyone's feelings have been taken into consideration and voices have been heard before acting."*
• Assertive, active, decisive • Likes to be in control of professional relationships and determine course of events • Quick to act • Enjoys challenges presented by difficult situations and people • Thinks in terms of the bottom line • Likes a quick pace and a fast track	• Allows others to feel important in determining direction of what's happening • Uses professional relationships to accomplish tasks, interaction is primary • Supportive, nurturing to colleagues and peers • Willingness to trust others' statements at face value • Intuition is regarded as truth • Team player, receptive to others' ideas, builds on ideas of others, noncompetitive

Source: "North, South, East, and West: Compass Points." Developed in the field by educators affiliated with NSRF. Adapted by Elisa MacDonald. http://www.nsrfharmony.org Reprinted with permission.

Resource 3.4

Hopes and Fears Exercise

Purpose: To surface expectations and concerns—help team members to see that their fears and hopes about collaborating as a team are shared by others and that they are out in the open and will be addressed.

Time allotted: 15–20 minutes.

Group format: Team (This can also be done with multiple teams at a school-wide PD)

Supplies: Yellow and green sticky notes, chart paper, and markers

Roles: Facilitator (can be the team leader)

THE EXERCISE

Team members silently write down on yellow sticky notes their own greatest fears for collaborating together: "If it's the worst experience you've had, what will have happened (or not happened)?" And on green sticky notes they write their own greatest hopes for collaborating together: "If this is the best experience you've had, what outcome(s) can you expect?" (3 minutes)

Team members share their hopes and fears with a partner. (3–5 minutes)

Facilitator labels two chart papers, one "fears" and one "hopes." Team members "popcorn" (call out at random) their hopes and stick them to the chart paper. If anyone on the team has named the same one a colleague has shared, that person stands up and shouts, "I'm with you!" As team members place notes on the chart paper, the facilitator can arrange them in categories and give them a title such as "Fear: loss of independence, or Hope: improved teaching." (Alternative: Facilitator names hopes and fears in marker on the chart paper.) (5 minutes)

Whole group reflection (5–7 minutes)

- Did you notice anything surprising/interesting while doing this activity?
- What group agreements can we make to prevent our fears and ensure our hopes?

Facilitator tip: Set the agreement so that all will withhold judgment. Avoid comments like, "Your hope is ridiculous" or "How can you be afraid of that? That won't happen." The only comment permitted is *"That's interesting."* Do not be fearful of having folks express their worst fears; it always makes things go better once expressed. Plus, we want to know what not to do!

Source: Adapted from the Woodrow Wilson Foundation Leadership Program for Teachers, 1999 Princeton–Rutgers Environmental Science Institute (www.woodrow.org/teachers/esi/1999/ princeton/online/activities1.html).

Resource 4.1
Adapted Consultancy Protocol

The Consultancy Protocol was developed by Gene Thompson-Grove, Paula Evans, and Faith Dunne as part of the Coalition of Essential Schools' National Re:Learning Faculty Program, and further adapted and revised as part of work of NSRF.

> *"A Consultancy is a structured process for helping an individual or a team think more expansively about a particular, concrete dilemma."*

Time: Approximately 50 minutes

Roles: Presenter (the person, whose dilemma or student work is being discussed by the group)

Facilitator Tip: Having the team leader be a presenter first can help set the stage for others to do so in the future.

PROCEDURE

Norms and Purpose (3 minutes): The facilitator overviews the protocol, reason for use, and team group agreements.

Dilemma (5 minutes): The presenter gives an overview of the dilemma with which he or she is struggling and frames a question for the team to consider. The framing of this question, as well as the quality of the presenter's reflection on the dilemma being discussed, are key features of this protocol. If the presenter has brought student work, educator work, or other "artifacts," there is a pause here to silently examine the work/documents. Participants silently listen and record notes and questions.

Recap and Questioning (5–10 minutes): Team members recap their understanding of what the presenter said, "I heard . . . I understand the problem to be . . ." and ask clarifying questions. When basic understanding is reached, participants have the opportunity to ask more probing questions to help define and isolate the issues more thoroughly. This is not the time to start giving feedback. When questioning is complete, the facilitator asks the presenter to restate his or her question for the team.

Discussion (15 minutes): The team talks with each other about the dilemma presented, while the presenter listens silently taking notes. The team references the presenter in the third person, creating an atmosphere where team members are free to talk openly and the presenter is able to listen like a "fly on the wall."

Possible questions to frame the discussion:

- What did we hear?
- What didn't we hear that they think might be relevant?
- What seems to be the root of the problem?
- What assumptions seem to be operating?
- What might we do or try if faced with a similar dilemma? What have we done in similar situations?

Members of the team sometimes suggest actions the presenter might consider taking. Most often, however, they work to define the issues more thoroughly and objectively.

Reflection (3 minutes): The presenter reflects on what she or he heard and on what he or she is now thinking, sharing with the group anything that particularly resonated for him or her during any part of the Consultancy. Team members are silent listeners.

Application (5 minutes): Each person on the team has the opportunity to share his or her take-aways from the adapted consultancy protocol. Possible questions to frame the discussion:

- What take-aways do you have from today's adapted consultancy protocol?
- How might you apply today's learnings to your own work?
- What dilemmas does today's discussion bring to mind for you?
- As a result of this discussion, what next steps in your own problems of practice are you considering taking?

Debrief (3 minutes): The facilitator leads a brief conversation about the group's observation of the Consultancy process. Possible questions to frame the discussion:

- How well did we keep to our group agreements?
- How did this protocol encourage rigorous discourse instead of stifle it? If it did seem to stifle our discourse, why?
- How might we improve our use of this protocol for future dilemmas?

Resource 4.2

Is Your School at Its Highest Leadership Capacity?

AN INFORMAL ASSESSMENT OF SHARED LEADERSHIP

Directions: Individually, mark each statement from one to five. One indicating strong disagreement, five indicating strong agreement. Then, as a team compare responses and discuss.

_____ 1. Everyone has a clear, shared vision and common sense of purpose.

_____ 2. The schoolwide focus is on both student *and* adult learning.

_____ 3. Schoolwide inquiry generates and discovers information that informs practice and decisions.

_____ 4. The principal facilitates learning and models his or her own learning.

_____ 5. Everyone (teachers, parents, students, etc.), not just formal leaders or small elite groups, is involved in leading.

_____ 6. Teaching and learning decision making is shared.

_____ 7. Roles are defined by the needs of the students and the broader school community.

_____ 8. Roles and responsibilities overlap, with each person taking personal and collective responsibility for the work of leadership.

_____ 9. Everyone is involved in skillful dialogue, inquiry, reflection, and problem solving.

_____10. There is collective responsibility among whole faculty for the learning of all students (not just those in my class).

_____11. Attitudes and beliefs shift from passivity to active engagement, from blame to responsibility, from cynicism to hopefulness.

_____12. Students proactively form learning plans, initiate requests for assistance, and assist other students with their work.

_____13. Staff, as a whole (not just recognized leaders), take responsibility for the implementation and evaluation of learning decisions.

_____14. One can move in and out of active leadership without condemnation.

_____15. The school will not crumble if a few individuals leave.

Score 50–75: High-leadership capacity

Score 25–50: Moderate-leadership capacity

Score 0–25: Low-leadership capacity

Source: Adapted from Lambert, L. (1998). *Building Leadership Capacity in Schools.* Alexandria, VA: ASCD.

Resource 5.1

Making the Shift From Seemingly SMART to SMART

ARE THESE GOALS SEEMINGLY SMART?

1. By November 1, 100% of science teachers will deliver all class notes in PowerPoint so that student engagement improves. Each teacher will develop and implement three PowerPoint presentations per unit. The science team will share strategies with the faculty. Success will be measured by the growth in number of teachers who use PowerPoint as a teaching tool.

2. By May, we will improve performance on the state test, summarizing and sequencing questions from an average of 43% correct to an average of 80% correct, and for each student to increase his or her performance by 40 percentage points, as evidenced by three practice tests given throughout the year.

3. For eight weeks, 90% percent of English language learners in Grade 6 will attend homework help four afternoons a week to improve their reading skills. Progress will be monitored through attendance records.

4. As of March 15, every child in Grades 3 through 5 will participate in school theater productions. Depending on personal interests, students will choose backstage work, set design, lighting design, acting, or directing. Volunteers will judge productions and award certificates to students who demonstrate creativity and ability to work as a team and award certificates to outstanding students.

Answer: All goals are Seemingly SMART except for Goal 2. Annotations on the following page explain why.

WHY ARE GOALS 1, 3, AND 4 SEEMINGLY SMART?

Annotations in parentheses explain what makes each goal Seemingly SMART.

1. By November 1, 100% of science teachers will deliver all content notes in PowerPoint so that student engagement improves. (Specifies PowerPoint, a teaching strategy, as the goal; assumes PowerPoint will improve engagement. Additionally, while engagement is a student outcome, it is not a learning outcome. Students can be engaged and still not improve in skills and knowledge they need. Goal does not specify the skills and knowledge this goal is intended to improve.) Each teacher will develop and implement three PowerPoint presentations per unit. The science team will share strategies with the faculty. Success will be measured by the growth in number of teachers who use PowerPoint as a teaching tool. (Even if the goal defined engagement in terms of skills and knowledge, it does not indicate any measurement tools to assess students' growth only teachers implementation. Goal is attainable, but the end result is a resource for teachers not measured gains in learning for students.)

2. For eight weeks, 95% of English language learners in Grade 6 will attend homework help four afternoons a week to improve their reading skills. (Specifies student activity over time, not the specific skills students will gain from attending the homework help and by how much each group of students will improve or what target each group will reach.) Progress will be monitored through attendance records. (Goal does not measure student growth or ability to demonstrate level of skill.)

3. As of March 15th, every child in Grades 3 through 5 will participate in school theater productions. (Specifies a student activity, not what students will learn from participation in the production.) Depending on personal interests, students will choose backstage work, set design, lighting design, acting, or directing. Volunteers will judge productions and award certificates to students who demonstrate creativity and ability to work as a team. (No specifics as to what students will know and do in each area or indication of how team will measure progress toward goal.)

What Could SMART Look Like?	
Seemingly SMART	**SMART**
1. By November 1, 100% of science teachers will deliver all class notes in PowerPoint so that student engagement improves. Each teacher will develop and implement three PowerPoint presentations per unit. The science team will share strategies with the faculty. Success will be measured by the growth in number of teachers who use PowerPoint as a teaching tool.	Currently, on average 80% of students are disengaged during class notetaking in science. When determining a cause, we discovered through a chapter quiz and student interviews that 15% of those students were comprehending next to nothing of the chapter when read independently, 40% were comprehending one third of the chapter and 25% were comprehending only half of the textbook chapter. We believed that improving students' understanding of what they read independently before teacher's class notes would improve their engagement in class. We set the goal: *By November 1, students' independent comprehension of each chapter will increase as measured by accuracy on teacher-generated chapter questions administered before teacher class notes are given. Specifically, 15% of students will comprehend one third of each chapter prior to teacher's notes. 40% of students will independently comprehend half of the text, and 25% of students will independently comprehend two thirds of the text.*
2. For eight weeks, 90% of English language learners in Grade 6 will attend homework help four afternoons a week to improve their reading skills. Progress will be monitored through attendance records.	Currently, two of nineteen English language learners in Grade 6 can identify the central idea in a nonfiction text at their grade level. We set the goal: At the end of an eight-week intervention (four afternoons per week), seventeen out of nineteen English language learner students will master common core standard RI.6.2, where they must determine the central idea from text details, as measured by a reading multiple-choice test given four times. One strategy for achieving this goal is to maintain a weekly 90% attendance rate so that students receive the direct instruction needed to improve.
3. As of March 15th, every child in Grades 3 through 5 will participate in school theater productions. Depending on personal interests, students will choose backstage work, set design, lighting design, acting, or directing. Volunteers will judge productions and award certificates to students who demonstrate creativity and ability to work as a team.	As of March 15th, every child in Grades 3 through 5 will demonstrate one level of growth in skills specific to one of the following: backstage work, set design, lighting design, acting, or directing, as measured by teacher-created rubrics. Volunteers will use rubrics to assess mastery of skills in an in-class production at the beginning of the year as well as an end-of-year production to determine growth by one point. Students who demonstrate mastery of skills or growth in all skills measured will receive awards.

Resource 5.2
SMA-H-RT Guiding Questions

SPECIFIC

- According to our analysis of the student data, which group of students will this goal benefit?
- What content, skills, or knowledge have they mastered? What are they ready to master next? By how much?
- Did we name a teaching strategy or student activity as our goal? If so, what student learning do we expect to achieve as a result of this strategy or activity?
- What additional goals or targets must we set for other groups of students?

MEASURABLE

- What information about students do we need as we work toward our goal? How will we get it? By when do we need it?
- What pre- and postassessment will tell us if students did or did not meet our goal?
- Do our assessments measure implementation of a teaching strategy? If so, what can we use that will instead give us information about students' learning and performance as a result of this strategy?

ATTAINABLE

- What support and resources do we have access to?
- What strategies are needed to attain this goal? Are these strategies sustainable?
- If our resources deplete, can we still attain our goal?

HEARTFELT

- Is each person fully invested in the achievement of this goal?
- Will this goal interfere with the "real" work of teaching? If yes, what is the "real" need of students that we must solve?
- Does this goal target a high-leverage standard or skill that if accomplished will help students and teachers succeed?

RESULTS ORIENTED

- What are our students going to be able to know and do as a result of our goal?
- If our goal results in a teaching resource, what results do we expect to see in students' work?

TIME-BOUND

- By when do students need to achieve this goal?
- How much time do we need to teach and assess this goal?
- What do we need to stop doing in order to utilize our time to achieve our goal?

Resource 5.3
Data Analysis Protocol

PHASE I: PREDICTIONS

Before a team observes data, they predict what they will see, thereby surfacing beliefs, assumptions, hunches, expectations, and questions.

Sentence stems: "I assume/I predict/I wonder . . ."

PHASE II: GO VISUAL

When the results of assessments are brimming over with information, a team leader can go visual to manage the information and help teachers see patterns and priorities emerge (i.e., scatter plots, bar graphs, pie graphs, etc.) on the wall.

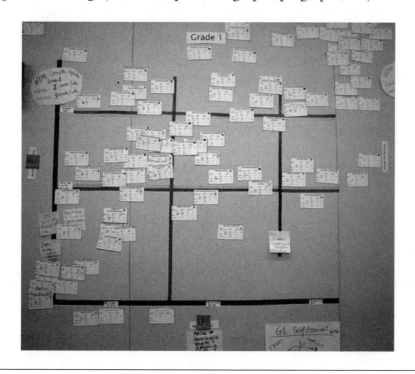

Photo by Lisa Lineweaver

PHASE III: OBSERVATIONS

Using the visuals from Phase II, a team can look for patterns, trends, surprises, and new questions.

> Sentence stems: "I observe/notice . . . ," "Some patterns/trends that I notice . . . ," "I can count . . . ," "I'm surprised that I see . . ."

PHASE IV: INFERENCES

Once a team spends sufficient time making observations, they generate hypotheses, inferring, explaining, and drawing conclusions. Defining new actions and interactions and the data needed to guide their implementation, building ownership for decisions.

> Sentence stems: "I believe the data suggests . . . because . . . ," "Additional data that would help me verify/confirm my explanations is . . . ," " I think the following are appropriate solutions/responses that address the needs implied in the data . . ."

Source: Adapted from Love, N. (2009). *Using Data to Improve Learning for All: A Collaborative Inquiry Approach.* Thousand Oaks, CA: Corwin.

Resource 6.1

Six Phases of Adopting Data-Driven Instruction

Challenging the test	*"Question #3 is poorly worded."* *"Answer 'b' is a trick answer."* *"The students made silly mistakes."*
Feeling inadequate or distrustful	*"How can two questions establish mastery?"* *"We don't teach it in this format."*
Confusion, overload	*"This is too much!* *How can I really use all of this?"*
Analytical but surface	*"Students do poorly on word problems, so we'll do more word problems."* *"We need more reading."*
Looking for causes	*"The wrong answers show that students can't tell the difference between a summary and a theme."*
Changing teaching practice and improving student learning	*"I need to write lesson plans for re-teaching that differentiate between the different needs of my student groups."*

Source: Copyright © 2010 The Achievement Network. Adapted from Trimble, S., Gay, A., & Matthews, J. (2005). Using Test Score Data to Focus Instruction. *Middle School Journal, 36*(4), 26–32. All rights reserved.

References

Ainsworth, L. (2003). *Power standards: Identifying the standards that matter most.* Englewood, CO: Lead+Learn Press.

Ainsworth, L., Almeida, L., Davies, A., DuFour, R., Gregg, L., Guskey, T., . . . Wiliam, D. (2007). *Ahead of the curve: The power of assessment to transform teaching and learning.* Bloomington, IN: Solution Tree Press.

Allison, E., Besser, L., Campsen, L., Cordova, J., Doubek, B., Gregg, L., . . . White, M. (Eds.). (2010). *Data teams: The big picture: Looking at data through a collaborative lens.* Englewood, CO: Lead+Learn Press.

Amabile, T., & Kramer, S. (2010, January/February). What really motivates workers: Understanding the power of progress. *Harvard Business Review, 88*(1), 44–45.

Amabile, T., & Kramer, S. (2011, May). The power of small wins. *Harvard Business Review, 89*(5), 82–89.

Argyris, C. (1993). *Knowledge for action: A guide to overcoming barriers to organizational change.* San Francisco, CA: Jossey-Bass.

Black, P., & Wiliam, D. (1998). Inside the black box: Raising standards through classroom assessment. *Phi Delta Kappan, 80*(2), 139–144.

Boston Public Schools. (2003). Coach Training Program. Boston Plan for Excellence, Author. www.bpe.org

Bovey, W. H., & Hede, A. (2001, May). Resistance to organisational change: The role of defence mechanisms. *Journal of Managerial Psychology, 16*(7), 1–15.

CES National. (April 1999). *Horace (15)*4, Author. Retrieved from http://old.essentialschools.org/cs/resources/view/ces_res/61

Champion, R. (1993). *Tools for change workshops.* Oxford, OH: National Staff Development Council.

Clinton, H. R. (1996). *It takes a village: And other lessons children teach us.* New York, NY: Simon & Schuster.

Collins, J. (2001). *Good to great: Why some companies make the leap . . . and others don't.* New York, NY: Harper Business.

Conzemius, A., & O'Neill, J. (2002). *The handbook for SMART school teams.* Bloomington, IN: National Educational Service.

Covey, S. (2004). *The 7 habits of highly effective people* (2nd ed.). New York, NY: Free Press.

Deal, T. E., & Peterson, K. D. (1999). *Shaping school culture: The heart of leadership.* San Francisco, CA: Jossey-Bass.

Dinham, S., & Scott, C. (2000). Moving into the third, outer domain of teacher satisfaction. *Journal of Educational Administration, 38*(4), 379–396.

Drago-Severson, E. (2004). *Helping teachers learn: Principal leadership for adult growth and development.* Thousand Oaks, CA: Corwin.

DuFour, R., & DuFour, R. (2005, December). *Critical priorities in building and sustaining professional learning communities.* Paper presented at the Northeast ASCD Affliate Conference, Boston, MA.

DuFour, R., & DuFour, R. (2007, Summer). What might be: Open the door to a better future. *Journal of Staff Development, 28*(3), 27–28.

DuFour, R., DuFour, R., Eaker, R., & Many, T. (2006). *Learning by doing: A handbook for professional learning communities at work.* Bloomington, IN: Solution Tree.

DuFour, R., Eaker, R. (1998). *Professional learning communities at work: Best practice for enhancing student achievement.* Bloomington, IN: Solution Tree.

Dweck, C. S. (2006). *Mindset: The new psychology of success* (2nd ed.). New York, NY: Random House.

Emberger, M., & McTighe, J. (2006). Teamwork on assessments creates powerful professional development. *Journal of Staff Development, 27*(1), 38–44.

Frey, N., Fisher, D., & Everlove, S. (2009). *Productive group work.* Alexandria, VA: ASCD.

Fullan, G. M. (1993). *Change forces: Probing the depths of educational reform.* London, England: Routledge.

Fullan, G. M. (1993, March). Why teachers must become change agents. *Professional Teacher, 50*(6), 12–17.

Fullan, M. (2001). *Leading in a culture of change.* San Francisco, CA: Jossey-Bass.

Fullan, M. (2006, November). *Change theory: A force for school improvement: Seminar series no. 157.* Victoria, Australia: Centre for Strategic Education. Retrieved from www.catalyst-chicago.org/sites/catalyst-chicago.org/files/michael_fullen_change_theory.pdf

Fullan, M. (2007, Summer). Change the terms for teacher learning. *Journal of Staff Development, 28*(3), 35–36.

Fullan, M. (2009, April 7). School leadership's unfinished agenda: Integrating individual and organizational development. *Education Week, 27*(31), 36–41.

Fullan, M., & Hargreaves, A. (1991). *What's worth fighting for in your school?* Toronto, Canada: Ontario Public School Teachers' Federation.

Fullan, M., & Rolheiser, C. (1997). *Breaking through change barriers.* Toronto, Canada: Ontario Institute for Studies in Education of the University of Toronto.

Garmston, R. (2004, Summer). Group work has its dangers, but facilitators have some helpful strategies. *Journal of Staff Development, 25*(3), 65–66.

Goleman, D. (2002). *Primal leadership.* Boston, MA: Harvard Business School Press.

Gwande, A. (2003). *Complications: A surgeon's notes on an imperfect science.* New York, NY: Picador.

Hargreaves, A. (1994). *Changing teachers, changing times: Teacher's work and culture in the post-modern age.* New York, NY: Teacher's College Press.

Heifetz, R. A., & Linsky, M. (2002). *Leadership on the line: Staying alive through the dangers of leading.* Boston, MA: Harvard Buisness School Press.

Helsing, D., Howell, A., Kegan, R., & Lahey, L. (2008, Fall). Putting the "development" in professional development: Understanding and overturning educational leaders' immunities to change. *Harvard Educational Review, 78*(3), 437–465.

Hord, S.M., Rutherford, W. L., Huling-Austin, L., & Hall, G. E. (1987). *Taking charge of change.* Alexandria, VA: ASCD.

Huffman, D., & Kalnin, J. (2003). *Collaborative inquiry to make data-based decisions in schools.* Retrieved from http://kuscholarworks.ku.edu/dspace/bitstream/1808/286/1/Nov%231620Huffman.pdf

Jacobson, S. (2011). Leadership effects on student achievement and sustained school success. *International Journal of Educational Management, 25*(1), 33–44.

Janis, I. L. (1972). *Victims of groupthink: A psychological study of foreign-policy decisions and fiascoes.* Boston, MA: Houghton Mifflin.

Kain, D. (2006, Summer). Choose colleagues before friends for teaching teams. *Education Digest, 72*(1), 53–56.

Kegan, R., & Lahey, L. L. (2009). *Immunity to change: How to overcome it and unlock the potential in yourself and your organization.* Boston, MA: Harvard Business Press.

Knight, J. (2007). *Instructional coaching: A partnership approach to improving instruction.* Thousand Oaks, CA: Corwin.

Lambert, L. (1998). *Building leadership capacity in schools.* Alexandria, VA: ASCD.

Lambert, L. (2000). Building leadership capacity in schools. [Monograph]. *APC Monrograph, 1,* 1–12. Retrieved from http://research.acer.edu.au/cgi/viewcontent .cgi?article=1000&context=apc_monographs

Lambert, L. (2003). *Leadership capacity for lasting school improvement.* Alexandria, VA: ASCD.

Lambert, L. (2005, Spring). What does leadership capacity really mean? *Journal of Staff Development, 26*(2), 38–40.

Lambert, L. (2009). Reconceptualizing the road toward leadership capacity. In A. M. Blankstein, P. D. Houston, & R. W. Cole (Eds.), *Building sustainable leadership capacity* (pp. 12–13). Thousand Oaks, CA: Corwin.

Larrick, R. P., Heath, C., & Wu, G. (2009). Goal-induced risk taking in negotiation and decision making. *Social Cognition, 27*(3), 342–364.

Leadership and Learning Center. (2012). On-site PD. Retrieved from www.leadandlearn.com/services/data-analysis/data-teams% C2%AE

Learning Forward. (2012). *Standards for professional learning.* Retrieved from www .learningforward.org/standards/learning-communities#.UEJfevWrOSo

Lehrer, J. (2012, January 30). Groupthink. *New Yorker.* Retrieved from www.newyorker .com/reporting/2012/01/30/120130fa_fact_lehrer

Leithwood, K., Louis, K. S., Anderson, S., & Wahlstrom, K. (2004, September). *How leadership influences student learning.* Ontario, Canada: Center for Applied Research and Educational Improvement, Ontario Institute for Studies in Education.

Lencioni, P. (2002). *The five dysfunctions of a team: A leadership fable.* San Francisco, CA: Jossey-Bass.

Lencioni, P. M. (2003, Summer). The trouble with teamwork. *Leader to Leader, 29,* 35–40. doi.10.1002/lt1.36

Lindsey, D. B., Jungwirth, L. D., Pahl, J. V., & Lindsey, R. B. (2009). *Culturally proficient learning communities: Confronting inequities through collaborative curiosity.* Thousand Oaks, CA: Corwin.

Locke, E. A., & Latham, G. P. (1990). *A theory of goal setting and task performance.* Englewood Cliffs, NJ Upper: Prentice Hall.

London, J. (1916, August 17). The Kanaka Surf. Retrieved from www.jacklondons.net/ writings/MakaloaMat/surf.html

Love, N. (2009). *Using data to improve learning for all: A collaborative inquiry approach.* Thousand Oaks, CA: Corwin.

Love, N., Stiles, K. E., Mundry, S., & DiRanna, K. (2008). *The data coach's guide to improving learning for all students: Unleashing the power of collaborative inquiry.* Thousand Oaks, CA: Corwin.

Lummis, B. (2001). *Turning points guide to collaborative culture and shared leadership.* Boston, MA: Center for Collaborative Education.

MacDonald, E. (2011, June). When nice won't suffice: Honest discourse is key to shifting school culture. *Journal of Staff Development, 32*(3), 45–51.

Mangin, M., & Stoelings, S. R. (2011, June). Peer? Expert? Teacher leaders struggle to gain trust while establishing their expertise. *Journal of Staff Development, 32*(3), 48–51.

Margolis, J. (2009, February). How teachers lead teachers. *Educational Leadership, 66*(5). Retrieved from www.ascd.org/publications/educational-leadership/feb09/v0166/num05/How-Teachers-Lead-Teachers.aspx

Marshall, K. (2006, April 14). *Interim assessments: Keys to successful implementation.* New York, NY: New Leaders for New Schools. Retrieved from www.marshallmemo.com/articles/Interim%20Assmt%20Report%20Apr.%2012,%2006.pdf

Marzano, R. J. (2009). *Designing and teaching learning goals and objectives.* Bloomington, IN: Marzano Research Laboratory.

Moss, C. M., & Brookhart, S. M. (2012). *Learning targets: Helping students aim for understanding in today's lesson.* Alexandria, VA: ASCD.

O'Connor, C. (1993). Resistance: The repercussions of change. *Leadership and Organization Development Journal, 14*(6), 30–36.

O'Connor, C., & Michaels, S. (2007). When is dialogue 'dialogic'? *Human Development, 50,* 275–285.

Ordóñez, L., Schweitzer, M., Galinsky, A., & Bazerman, M. (2009). Goals gone wild: The systematic side effects of overprescribing goal setting. *Academy of Management Perspectives, 23*(1), 6–16.

Pappano, L. (2010). *Inside school turnarounds: Urgent hopes, unfolding stories.* Cambridge, MA: Harvard Education Press.

Parker-Boudett, K., City, E. A., & Murnane, R. J. (2006). *Data Wise.* Cambridge, MA: Harvard Education Press.

Pfeffer, J., & Sutton, R. I. (2000). *The knowing-doing gap: How smart companies turn knowledge into action.* Boston, MA: Harvard Business School Press.

Radmacher, M. A. (n.d.). *Courage doesn't always roar.* Retrieved from http://maryanneradmacher.com/?3e3ea140

Reeves, D. (2010). *Transforming professional development into student results.* Alexandria, VA: ASCD.

Richardson, J. (1999, August/September). Norms put the golden rule into practice for groups. *Journal of Staff Development, 3*(1), 1–2. Retrieved from http://wvde.state.wv.us/ctn/Informational%20Documents/Developing%20Norms%20%28NSDC%29.pdf

Riggio, B. (Winter, 2008). An interview with Ronald Heifetz. *Leadership Review* (8). Claremont: CA: Claremont McKenna College Kraivs Leadership Institute. Retrieved from http://www.leadershipreview.org/2008winter/

Sarason, S. B. (1971). *The culture of the school and the problem of change.* Boston, MA: Allyn & Bacon.

Scharff, H. A., Deidre A. DeAngelis, D. A., & Talbert, J. E. (2010). Starting small for big school improvement. *Principle Leadership, 10*(8), 58.

Schein, E. H. (1985/1992). *Organizational culture and leadership.* San Francisco, CA: Jossey-Bass.

Schein, E. H. (2009). *Helping: How to offer, give and receive help.* San Francisco, CA: Berrett-Koehler.

Schmoker, M. (1999). *Results: The key to continuous school improvement* (2nd ed.). Alexandria, VA: ASCD.

Schmoker, M. (2003). First things first: Demystifying data analysis. *Educational Leadership, 60*(5), 22–24.

Schmoker, M. (2006). *Results now: How we can achieve unprecedented improvements in teaching and learning.* Alexandria, VA: ASCD.

Senge, P., Kleiner, A., Roberts, C., Ross, R. B., & Smith, B. J. (1994). *The fifth discipline fieldbook: Strategies and tools for building a learning organization.* New York, NY: Crown Business.

Sharma, R. R. (2007). *Change management: Concepts and applications.* New Delhi, India: Tata McGraw-Hill.

Smiley, M. (2005). Collective responsibility. In E. N. Zalta (Ed.), *The Stanford encyclopedia of philosophy* (Fall 2011 ed.). Retrieved from http://plato.stanford.edu/entries/collective-responsibility/

Stiggins, R. (2002, June). Assessment crisis: The absence of learning. *Phi Delta Kappan, 83*(10), 758–765.

Stone, D., Patton, B., & Heen, S. (1999). *Difficult conversations: How to discuss what matters most.* New York, NY: Penguin Books.

Talbert, J. (2011). Collaborative inquiry to expand student achievement in New York City schools. In J. O'Day, C. Bitter, & L. Gomez (Eds.), *Education reform in New York City: Ambitious change in the nation's most complex school system.* Cambridge, MA: Harvard Education Press.

Talbert, J., Scharff, N., & Lin. W. (2008, March). *Leading school improvement with data: A theory of action to extend the sphere of student success.* A paper presented at the Annual Meeting of the American Educational Research Association, New York, NY.

Teachers aren't in it for the money. (2010, May/June). *American Teacher, 94*(6), 7. Retrieved from www.aft.org/pdfs/americanteacher/at_mayjune10.pdf

Timperley, H. (2005). Distributed leadership: Developing theory from practice. *Journal of Curriculum Studies, 37*(4), 395–420.

Trimble, S., Gay, A., & Matthews, J. (2005). Using test score data to focus instruction. *Middle School Journal, 36*(4), 26–32.

Tuckman, B. W. (1965). Developmental sequence in small groups. *Psychological Bulletin, 63*(6), 384–389.

Wagner, T., Kegan, R., Lahey, L., Lemons, R. W., Garnier, J., Helsing, D., . . . Rasmussen, H. T. (2006). *Change leadership: A practical guide to transforming our schools.* San Francisco, CA: Jossey-Bass.

Wahlstrom, K. L., Louis, K. S., Leithwood, K., & Anderson, S. E. (2010). *Investigating the links to improved student learning: Executive summary of research findings.* Ontario, Canada: Center for Applied Research and Educational Improvement, Ontario Institute for Studies in Education.

White, M. (2010). The real value of data teams. Englewood, CO: Leadership and Learning Center. Retrieved from http://tinyurl.com/dyrz2yt

Whitworth, L., Kimsey-House, K., & Kimsey-House, H. P. (2007). *Co-active coaching: New skills for coaching people toward success in work and life.* Mountain View, CA: Davies-Black.

Williams, R. (2011, April 11). Why goal setting doesn't work [Blog post]. Retrieved from http://business.financialpost.com/2011/04/13/why-goal-setting-doesnt-work/?__lsa=303c4066

Index

CORWIN

A SAGE Company

The Corwin logo—a raven striding across an open book—represents the union of courage and learning. Corwin is committed to improving education for all learners by publishing books and other professional development resources for those serving the field of PreK–12 education. By providing practical, hands-on materials, Corwin continues to carry out the promise of its motto: **"Helping Educators Do Their Work Better."**

Advancing professional learning for student success

Learning Forward (formerly National Staff Development Council) is an international association of learning educators committed to one purpose in K–12 education: Every educator engages in effective professional learning every day so every student achieves.